Christoph Schlingensief:
Art Without Borders

Christoph Schlingensief:
Art Without Borders

Edited by Tara Forrest and Anna Teresa Scheer

intellect Bristol, UK / Chicago, USA

First published in the UK in 2010 by Intellect,
The Mill, Parnall Road, Fishponds, Bristol, BS16 3JG, UK

First published in the USA in 2010 by Intellect, The University of Chicago Press,
1427 E. 60th Street, Chicago, IL 60637, USA

A catalogue record for this book is available from
the British Library.

Cover design: Holly Rose
Copy-editor: Emma Rhys
Typesetting: John Teehan

ISBN 978-1-84150-319-6

Printed and bound by Gutenberg Press, Malta.

Contents

ACKNOWLEDGEMENTS

We would like to thank Christoph Schlingensief for finding time in his busy schedule for the interview and for his kind permission to reproduce the images for which he holds copyright in the book. We extend our thanks to Meike Fischer and Patrick Hilss for their help in securing the images, and we are grateful to Matthias Horn for permission to include two of his photographs in the book.

Many thanks to Alexander Kluge for kindly writing the 'Foreword', and to Beata Wiggen for her enthusiastic support of the project. We also gratefully acknowledge the assistance of Sabine Zolchow and the staff of the Akademie der Künste in Berlin for the resources and generous assistance they have provided us with at various points during our research. We are grateful to Florian Malzacher for conducting and transcribing the interview and to Michael Turnbull for translating two of the chapters. Thanks also to Demetrios Douramanis for his support, advice, and assistance on the project, and to Gudrun Herrbold for generously providing Anna with the use of her apartment in Berlin during an extended research trip in 2009.

Finally, the book could not have been completed without the generous financial assistance of the Faculty of Arts and Social Sciences, University of Technology, Sydney. This publication is also supported by a grant from the Research and Research Training Committee, Faculty of Arts, The University of Melbourne. We thank them for their support.

LIST OF TITLES

The following pages list the English translations of Schlingensief's works as cited throughout the book, followed by the original German titles.

Films

Hey Mummy, we're making a movie/*Mensch, Mami, wir dreh'n 'nen Film* (1977)

Phantasus Must Be Different: Phantasus Go Home/*Phantasus muss anders werden: Phantasus Go* Home (1983)

The Nonchalant Ones Are Coming – What Happened to Magdalena Jung?/*Die Ungenierten kommen – What happened to Magdalena Jung?* (1983)

Tunguska – The Crates Are Here/*Tunguska – die Kisten sind da* (1983–84)

Menu Total (1986)

Mother's Mask/*Mutters Maske* (1987–1988)

100 Years of Adolf Hitler: The Last Hour in the Führer's Bunker/*100 Jahre Adolf Hitler: Die letzte Stunde im Führerbunker* (1988–89)

The German Chainsaw Massacre: The First Hour of Reunification/*Das deutsche Kettensägenmassaker* (1990)

Terror 2000 – Intensive Care Unit Germany/*Terror 2000 – Intensivstation Deutschland* (1992)

United Trash (1995)

The 120 Days of Bottrop/*Die 120 Tage von Bottrop* (1997)

Freakstars 3000 (2003)

Theatre and Opera

100 Years of the Christian Democratic Union: Game Without Limits/*100 Jahre CDU: Spiel ohne Grenzen* (1993)

Kühnen '94: Bring Me the Head of Adolf Hitler/*Kühnen '94: Bring mir den Kopf von Adolf Hitler* (1993)

Rocky Dutschke, '68 (1996)

Hamlet (2001)

Quiz 3000 – You are the catastrophe!/*Quiz 3000 – Du bist die Katastrophe!* (2002)

ATTA ATTA – Art Has Broken Out!/*ATTA ATTA – die Kunst ist ausgebrochen!* (2003)

Bambiland (2003)

Atta-Bambi Pornoland (2004)

Parsifal (2004)

Art and Vegetables, A. Hipler/*Kunst und Gemüse, A. Hipler* (2004)

Area 7– St. Matthew's Expedition/*Area 7– Matthäusexpedition* (2006)

Joan of Arc – Scenes from the life of St. Joan/*Jeanne d'Arc – Szenen aus dem Leben der Heiligen Johanna* (2008)

The Current State of Things/*Zwischenstand der Dinge* (2008)

A Church of Fear for the Stranger in Me/*Ein Kirche der Angst vor der Fremden in Mir* (2008)

Mea Culpa: A ReadyMade Opera/*Mea Culpa: ein ReadyMadeOper* (2009)

'Actions' and Installations

My Felt, my Fat, my Hare!/*Mein Filz, mein Fett, mein Hase!* (1997)

Passion Impossible: 7 Day Emergency Call for Germany/*Passion Impossible: 7 Tage Notruf für Deutschland* (1997)

Chance 2000 – Election Campaign Circus '98/*Chance 2000 – Wahlkampfzirkus '98* (1998)

Chance 2000 – Bathing in Lake Wolfgang/*Chance 2000 – Baden im Wolfgangsee* (1998)

Please Love Austria: First Austrian Coalition Week/*Bitte liebt Österreich: erste österreichische Koalitionswoche* (2000)

Action 18/*Aktion 18* (2002)

Church of Fear (2003)

The Animatograph, Iceland Edition: House of Obsession/*Der Animatograph, Island Edition: House of Obsession* (2005)

The Animatograph, German Edition: Odin's Parsipark/*Der Animatograph, Deutschland Edition: Odins Parsipark* (2005)

The Animatograph, Africa Edition: The African Twin Towers/*Der Animatograph, Afrika Edition: The African Twintowers* (2005)

Kaprow City (2006)

Trem Fantasma – First Prototype for an Operatic Ghost Train/*Trem Fantasma - Erster Prototyp einer Operngeisterbahn* (2007)

18 Images per Second/*18 Bilder pro Sekunde* (2007)

Cross-mutilation/*Querverstümmelung* (2008)

The King Lives Within Me/*Der König wohnt in mir* (2008)

To Burn Oneself With Oneself – The Romantic Damage Show (2008)

Television Programs

Talk 2000 (1997)

U-3000 (2000)

Freakstars 3000 (2002)

The Pilots – 10 Years of Talk 2000/*Die Piloten – 10 Jahre Talk 2000* (2007)

Radio Plays

Radio P.S.1 Radio show (1999)

Camp without Limits/*Lager ohne Grenzen* (1999)

Rosebud (2002)

18 Radio plays in one Second/*18 Hörspiele in einer Sekunde* (2006)

Book

Heaven Can't Be as Beautiful as Here: A Cancer Diary/*So schön wie hier kanns im Himmel gar nicht sein: Tagebuch einer Krebserkrankung* (2009)

Alexander Kluge

My friend Christoph Schlingensief is a unique artist. One of his central qualities (which remains constant with the continual alternation of his themes and artistic means) is his CAPACITY FOR COMMITMENT: the firm will, regardless of what is produced as a result, to be authentic, to abandon oneself directly to an experience and to react immediately. As they say in the German classics: 'and if you don't risk your life, you won't win it'.

Such a stance is a radical character trait of the modern as propagated by Joseph Beuys, whom Schlingensief artistically follows. Schlingensief is open to all postmodern expressive forms, he likes to draw on this reservoir, but he grinds it through the mills of the modern. What emerges is the new raw material with which he works.

I am writing this preface on the morning after Schlingensief's phenomenal success at the Burgtheater in Vienna, where he staged his play *Mea Culpa*, which he describes as a 'Ready-Made-Opera'. It deals with a theme that drives him: death. Since the baroque, it has been a central theme of art. If one looks at Schlingensief's earlier work, one notices that he has always been preoccupied with this theme, and not only now as a result of his illness with cancer. As is the case with his earlier work, in this new piece Schlingensief is also concerned with the deconstruction of death through jokes, chaos, and the demise of a diametrically opposed kind of theatre experience. This double strategy, to place a visceral theatre ['*Theater der Handgreiflichkeit*'] next to a theatre of art, is characteristic of Schlingensief's work. It connects, for example, the formal world of Richard Wagner with the comedies of Ferdinand Raimund or Jacques Offenbach. Above all, Schlingensief continues in the tradition not only of Beuys, but also of that north German hero Till Eulenspiegel, whose principle works have unfortunately not been passed down.[1]

I met Christoph Schlingensief, whose artistic standing was already familiar to me, some fifteen years ago at the burial of our shared friend and colleague, the actor Alfred Edel. We both delivered eulogies. Alfred Edel had acted in my films and in the films and revues of Schlingensief. Edel was an icon of the German *Autoren* Films and is now also – posthumously – an intermediary when I have an argument with Schlingensief.

1

Initially I exchanged ideas with Schlingensief about his films. *The German Chainsaw Massacre* and *Terror 2000* have become famous. They were based on earlier films such as *Tunguska* (with Alfred Edel) and *Mother's Mask* (with Helge Schneider). The ground covered in each of these films leads to a wealth of other films. To single out *Mother's Mask*: In a similar vein to the films of Rainer Werner Fassbinder, Schlingensief unites elements of the *Autoren* films with his interest in and admiration for the old UFA film. *Mother's Mask* copies in a baffling way the plot of a 1944 film by Veit Harlan about a novella by Rudolf Binding with the title *Opfergang* [*The Great Sacrifice*]. This strange film reflects, at the end of the Second World War, a highly tense, romantic, atmosphere of death during which time a 'Blitzkrieg in reverse' is taking place. Schlingensief completely turns the original on its head: whereas in Harlan's film the gentleman rider Willi Birgel rode on his noble steed, now a girl circles around on a pony in a meadow in North Rhein-Westphalia, where pathos once existed, there is now only the grotesque, where the Third Reich charged ahead via means of sentimental propaganda, there is Dada.

One does not meet with Schlingensief to babble, rather cooperation immediately comes into play. Over the years, this is how we produced twenty-nine films, or rather television programs, together. They reflect the changes in Schlingensief's preferences and themes better than any description in written form. The theme is always the same: in the midst of life we are surrounded by death –but also by the necessary and always recurring breakout attempts via which life's vitality [*Lebendigkeit*] defends against death. What is essential for Schlingensief's work is that he is never just concerned with a theme or its modification. Rather, what is equally important is that the artistic means, the forms of expression change, are renewed in surprising ways, and are spun around helter skelter.

Schlingensief works with a new, boundary-breaking kind of medium, colonized from the theatre or the anti-theatre, with the support of film, video and music. It has the following characteristics:

1. At the heart of Schlingensief's élan lie conservative values and desires. Parents as authority figures, art as a challenge whose rules are to be protected and at the same time broken, the tradition of disobedience, and while that, over time, becomes boring, the reconstruction and reestablishment of artistic moments. In the middle of the chaos of a revue, moments of concentration, art.

2. There are no boundaries between genres. Is a work by Schlingensief an installation, an opera, a series of numbers, a total work of art, a working through of reality, a piece of theatre, an intermission or backstage activity? They are all interventions, transcriptions, transliterations, continuations.

3.   The works for theatre, the films and his published texts are all types of musical theatre. The way in which music moves constitutes the essential form of his dramaturgy.

4.   The works are cooperative. His dramaturge Carl Hegemann, his ensemble, which comprises scores of non-actors, are a part of who he is, and are held together by him. When he was operated on, the production work for the opera *Joan of Arc* at the German Opera in Berlin went ahead, because his team took over the production by following his directions on the telephone. Directing an opera via telephone was up until then unheard of.

5.   All of Schlingensief's work has to be risky: on the knife's edge. That is what makes or breaks it. Otherwise it doesn't please him.

In his mind, Schlingensief is already on his way to Africa. There, in the green hills of Africa, a new opera house will be built without plush on the Bayreuthian hill. A cathedral of music made out of clay. Schlingensief has already prepared himself for the backlash that is hinted at in *Mea Culpa*: he believes that his work on Richard Wagner's *Parsifal* is responsible for his illness. Wagner, he claims, disseminates a deadly poison via his suggestive music. It is thus imperative to not only construct but also to deconstruct Wagner. I would argue that Schlingensief, in this dialectical manner, will move in the direction of Alban Berg, Wagner's modern successor, or else towards a more pure modernity in the form of Meyerbeer and Verdi. I believe that the deeper he penetrates into the mines of the classics, the more free, wild, visceral and contemporary his musical theatre will be.

– Translated by Tara Forrest

Endnotes

1   *Translator's Notes*:
Thanks to Anna Teresa Scheer for feedback on the translation.
Till Eulenspiegel was, according to Paul Oppenheimer, 'Europe's most famous jester': a figure who, since the publication of his stories in 1510–11, has taken on legendary status in Germany. These stories—which have been published in English as *Till Eulenspiegel: His Adventures*—recount the fourteenth century trickster's various pranks; the majority of which were socially critical of the hypocrisies and injustices characteristic of the society in which he lived. According to Oppenheimer,

these pranks and tricks were driven by Eulenspiegel's 'contempt' for, among other figures, 'dishonest' Christians, officials, nobles, citizens, doctors and politicians. Oppenheimer, P. (2001), 'Introduction', in *Till Eulenspiegel: His Adventures* (trans. Paul Oppenheimer), London and New York: Routledge, pp. xxi and xxxi–xxxii.

Background, Inspiration, Contexts

Tara Forrest and Anna Teresa Scheer

By the end of the 1990s, Christoph Schlingensief had attracted as much media attention in Germany as pop stars, leading politicians, and film celebrities. The fact that he was an artist, an independent film-maker, and one of the in-house directors of the Volksbühne in Berlin made his media profile a little more unusual. One of the defining features of Schlingensief's work is the manner in which it intervenes in the politics of the day and, throughout his career, he has actively sought to mobilize public debate about a diverse range of topics and issues including, to cite just a few examples: the recent success of far-right parties across Europe; the indignities of unemployment and homelessness; the lack of visibility of disabled people in the media; the politics of fear in the post 9/11 period; and the legacy of the Nazi past in contemporary Germany.

Schlingensief's work is thus highly political in its focus. This, however, is not to suggest that it pushes a particular political agenda. Indeed, as attested by the open, ambiguous character of his work, Schlingensief is not interested in pedagogically instructing the audience on the 'best way' to approach the topic at hand. On the contrary, he is much more interested in developing complex, multilayered productions that provoke the audience to think for themselves, and to approach the topic from multiple angles.[1] Schlingensief himself has described this active, exploratory mode of engagement as a form of 'self-provocation'[2], and it is precisely because of the confronting manner in which his work undermines stereotypes and challenges the status quo that it has attracted so much media attention.

The heated media debates that are often sparked by his productions do not, however, engage in any detail with their content, and often disregard the complex manner in which Schlingensief foregrounds ambiguity and a pluralistic approach to the generation of meaning. Although his work has attracted much international attention, outside of the German-speaking countries, access to Schlingensief's highly challenging productions has been hampered by the fact that very little has been published on his oeuvre in the English-speaking world.

The aim of the book is thus to provide the reader with a comprehensive introduction to Schlingensief's work in film, theatre, television, activism, art and opera. While it would be near impossible to analyze Schlingensief's entire oeuvre in one volume, the work explored in detail in the book (which spans from 1983 to 2009) provides a fascinating overview of the key issues, themes, concerns, and preoccupations that have driven and inspired the development of Schlingensief's highly eclectic body of work over a period of some 25 years.

Career overview

Christoph Schlingensief was born in 1960 in Oberhausen, Germany. He began making films using Super 8 at an early age and by 22 had made twelve films of varying length and genre inspired by film-makers such as Luis Bunuel, Werner Herzog, Rainer Werner Fassbinder and Werner Schroeter. In 1983, following the early termination of his University studies in German Philology, Philosophy and Art History, Schlingensief

Figure 1: Christoph Schlingensief and friends on a location shoot. © Christoph Schlingensief.

became the assistant to experimental film-maker Werner Nekes after being rejected twice by the Munich School for Film and Television. He continued to make independent, low-budget films throughout the 1980s, before starting work on his *Deutschlandtrilogie/ German Trilogy* (1989–1992).[3]

The films that constitute the trilogy deal with significant moments in twentieth century German history and reveal themes to which Schlingensief obsessively returns in many of his later works, including: the legacy of the Third Reich and Adolf Hitler; the difficulties faced by Germany in dealing with its National Socialist past; the end of the 1968 revolutionary movement following the violent excesses of the Red Army Faction (RAF); and the many challenges posed by the post 1989 reunification period. The films themselves are excessive in their graphic imagery and trashy aesthetics, yet demand a closer reading as documents of their times.

Although Schlingensief has described himself as working in the tradition of the New German Cinema, he states that once the movement lost impetus, his response was to produce films that enacted a '75 minute fist against the screen'.[4] Although Schlingensief's early films never achieved recognition beyond an underground cult status, in 2005 he was awarded a film prize by the city of Hof. In 1993, Schlingensief was invited by Matthias Lilienthal—then head dramaturge at the Volksbühne, one of Berlin's most renowned and successful theatres—to direct a production of his own devising, and he made his theatre debut soon after with *100 Years of the Christian Democratic Union, Game Without Limits* (1993). The productions that followed won him as many supporters as detractors for the way in which they dealt with controversial issues in provocative ways. For example, the title of his second production *Kühnen 94, Bring me the head of Adolf Hitler* (1993) takes its name from Michael Kühnen (a notorious neo-Nazi leader up until his death in 1991), while his 1996 production *Rocky Dutschke, '68* sought to engage, in part, with the life and ideas of Rudi Dutschke: a prominent leader of the 1968 German student movement.

The sixties 'happening' format of the latter production demanded the active, creative participation of the audience, and Schlingensief employed a megaphone (since then a regular feature of his events) to make himself heard above the melee. *Rocky Dutschke, '68* was also the first performance in which Schlingensief brought actors together with lay and handicapped people as a performance ensemble. This strategy of working with performers of diverse ages and backgrounds has since become a feature of his work, with the same group or 'family' involved in many of Schlingensief's productions.[5]

In 1996, Schlingensief was offered a position as in-house director at the Volksbühne where he directed intermittently until 2006. During this period, he was also very active in a diverse range of media producing, in addition to more than 25 theatre, opera, and public performances: three feature length films[6]; several radio plays[7]; four television series; and a number of interactive installations. It was, however, via his work as a director and host of a series of controversial television programs that Schlingensief became a household name in Germany. The first of these programs, *Talk 2000*, screened

Figure 2: Schlingensief and guests in the Berlin underground recording *U3000*. Photo: David Baltzer.

on SAT 1, RTL, Kanal 4, and ORF in 1997[8], and consists of eight episodes in which Schlingensief interviews a diverse group of guests, including well-known personalities from the German art, media, and popular culture spheres. The show digressed from the standard talk show format when the host spontaneously began wrestling with certain guests, lampooned others, discussed his own personal problems, and announced short naps that were broadcast live on television.

Talk 2000 was followed three years later by *U3000*—a talk show of sorts that screened on MTV in 2000, and which consists of eight episodes that were shot in a train as it raced through Berlin's underground railway network. Part talk show and part performance event, *U3000* featured Schlingensief—in an increasingly frenzied state—moving through the tightly packed carriages which contained, in addition to a diverse group of guests: a camera crew, a studio band, books and handouts for discussion, religious and political posters, barking dogs, and a live 'studio' audience.

In 2000, Schlingensief stepped outside the variety talk show format to produce *Freakstars 3000*: a six-part television series that screened on VIVA and that was modelled on the casting show format made popular by programs such as *Popstars* and *Deutschland sucht den Superstar/Germany searches for a Superstar*. What distinguished *Freakstars 3000* from these programs, however, was that it was structured as a casting show for people with disabilities: a format that enabled Schlingensief to explore the lack of visibility of disabled people in the German media, and to encourage viewers to reflect on the degree to which certain National Socialist ideals persist in the contemporary media and popular culture spheres.[9]

Figure 3: *Chance 2000* members assembled for a campaign event. Photo: Bettina Blämer.

This emphasis on drawing public attention to the limited, exclusionary nature of the media and public spheres was also a key factor driving Schlingensief's production *Chance 2000* (1998). As a part of this complex, multifaceted event (which was staged in the lead-up to the German federal election) Schlingensief founded a political party with the aim of supporting disabled, unemployed, and other marginalized people to become independent electoral candidates. Employing slogans that echoed the work of Joseph Beuys (whose influence on Schlingensief will be explored in the following section), the party encouraged self-representation by urging participants to 'Vote for Yourself!' and 'Prove your existence!'.[10]

Chance 2000 is just one of many public 'actions' staged by Schlingensief since 1997 in which the line between art and politics has been consistently blurred. Other productions in this vein include, among others: *Passion Impossible: 7 Day Emergency Call for Germany* (1997); *Please Love Austria: First Austrian Coalition Week* (2000); and *Action 18* (2002). Each of these events generated substantial media attention and were highly successful in mobilizing debate about homelessness, immigration and—in the case of *Action 18*—then German politician Jürgen Mölleman's perceived targeting of the far right, anti-Semitic vote. In a similar vein to Schlingensief's theatre work, each of these actions were open, multilayered, and ambiguous in their structure, and encouraged viewers to become active participants in the meaning-making process that was initiated but not foreclosed by Schlingensief himself.

Schlingensief's first foray into the classical repertoire took place in 2001 when he staged Shakespeare's *Hamlet* at the Schauspielhaus in Zurich and at the Theatertreffen in Berlin. In this highly controversial production, 'the players' in the famous mousetrap scene were played by neo-Nazis, who had expressed a desire to leave the far-right scene. In what resulted in a direct intervention into Swiss politics, the play itself became the backdrop for the supposition that, in 2001, 'something rotten' was afoot in Switzerland and neighbouring European countries, given the increasing approval rates enjoyed by far-right populist parties.

Between 2003 and 2004, Schlingensief engaged with debates and media discourses pertaining to terrorism and the events of 9/11 that resulted in a series of interrelated works starting with the theatre production *ATTA ATTA, Art has Broken Out!* (2003). This was followed by a mobile art and activist project entitled *Church of Fear* (2003) (which travelled to Venice, Cologne and Frankfurt) and—after directing *Bambiland* by Elfriede Jelinek in Vienna—Schlingensief went on to produce a theatre production entitled *Atta-Bambi Pornoland* (2004). The latter multimedia works—which were very multilayered in their structure—encouraged the audience to engage critically with the media's representation of modern warfare, with its 'safe bombs', embedded journalists, and its aestheticization of violence and destruction.

This emphasis on generating an interactive mode of engagement was, however, taken to new lengths with the production of Schlingensief's 'Animatographs': large-scale

Figure 4: *Hamlet*: the arrival of the Players onstage. *Schauspielhaus*, Zurich, 2001. Photo: David Baltzer.

rotating 'carousels' that serve as blank projection surfaces for a diverse collection of footage.[11] These animatographs—which developed out of the rotating stage employed in Schlingensief's 2004 production of Richard Wagner's opera *Parsifal* (2004)[12]—were staged at various festivals and events in Iceland, Germany, Namibia and Austria[13]. For example, in Schlingensief's production, *Area 7—St. Matthews Expedition* (2006), the ground floor seating was removed from the Burgtheater in Vienna and replaced with a massive installation featuring an animatograph at its centre. Instead of 'viewing' the production from the auditorium, audience members were invited to wander through the theatre and to interact with the diverse collection of materials (including signs, images, blackboards, projections, and found objects) out of which the installation was constructed.

Although Schlingensief participated in three art exhibitions in 2008[14], since 2007 his energies have been largely focused on the development of a series of theatre and opera productions; the most recent of which deal directly with his illness and treatment since being diagnosed with lung cancer at the start of 2008.[15] As foreshadowed in the third part of his 'cancer trilogy'—*Mea Culpa: A ReadyMade Opera* (2009)—Schlingensief's latest ongoing project revolves around the construction of an opera house in Africa: a venture which, according to Schlingensief, was conceived not as an artwork that seeks to 'show Africans what German culture can do, but as a blank [*blasses*] European page' that—in the tradition of his animatographs—provides a surface of 'illumination for Africa'.[16]

Inspiration, influences, affinities

Schlingensief's work has been heavily influenced by the historical avant-garde, and by the emphasis placed by the Dadaists and the Surrealists on critiquing and disrupting the social etiquette and artistic practices of their day. As revealed by the chapters contained in the book, Schlingensief's influences are wide-ranging, spanning figures and groups as diverse as Rainer Werner Fassbinder, Werner Herzog, and the New German Cinema, the Vienna Actionists, Dieter Roth, Arnold Schönberg, Joseph Beuys and Allan Kaprow.

The significance of an art practice that emerges from the social sphere—and that develops, in part, out of the active, creative participation of the viewer/audience—was a key concept driving artists such as Kaprow and John Cage around whom the Fluxus movement developed in New York in the late 1950s. Constituted by a loose collective of international artists (including, among others, George Brecht, Joseph Beuys, Nam June Paik, Wolf Vostell and Yoko Ono) the Fluxus network sought—in multifarious ways—to transform our understanding of both the role of art and the possibilities and limitations of the present. The consolidation of their various interests in narrow political terms was, however, rejected by the group, whose emphasis on 'intermedia' challenged conventional delineations of artistic practice according to categories such as theatre, music, poetry, performance and sculpture, and instead encouraged a process-based model that was not driven by the desire for a fixed outcome.[17] As Mike Sell notes of the active, participatory mode of engagement facilitated by the experimental work produced by Fluxus members: 'Happenings and Fluxus events allowed themselves to be altered and reconfigured by the spectator, to be "put forth as a force" in the world'.[18]

This emphasis on facilitating an active, creative mode of engagement is one of the key characteristics of Schlingensief's work. It is also one of the defining features of the work of Joseph Beuys which—in its complex blending of sculpture, objects, performance and activism—had an important influence on the aesthetic form and political ambitions of Schlingensief's work. Beuys' 'expanded' concept of the role of art, which he described as 'social sculpture', was driven by the desire to produce work that would facilitate the active, creative participation of the viewer. 'My objects', he writes:

> are to be seen as stimulants for the transformation of the idea of sculpture, or of art in general. They should provoke thoughts about what sculpture can be and how the concept of sculpting can be extended to the invisible materials used by everyone.[19]

For Beuys, foremost among these 'invisible materials' are the thoughts and ideas that are generated when people are provided with the opportunity to actively participate in shaping the formation of opinions and policies that impact on the world in which they live. In an attempt to undermine the commonly held assumption that we live in a world where people are either 'artists' or 'non-artists'[20], Beuys famously declared that 'every human being is an artist!'[21] because 'thinking is practically a sculptural process'[22]. Within this schema, the aim of 'social sculpture' is thus to stimulate debate and, in doing so, to open up a space within which the viewer is encouraged to become an active, creative participant in the democratic process.

To this end, in 1971, Beuys founded the 'Organization for Direct Democracy by Referendum', which proposed increased political power and social justice for individuals.[23] In an attempt to promote his ideas, Beuys distributed 'shopping bags printed with a multicolored diagram of the Organization for Direct Democracy program' on a main thoroughfare in Cologne while, in 1972, he established an 'Information Office' at the Kassel Documenta 5 exhibition where he participated—for a period of 100 days—in discussions with visitors about issues pertaining to society, politics, and the arts.[24]

The title of Schlingensief's Kassel Documenta project, *My Felt, My Fat, My Hare: 48 Hours of Survival for Germany* (1997), clearly references some of the signature materials and motifs used in—and characteristic of—Beuys' work. The subtitle of the project— *What are 7000 Oak Trees Compared to Six Million Unemployed?*—also references Beuys' last action at Documenta that involved planting seven thousand oak trees around the city of Kassel in an attempt to promote ecological awareness. In *My Felt, My Fat, My*

Hare, Schlingensief and his ensemble installed themselves in the Hybrid Workspace at Documenta X, barricaded in by large sandbags where they resided for a period of 48 hours. The significance of the sandbags was highlighted by Schlingensief in the flyer, which asked people to imagine Germany metaphorically as a 'gigantic theatre performance' with then conservative Chancellor Helmut Kohl as its 'director'[25], explaining that the sandbags represented 'der Obersandsack'[26] or 'head sandbag' Kohl over which people would have to climb in order to bring about social change. The action concluded with Schlingensief's arrest after he posted a sign on the door that read 'Kill Helmut Kohl' and announced to visitors: 'in one hour we will begin to destroy artworks'.[27] A nationwide media scandal ensued, with the tabloid newspapers denouncing Schlingensief as a 'provocateur' and an 'enfant terrible'[28]—titles that have since become firmly attached to his name.

Figure 5: Schlingensief and his team (including Bernhard Schutz and Carl Hegemann) in the Hybrid Workspace at Documenta X, Kassel, 1997. © Christoph Schlingensief.

However, despite these claims, it is clear that Schlingensief is not driven by a desire to produce work that seeks to shock, or provoke anger in his audience. As Mark Siemons suggests, the 'provocateur' label would appear to sit more comfortably as a description of someone who starts out with a clear conception of the kind of reaction he is aiming to provoke[29]. As noted previously, however, Schlingensief is not interested in producing a particular political or pedagogical outcome, but in generating work that is fluid and open in its structure, and that encourages the audience to think critically and creatively for themselves.

While Schlingensief's productions (and his public 'actions' in particular) clearly resonate with the work of Beuys in this regard, they also share a number of affinities with the work of Alexander Kluge, whose experimental films and television programs are constructed in a manner that seeks to maximize the active, imaginative participation of the audience.[30] 'Film', Kluge argues, 'is not produced by auteurs alone, but by the dialogue between spectators and authors'[31]—a dialogue that is not manifested in the film itself, but in the associations cultivated in 'the spectator's head' by 'the gaps [...] between the disparate elements of filmic expression'.[32] Schlingensief, too, places great emphasis on the open, 'unfinished' structure of his work.[33] In a comment that takes Kluge's analysis a step further, Schlingensief has stated: 'I've had the idea of producing a film by me on CD-ROM, where the speech, the images and the music are separate. And each person can put it together on the computer. Each person can make their own film'.[34]

Schlingensief's work in television, theatre, installation, and opera is similarly open and ambiguous in its structure and—in keeping with the emphasis on 'intermedia' characteristic of the work produced by Fluxus—is not always easy to categorize according to traditional art and media forms. Was *Please Love Austria*, for example, a reality television program, a public protest, an installation, or all of the above? Was the *Church of Fear* an art project, an internet community, or a secular church? According to Schlingensief: 'All works are fluid. Therefore, the *Church of Fear* also crops up in *Parsifal* 2004, and therefore *Parsifal* crops up in *The Animatograph*, and therefore a model of the *Animatograph* stands on the stage of *Parsifal* 2005'.[35]

The highly fluid, intermedial nature of Schlingensief's work is explored in detail in the book. Although each of the chapters focuses on a specific work (and the particular political, historical, and/or biographical conditions in which its production was embedded), when read together, they illuminate some of the many resonances and connections that exist between the films, television programs, theatre productions, public actions, animatographs, and operas that Schlingensief has developed throughout the course of his career. The aim of this book is not only to amplify some of these resonances, but to encourage the reader to generate their own connections: a process that will hopefully inspire further thinking about Schlingensief's extraordinary body of work.

Chapter Summaries

The book is organized in a chronological fashion and begins with an exploration of Schlingensief's work as a film-maker with the first two chapters focusing on the film trilogies he completed in 1984 and 1992 respectively. Richard Langston argues in the first chapter that, far from being an immature work, Schlingensief's early trilogy (begun when he was just 23 years old) sets out an aesthetic and political agenda that has preoccupied him throughout his career. Langston accords the film *Tunguska—The Crates are Here* (1984), in particular, the status of a manifesto and draws attention to its connections with the historical avant-garde's ambitions to subvert the boundaries between art and life.

In her examination of Schlingensief's *Deutschlandtrilogie*—which covers the period immediately prior to and post Germany's reunification in 1989—Kristin T. Vander Lugt explores the provocative manner in which the trilogy engages with post-war Germany and its cultural processes of coming to terms with both the past (*Vergangenheitsbewältigung*) and the present (*Gegenwartsbewältigung*). She argues that Schlingensief is driven by a desire to unveil the hypocrisies, discriminatory practices and repressed violent tendencies that are masked by post-war Germany's desired vision of itself as a post-fascist liberal democracy.

In Chapter 3, Sandra Umathum discusses Schlingensief's early works in the theatre and, in particular, his attempts to break down the fourth wall which—in the context of conventional theatre—separates the audience from the activities of the performers onstage. The 1996 production, *Rocky Dutschke '68*, is the main focus of her chapter and she locates its open, ambiguous structure within the framework of 'post-dramatic theatre' as theorized by Hans Thies-Lehmann. Her personal approach provides an insight into the active spectatorial relationship facilitated by Schlingensief's highly challenging theatre productions, and highlights how his work attempts to elide theatrical convention by means of its radical aesthetic.

The subsequent three chapters follow on from Umathum's analysis of the active, participatory mode of engagement facilitated by *Rocky Dutschke* by examining the reinscription of the audience as performers in a series of radical and political projects that took place—for the most part—in the public realm beyond the theatre. Focusing on *Passion Impossible* (1997), *Chance 2000*, and *Please Love Austria*, each of the chapters explores how—and with what effects—Schlingensief has sought to mobilize the public sphere.

In Chapter 4, Anna Teresa Scheer investigates Schlingensief's co-optation of public spaces for political action via an analysis of his socially engaged project *Passion Impossible* in Hamburg. Here, Schlingensief abandoned the theatre in favour of setting up a mission for homeless people and drug addicts whilst encouraging them to participate in a series of activist events at key locations in the city. Drawing on Erving Goffman's application of theatrical principles to social interaction, Scheer contends that by rejecting a theatre venue in favour of a series of public events, Schlingensief was—in line with Goffman's ideas—attempting to re-stage reality for socially critical purposes.

Schlingensief's interventions into the German federal election campaign of 1998 are the focus of Solveig Gade's study in Chapter 5 which outlines the events surrounding the founding of Schlingensief's own political party: *Chance 2000*. Through an exploration of his inclusion of the unemployed and disabled as electoral candidates, Gade argues that *Chance 2000* sought to create a utopian and universal public sphere that both encouraged and enabled direct participation in political events, and facilitated public reflection on the shortcomings of the activities and policies of the established political parties.

In Chapter 6, Denise Varney explores *Please Love Austria* a decade after its inception. The most well-known of Schlingensief's projects outside the German-speaking world, *Please Love Austria* (which was inspired by the *Big Brother* television series) created international controversy by not only placing asylum-seekers in a shipping container in the centre of Vienna, but by encouraging Austrians to vote online for the foreigners/contestants they would like to see deported. After carefully summarizing previous literature on the project, Varney offers a reading of this highly complex, multimedia work in terms of Bertolt Brecht's concept of *Gestus*, positing that Schlingensief's project can be seen as a revitalization of Brecht's epic theatre.

Continuing this focus on Schlingensief's reworking of popular television programs in an attempt to mobilize debate about contemporary politics, in Chapter 7 Tara Forrest explores *Freakstars 3000*: a reality television series (and subsequent film) that draws on the casting show format. Focusing on Theodor Adorno's writings on mass culture and the enabling effects of Schönberg's atonal music, Forrest argues that Schlingensief's 'atonal re-enactment' of the casting show format as a contest for people with disabilities, produces a sense of discord that challenges the audience to question why—and with what effects—disabled people are largely excluded from the public sphere generated by the media.

The following two chapters focus on two intermedial theatre productions that were produced in response to the events of 9/11 and the subsequent wars in Afghanistan and Iraq. In Chapter 8, Brechtje Beuker concentrates on *ATTA ATTA, Art has Broken Out!* (2003): a production that developed out of ideas explored in a seminar on art and terrorism at the Volksbühne in 2002. As Beuker makes clear, far from providing the audience with a clear-cut statement on terrorism and the events of 9/11, this complex, multilayered production (which draws on and recycles media images of violence, Christian and Islamic symbols, and the work of Beuys and the Vienna Actionists) encourages the audience to critically examine their own investment in 'fictions of violence'.

As revealed by Morgan Koerner in the following chapter, this process of self-reflection is also prompted by Schlingensief's *Bambiland* (2004), which is similarly preoccupied with images of violence and, more specifically, with the televisual representation of the Iraq war. In this highly complex stage production—which mixes video footage of violence and destruction with (quotations of) avant-garde performance—Koerner argues that Schlingensief prompts the audience to critically reflect on the connections between—and spectatorial effects generated by—sensationalist news programs, infotainment and pornography.

The development of Schlingensief's 'Animatographs' across a range of different contexts is the focus of Roman Berka's study in Chapter 10, which provides a detailed analysis of a number of large-scale, site-specific installations that Schlingensief produced between 2004 and 2007. For Berka, the animatographs (which were inspired, in part, by the work of Beuys and Dieter Roth) mark an important point in the development of Schlingensief's career, not only because they are constructed out of an amalgam of practices, materials, and ideas gleaned from theatre, film, installation, art, performance and opera, but because they also mark Schlingensief's entry into the art gallery and the museum.

In Chapter 11, Florian Malzacher provides a detailed analysis of Schlingensief's 'cancer trilogy', which consists of three works that he produced after being diagnosed with cancer in 2008. While Schlingensief's illness is very much the driving force—and central focus—of these productions, Malzacher notes that a 'fascination with illness and death' also features prominently in Schlingensief's early films, and in more recent theatre productions such as *Art and Vegetables, A. Hipler* (2004) which focused, in part, on an exploration of the debilitating effects produced by ALS (Amyotrophic Lateral Sclerosis).

Schlingensief's battle with cancer is also explored in detail in Chapter 12, which consists of an interview conducted by Malzacher, in which Schlingensief discusses, among other topics: the conditions which led to the development of his 'cancer trilogy'; his relationship to his parents and the broader 'family' with which he works; his early influences as a young film-maker; the relationship between art and politics; his initial impressions of working in theatre; and his recent fascination, and preference for working, with opera. Finally, a scholarly reading list of English and German language sources is contained at the end of the book. While not exhaustive, like the book as a whole, its inclusion was driven by the desire to provide a point of departure for further research on Schlingensief's work.

Endnotes

1. 'One must', Schlingensief notes in a television interview with Alexander Kluge, 'look at things from multiple aspects, and the person who doesn't is probably well placed in politics but, unfortunately, no longer in life'. Kluge, A. (2003), 'Das Zelt ist der Gedanke des Nomaden/Christoph Schlingensief über die Kunst als Speerspitze des Terrors', *News & Stories*, SAT 1, 7 December. All translations are, unless otherwise noted, our own.

2. Schlingensief quoted in Anon., 'Keine Wiener-"Konzentrationswoche"' (2000), *Die Presse*, 7 June.

3.   The trilogy consists of: *100 Years of Adolf Hitler* (1988–89); *The German Chainsaw Massacre: The First Hour of Reunification;* (1990) and *Terror 2000—Intensive Care Unit Germany* (1992).

4.   Schlingensief quoted in Seeßlen, G. (1998), 'Vom barbarischen Film zur nomadischen Politik', in J. Lochte and W. Schulz (eds.), *Schlingensief! Notruf für Deutschland. Über die Mission, Das Theater und die Welt des Christoph Schlingensief*, Hamburg: Rotbuch Verlag, p. 42.

5.   This 'family' consists of, among other members: Achim von Paczensky (who died in 2009), Kerstin Grassmann, Helga Stöwhase, Horst Gelloneck, Mario Garzaner and family, Dietrich Kuhlbrodt, Werner Brecht (who died in 2003), former Fassbinder actresses Irm Hermann and Margit Carstensen, and Schlingensief's regular dramaturge Carl Hegemann.

6.   These include *United Trash* (1995) and *The 120 Days of Bottrop* (1997), the latter a pastiche of Pier Paolo Pasolini's 1975 film *Salo, or the 120 Days of Sodom*. During this period, Schlingensief also directed *Freakstars 3000* (2003) which served as a feature length documentation of his 2002 television series of the same title.

7.   These include *Rocky Dutschke '68* (1996), *Radio P.S.1 Radioshow* (1999), *Camp without Limits* (1999), *Rosebud* (2002), and *18 Radio plays in one Second* (2006).

8.   Gilles, C. (2009), *Kunst und Nicht Kunst: Das Theater von Christoph Schlingensief*, Würzburg: Königshausen & Neumann, p. 62.

9.   In 2007, Schlingensief also produced *Die Piloten* which, in a similar vein to *Talk 2000*, features Schlingensief in conversation with a diverse group of guests. Although the program has not, to date, been broadcast on television, Cordula Kablitz-Post has produced a feature length film that documents the production of the 'pilot' episodes: *Christoph Schlingensief—Die Piloten* (2009).

10. Schlingensief, C. and Hegemann, C. (1998), *Chance 2000: Wähle Dich Selbst*, Cologne: Kiepenhauer & Witsch, p. 18 and p. 73.

11. Schödel, H. (2006), 'Blubbernde Animatografen', *Süddeutsche Zeitung*, no. 19, 24 January, p. 12.

12. This production was staged at the *Bayreuther Festspiele*. Subsequent productions appeared at the same festival in 2005, 2006 and 2007.

13. These include: *The Animatograph, Iceland Edition: House of Obsession*, Reykjavik, Iceland (2005); *The Animatograph, German Edition: Odin's Parsipark*, Schloss Neuhardenberg, Germany (2005); *The Animatograph, Africa Edition: The African Twin Towers*, Namibia (2005); and *Area 7, St. Matthew's Expedition*, Burgtheater, Vienna (2006).

14. These exhibitions include: *Double Agent* (group exhibition), Institute for Contemporary Arts, London; *Christoph Schlingensief: The King lives within Me* (solo exhibition), Kunstraum Innsbruck; and *To Burn Oneself with Oneself—The Romantic Damage Show* (group exhibition), De Appel, Amsterdam.

15. These include: *The Current State of Things* (2008); *A Church of Fear for the Stranger in Me* (2008); and *Mea Culpa—A ReadyMadeOpera* (2009). The second production, *A Church of Fear,* was described by Schlingensief as 'A Fluxus Oratorio'—a description which also signals his direct connection to that movement. See http://www.kirche-der-angst.de/. Accessed 28 August 2009. Throughout his treatment, Schlingensief recorded feelings, thoughts, and experiences on a dictaphone that were later published in the form of a book: Schlingensief, C. (2009), *So schön wie hier kanns im Himmel gar nicht sein: Tagebuch einer Krebserkrankung*, Köln: Kiepenheuer & Witsch.

16. Schlingensief, C., 'Festspielhaus Africa: Einführung', http://www.festspielhaus-afrika.com/weblog/?page_id=2, 25.01.2009. Accessed 24 August 2009.

17. Sell, M. (2005), *Avant-Garde Performance and the limits of criticism*, Ann Arbor: University of Michigan Press, p. 177.

18. Sell, M. (2005: 150). Sell is quoting Roland Barthes.

19. Harlan, V. (2007), 'Conversation with Joseph Beuys', in *What is Art?: Conversation with Joseph Beuys*, Forest Row: Clairview Books, p. 9.

20. Harlan, V. (2007: 21).

21. Beuys quoted in Harlan, V. (2007), 'A Note on the Text', in *What is Art?: Conversation with Joseph Beuys,* p. 2.

22. Harlan, V. (2007), 'Conversation with Joseph Beuys', p. 17.

23. Stachelhaus, H. (1991), *Joseph Beuys* (trans. D. Britt), New York: Abbeville Press, p. 108.

24. Stachelhaus, H. (1991), p. 109.

25. See Seeßlen, G. (1998), p. 58.

26. See Schlingensief, C. (1998), 'Wir sind zwar nicht gut, aber wir sind da', in J. Lochte and W. Schulz (eds.), p. 30.

27. Koberg, R. (1998), 'Das Schlingensief Theater', in J. Lochte and W. Schulz (eds.), p. 156.

28. Anon. (1996), 'Rattenfänger von Berlin', *Focus Magazin,* no. 27/07, http://www.focus.de/politik/deutschland/theater-rattenfaenger-von-berlin_aid_159968.html. Accessed 12 August 2009.

29. Siemons (2000) notes: 'He who wants to provoke is himself sure about his means and his goals. He knows how the world is and how it should be'. 'Der Augenblick, in dem sich das Reale zeigt. Über Selbstprovokation und die Leere', in M. Lilienthal und C. Philipp (eds.), *Schlingensiefs Ausländer Raus. Bitte Liebt Österreich*, Frankfurt am Main: Suhrkamp Verlag, p.120.

30. The many television interviews that Alexander Kluge has conducted with Schlingensief over the past fifteen years are exemplary for the dynamic way in which Kluge as interviewer seeks to engage both Schlingensief and the audience in a conversation that moves imaginatively between a diverse range of issues and ideas while seeking to address the complexity of the topic in question. See, for example, Kluge, A. (2007), 'Im erster Linie bin ich Filmemacher: Begegnung mit Christoph Schlingensief', in S. Huber and C. Philipp (eds.), *Alexander Kluge: Magazin des Glücks*, Wien: Springer-Verlag, pp.109–114. The full discussion can also be viewed on the DVD that is contained in the book.

31. Dawson, J. (1977), 'But why are the questions so abstract: An Interview with Alexander Kluge', in J. Dawson, *Alexander Kluge and the Occasional Work of a Female Slave*, New York: Zoetrope, p. 37.

32. Reitz, E., Kluge, A. and Reinke, W. (1988), 'Word and Film', trans. M. Hansen, *October*, 46, Fall, p. 87.

33. See Schlingensief, C. (1998), 'Wir sind zwar nicht gut, aber wir sind da', p. 27.

34. See Schlingensief, C. (1998), p. 35.

35. Schlingensief, C. and Koegel, A. (2005), 'Just a brushstroke...', in A. Koegel and K. König (eds.), *AC: Christoph Schlingensief: Church of Fear*, Köln: Museum Ludwig and Verlag der Buchhandlung Walther König, p. 39.

THE TUNGUSKA MANIFESTO: SCHLINGENSIEF'S CRITIQUE OF FILM AND THE RESITITUTION OF EXPERIENCE

Richard Langston

At the age of seven, Christoph Schlingensief visited his first film festival in the spring of 1968: the scandal-ridden fourteenth annual 'International Short Film Festival' held in his hometown of Oberhausen. A year when vanguard films and politically radicalized film-makers disrupted film festivals throughout Europe, when 'underground' became the locus of cutting-edge cinematic creativity, and when attributes like 'structural', 'material', 'expanded' and 'lyrical' shaped experimental film aesthetics. 1968 was also when the 7-year-old Schlingensief shot his first 8mm film. Amidst this flurry of filmic innovation in the Federal Republic of Germany, Schlingensief cycled through the gamut of cinematic modes (narrative, documentary and experimental film) with the help of family members and peers before taking his college entrance exams. After two failed attempts beginning in 1980 to matriculate into Munich's University of Television and Film, he found himself back at square one: an outsider of West Germany's fledgling institutions of experimental film. After brief mentorships under mainstream director Franz Seitz and then experimental film-maker Werner Nekes, Schlingensief produced between 1983 and 1984, a programmatic film trilogy comprised of two 16mm shorts and a 16mm feature film that he dubbed his 'Critique of Film—Film as Neurosis'. Often overshadowed by his second widely received topical trilogy, the infamous *Deutschlandtrilogie/German Trilogy* (1989–92), the long history of Schlingensief's unrelenting efforts to gain entry into film-making culminated in this first largely overlooked trilogy. Upon close inspection, Schlingensief's 'Trilogy on the Critique of Film' reveals not only the aesthetic and political dimensions of Schlingensief's films, but also the grounds on which he rejected the many institutions of cinema which he had for so long observed, studied and suffered. Often thought of as a decade of unprecedented postmodern heterogeneity in German experimental film, the early eighties were for Schlingensief that decisive moment when he officially laid claim to his own brand of politicized film-making.[1] As will be demonstrated in this chapter, Schlingensief's first trilogy—a manifesto whose relevance arguably lingers on well into his present post-cinematic work—sets its crosshairs on experimental cinema's self-absorption after 1968, its growing remove from social reality, as well as its alienation of quotidian experience.

Although never explicitly designated by Schlingensief or his critics as comprising a programmatic manifesto of sustained importance for his career, his 'Trilogy on the Critique of Film' not only operates with the bravado of the 'high' manifestos of the historical avant-garde but also seeks, at the very least, to trace the contours of how to change the world in which we live for the better. The most evolved manifestos, explains Mary Ann Caws, must by definition exert a manipulatory force intent on disabusing a public of its dominant assumptions, values and knowledge.[2] Oppositional, crazed, noisy and excessive, manifestos assign the immediate transformation of the world unparalleled urgency and, to this end, call upon their audiences to bring about this change, often not without some form of violence. For Schlingensief, the linchpin of this transformation is experience. Long a central concern for both German artists and philosophers alike, the status of modern experience has continued to garner bleak diagnoses. According to practitioners of the Frankfurt School, for example, the cornerstone of modernity has always been the poverty of experience; the world of modern progress stunts human experience by rendering it solipsistic, amnesiac, and thus isolated, both spatially and temporally. In contradistinction to lonely individual experiences (*Erlebnisse*) endemic to life in an administered society, thinkers like Walter Benjamin and Theodor Adorno sought to facilitate through aesthetic experiences the restitution of authentic, undamaged, trans-historical experience (*Erfahrung*) shared within a collective.[3]

Lightning rods during the rebellious late sixties, Benjamin and Adorno exert, however, little influence over Schlingensief in the early eighties. Instead of the melancholy science of negative dialectics, Schlingensief opts for another more jovial approach for restoring experience (as will be clarified shortly). Nevertheless, he is in agreement with the masters of Critical Theory that works of art are indeed capable of rejuvenating quotidian experience today in the name of the public sphere. And yet Schlingensief refrains from awarding the work of art an exclusive and unassailable power to reinvigorate experience. As will be demonstrated, regaining lost experience is a function of the unpredictable collisions between Schlingensief's works, be they cinematic or theatrical, and the reality into which they are inserted. In keeping with the manifestos of the historical avant-garde, art for Schlingensief may still very well be able to unseat dominant reality and its sway over experience. Far more likely, however, is reality's ability to foil or even destroy insurrectionist art by unexpectedly expanding its playing field under the demands of art, rendering itself transparent or sidestepping art's volleys altogether. In either scenario, affirmative experience (in the sense of *Erlebnis*) is made alien in public with the hope that it will undergo a collective transformation for the better (in the sense of *Erfahrung*).

Attributed by Schlingensief and his critics as a defining feature of his theatrical turn *Störfaktor Realität/Disruption Factor Reality* (1993)—properly understood as both the disruption of reality *and* reality as disruption—is the name of this collision between reality and art that potentially remakes collective experience, and it is as much at work in Schlingensief's debut film trilogy as his more recent theatrical productions.[4] Grasped retrospectively from his current twenty-first century post-cinematic standpoint, the cornerstone of Schlingensief's 'Trilogy on the Critique of Film' reads today more clearly than ever as a manifesto that has continued to subtend everything the artist has accomplished as a film-maker, television host, radio playwright, action artist, and theatre and opera director.[5]

Film about film: The story of *Tunguska*

Making sense of Schlingensief's 'Trilogy' is no easy task.[6] Only nine minutes long, the first of the three films is a dizzying non-narrative short entitled *Phantasus Must Be Different: Phantasus Go Home* (1983). Also completed in 1983, the follow-up was the second twelve-minute short *The Nonchalant Ones Are Coming: What Happened to Magdalena Jung?* The apogee of the trilogy, the feature film *Tunguska—The Crates Are Here* (1984), was first screened in September 1984 and took third place in the 1985 North Rhine-Westphalian young film-maker awards. Increasingly story-driven with each installment, Schlingensief's trilogy lacks any and all obvious cohesion; how the more accessible *Tunguska* builds upon its more experimental predecessors is anything but clear. Deciphering each film is equally challenging. The course taken below thus begins in reverse by fleshing out the story of *Tunguska* with the intention of eventually weaving all three films together into the coherent conceptual whole that is Schlingensief's manifesto.

Tunguska—we spectators are told in the scrolled back-story that opens the film—refers not to that mysterious cataclysmic explosion that flattened over two thousand square miles of Siberia in June 1908. No, *Tunguska* marks the title of a mysterious film that debuted in 1967 and was scrapped shortly thereafter. Its creators, a trio of mad avant-garde researchers, soon discovered in the film's wake, 'new aspects of zeitgeist and filmic language'. What we spectators are not told is the fact that the researchers' subsequent sixteen years were a complete failure. In spite of their revolutionary discoveries, their ambitions to expose indigenous peoples inhabiting the Arctic Circle to avant-garde films were foiled when their plane crashed in Siberia. Unable to execute their anthropological study of a first contact between avant-garde cinema and 'primitive' peoples, Ireen Fitzler (Anna Fechter), Lossowitsch (Vladimir Konetzny) and ringleader Roy Glas (Alfred Edel) bided their time screening avant-garde films together in an austere Siberian ruin while chanting 'Strength and Power!' Over the years, the researchers, alone and lonely, suffered from a lack of subjects on which to exercise their quest for power and therefore switched gears from innovation to critique. The institution of film has grown hysterical, Glas asserts in his manifesto that opens the film, and is purportedly included in an imaginary anthology from the future (printed in the Orwellian year 1984) called 'The Spectator as Film'. The institution of film is anything but avant-garde, Glas decrees. Film, he insists, is inherently neurotic and this neurosis must be disavowed if it is ever to be truly avant-garde.

As simple as the story may seem thus far, it fills its spectators rather full of seemingly unanswerable questions. Why do the researchers resolve to stay in Siberia? Why are lovebirds Rolf (Mathias Colli) and Tina (Irene Fischer) travelling on holiday through this barren Siberian landscape and, moreover, why do they waste their last drops of gasoline driving into the fortified clutches of the three seemingly mad avant-gardists? Who is the parentless and nearly unintelligible recluse Mr Norbert (Norbert Schliewe) who finds moving images of Rolf and Tina tucked away in the heads of wild mushrooms?

Figure 1: A collage of stills from *Tunguska*—Tina wanders through the Siberian forest. Mr Norbert peeks at Tina and Rolf in a mushroom cap. The avant-garde researchers march to their lair.

Who is the affected Major Father Help (Christoph Schlingensief) who orchestrates a fiery symbol of hopeful redemption for all humanity only then later to be crushed to death by Mr Norbert? How do the eponymous crates full of provisions suddenly appear outside the lair of the avant-gardists? Does Tina undergo a psychic transformation while being forced to watch Kenneth Anger's film *Eaux d'Artifice* (1953)? And what does her fairytale about a dance teacher from Tunguska have to do with Oskar Fischinger's abstract animated short *Komposition in Blau* (1935), which is shown in its entirety shortly before her untimely death? Does Tina really die or is the image of her funeral pyre an illusion? Does Rolf really trade places with the avant-gardists at the close of the film, when the researchers carjack their way out of Siberia, or are they too locked inside the compound, as were Rolf and Tina at the outset of the film? What exactly is this vertiginous film featuring mad film-makers and innocent filmgoers about, and what—if anything—does that have to with the two preceding shorts? In order to make sense of *Tunguska*, viewers must obviously be prepared for the gaps and jumps in the film's fragmented storylines that forestall any single narrative arc from emerging. Similarly, viewers must account for the myriad formal experiments that punctuate and disrupt the film at regular intervals. A thorough analysis of the film must therefore acknowledge how *Tunguska* struggles to tell a (fragmentary) story (reliant on multiple genre conventions like the fairy tale, the horror film, and the morality play) *and* reflects simultaneously on the medium of film (much like the structural film experiments from the previous decade).

Magdalena Jung, reality, experience

As the preceding summary makes clear, *Tunguska* is an allegorical film about film. It devotes its attention to both the medium of film as well as the institutions of experimental film-making, which, according to Glas's back-story scrolled at the outset of the film, claims to explore 'new aspects of [...] filmic language'. Forging a new film language would naturally assume one knows first what exactly film was, is, and could possibly become. Avant-garde researcher Roy Glas is certain of this. In his manifesto, which opens *Tunguska*, Glas writes: 'The hysteria of the last couple of years must be laid bare and its characteristics recognised: Film as a form of neurosis'. According to Sigmund Freud's foundational definitions of neurosis, the neurotic individual evinces a disturbed relationship to external reality insofar as reality incurs loss and symbolic substitution; cogent of reality's existence, the neurotic nevertheless ignores or allegorizes particular features of reality, especially those responsible for triggering the unsuccessful repression of instinctual drives that in the end bring forth hysterical symptoms.[7] This departure from reality, which Schlingensief also calls 'neurosis', runs to the core of his trilogy. Neurosis manifests itself quite differently, however, in Schlingensief's other two films. In *Phantasus*, loneliness is the sign of this neurosis and is identified as the cornerstone

27

of humankind's unfortunate modern condition. The connective tissue between the first and last film, *What Happened to Magdalena Jung?* equates neurosis with a poverty of everyday experience engendered by the dour institutions of film that dominate the cinematic landscape of the Federal Republic. But unlike the capstone of the trilogy that holds dominant cinema responsible for fomenting misery, *Magdalena Jung* serves up a cinematic solution.

'On November the twelfth, nineteen eighty-two, Ladies and Gentlemen'—news anchor Mrs Air (Martina Wolfs) explains at the beginning of *What Happened to Magdalena Jung?*—'Magdalena Jung leaves the firm ground of reality and declares she can fly'. The only individual invested in Jung's neurotic declaration is a film school instructor, Mr Search (Rudolf Färber), who otherwise '[sits] with guitar, sunglasses, and hat on the endless beach of [cinema's] prairie'. Lena's arrival has had nothing less than an earth-shattering effect on the instructor and his preconceived notion of reality. Certain of the 'magnitude and value of German cinema' and a firm believer in scientifically verifiable laws of nature, Mr Search witnesses Lena leap 20 metres from an overpass and then fly onto the hood of his car. Unscathed by her flagrant disregard of the laws of gravity, she runs away, leaving him dumbfounded. After two more unbelievable sightings, he nearly apprehends Lena in a wintry field at the close of the short, charging her with disavowing the laws of nature before she flies away once again. 'Oh, that's okay', remarks blue-blooded Mr Colli (Mathias Colli) who, like Mrs Air, intermittently interposes the story of Lena and Mr Search with haughty commentary. If neurosis is marked by a (partial) disavowal of the laws of reality, then Lena is thoroughly neurotic. And yet the film instructor is as well, for his own hysterical outbreak at the close of the film makes evident the fictional status of those natural laws that presumably necessitate aviation technologies for human flight. The crucial distinction between Lena's and Mr Search's neuroses lies in the fact that he disavows the very existence of his own neurotic anxieties.[8]

Anything but a denial of gravity itself, *What Happened to Magdalena Jung?* likens the laws of film-making existent in its own day with those irrefutable universal laws of nature. Lena's declaration of flight—later paralleled by a hysterical young film-maker's act of launching his (fake) camera off an office building's roof—scoffs at the film school instructor's unwavering narrow-minded grasp of film-making wedded to deadly serious fundamental rules (allegorized as gravity) and excessive production teams (allegorized as a flight crew). All this filmic baggage results in impotence that Schlingensief's short reacts against, insofar as it repeatedly professes to accrue a power otherwise overlooked by the German film establishment. In an English voiceover accompanying an intertitle of the original German of Ernst Jünger's reworked *The Adventurous Heart*, Schlingensief introduces his audience early on to an archaic form of power Jünger calls *désinvolture*. Rendered in German roughly as '*Ungeniertheit*' and in English as 'casualness' or 'nonchalance', *désinvolture* marks the unquestionable attitude of the almighty sovereign, someone who administers power without second thought or reservation. Akin to arbitrary luck or supernatural magic, this power, says Jünger, is 'a special form of joviality' that acts like 'divine armour' capable of withstanding 'the horror of destruction'.[9] The destruction in question in Schlingensief's second short is that of film itself (thanks, in part, to the values upheld by Mr Search). Conversely, Lena the *désinvolture* embodies the very attitude capable of withstanding this ruination by virtue of the fact that she openly embraces her disavowal of reality.

Widely dismissed as a dyed-in-the-wool fascist, Ernst Jünger will certainly strike many a spectator as a not-so-unproblematic paragon for Schlingensief's emergent cinema.[10] Yet Schlingensief's progressive re-animation of Jünger in 1983 is anything but untimely. That same year Peter Sloterdijk published his *Critique of Cynical Reason*, in which he declared the exhaustion of Critical Theory's prescription for remedying the poverty of modern experience, in general, and its mandate that all critique must evince negativism and suffering, in particular. Counter to the malaise of postmodern cynical reason, Sloterdijk champions instead a not-so-new cheeky temperament endowed with the power of revitalizing reason. Not unlike Sloterdijk's figure of the kynical Diogenes who pisses in the public marketplace, Lena's joviality not only repudiates Mr Search's dour convictions about film-making but also functions as an allegory of a generative power with which another kind of emancipated film-making—one not consumed by itself—can emerge.[11] For Jünger, the aesthetic dimension is the privileged space where intoxicating pleasures of sovereign experience can unfold. Only when rendered sensuously and excessively can aesthetic reflection free itself from the clutches of a reality mired in oppressive narratives (like those propagated by Mr Search) and verge on an autonomous experience somewhere between astonishment and rapture.[12] Schlingensief thus brings to bear Jünger's concept of 'stereoscopic pleasure' in the disorienting formal construction of his second short by doubling, splitting, and flipping characters, languages, and even the screen itself.

Tunguska, terror, loneliness

Quoting Goethe's starry-eyed Faust before his encounter with Mephistopheles, *What Happened to Magdalena Jung?* closes with its gravity-defying heroine scurrying onward toward a 'new day' and 'new shores' while Mr Search lies prostrate and flummoxed in the industrial landscape of Mülheim. As the film fades to black it flashes its last subtitles, reminding viewers that Lena's sprightly dash forward stands in stark opposition to the handicraft of dominant (experimental) film-making. Looking back two decades later, Schlingensief leads us to believe that Mr Search as well as the three crazed avant-garde researchers in *Tunguska* are stand-ins for his own mentor, Werner Nekes. 'After these two films [*Phantasus* and *Magdalena Jung*] I naturally developed a latent rage against Nekes', Schlingensief explains in Frieder Schlaich's 2005 documentary. 'I thought, why should I become Nekes? What's with all this crap? [...] I wanted to separate myself [from him] and then I made the film [...] *Tunguska—The Crates are Here*.'[13] Best known for his unparalleled collection of proto-cinematic toys, Nekes, an established experimental film-maker in his own right, is never named outright in Schlingensief's trilogy. Yet avant-garde ringleader Roy Glas who opens *Tunguska* certainly seems to ventriloquize Nekes. Conjecture or not, Glas's 'new', albeit undisclosed, 'aspects' of 'filmic language', to which he alludes in his opening manifesto, are remarkably akin to Nekes's own declarations about the unique grammar of film, its reducibility down to the 'smallest unit[s] of filmic language', film's ever-evolving 'time/space relations', as well as its pure 'visual motion'.[14] Speculative resemblances between Glas and Nekes aside, Schlingensief's *Tunguska* shifts gears markedly when compared to *Magdalena Jung*; whereas the preceding short begins to envision a new film-making practice free from dogma, *Tunguska* ventures backward to territory first mined in the first short of his trilogy, *Phantasus Must Be Different*, namely that of cinema's badly mistreated spectator.

Tunguska is primarily a moralizing story about torture and disfigurement. It casts the history of avant-garde and experimental film-making as a story of grossly abused power. It not only tells but also shows viewers how the vanguard exploration and development of film's unique visual language has resulted in a crude biological objectification of spectators, in general, and of female spectators, in particular. It also illustrates, with its tragic narrative about Rolf and Tina, how the entire tradition of non-narrative cinema is a dead end set with a lethal trap. This terrorism of experimental cinema rears its head initially as a ruse. After their run-ins with the recluse, Mr Norbert and the hysterical semiotician Major Father Help, Tina and Rolf take refuge in the seemingly abandoned lair of the avant-garde researchers. Right when they think the coast is clear, Ireen Fitzler raps unexpectedly at the door and summons the couple's help. An accident has occurred. Fischer, a biologist specializing in 'phenomenological objects and related phenomena like [...] [the] constriction of the body', employs Rolf and Tina to drive her and Lossowitsch to the first of two large wooden crates that appear in the film. Seen through the passenger window of Rolf's car, Fitzler fishes out a bottle of wine from the crate; the emergency turns out to be an overdramatic liquor run. Despite having witnessed Fitzler and Lossowitsch's hedonistic indulgences firsthand, Rolf and Tina remain unenlightened as to the function and contents of the crates. After a second jaunt to another crate full of soup cans, chicken and ham, they still remain baffled.

'The crates that the researchers bring along [on their aborted expedition]', Schlingensief's alter ego Christopher Krieg explains in the publicity packet produced by his studio DEM Film, 'represent every single frame [...]. It can contain new contents if the spectator is in the position to forget the director'.[15] To be sure, there are two concatenated sets of crates at work in *Tunguska*, those the researchers serve up to Rolf and Tina, and those Schlingensief allows us spectators to feast on. As for the former, they are, on the one hand, a source of basic nutrients and, on the other hand, a path toward intoxication. While the preciousness of the crates is self-evident to the researchers, their mundanity fails to entice Rolf and Tina. As they are unaware of the 'joys' within the researchers' crates—obvious metaphors for the researchers' experimental films—Fitzler collects her primitive surgical utensils and Glas and Lossowitsch prepare the screening room. 'Fischinger or Eggeling?' Glas asks the clueless Rolf, referring to two early European pioneers of abstract film. After Fitzler explains how she uses an ordinary fork to perform tiny operations on the corneas of film spectators that constrict their field of vision, Rolf and Tina are straddled alongside a 16mm projector and forced to watch Lossowitsch, shrouded in a white sheet, dance in front of a projection of Kenneth Anger's *Eaux d'Artifice*. Soon the ominous acousmatic organ soundtrack returns and the performative spectacle gives way to a flurry of psychedelic in-camera and post-production distortions. Following a woman's off-screen high-pitched scream and a simulated glitch with the projector that leads us to temporarily believe that the film has been damaged, we then see a now rabid Tina who has fully succumbed to Glas's manipulations.

Just how penetrating and detrimental Glas' will to 'strength and power' is becomes clear when Rolf and Tina retire to their dishevelled bedroom for the night. Rolf collapses in Tina's arms in bed and she begins to tell a macabre fairytale-cum-cartoon while evincing signs of a nascent psychiatric disorder: 'A long, long time ago there lived a very bad dance instructor in Tunguska...'. Tina's violent story about the legendary explosion in Tunguska ends happily; although a mob of animated blue building blocks murders its creators in the course of the story, the aforementioned dance instructor manages to avoid a similarly gruesome fate. 'And if he hasn't died yet', Tina says, using only the first half of the traditional German fairytale ending, leaving us wondering whether he is still alive and, if so, where he lives today. Certainly not dead, the story's dance instructor is but a prior incarnation of the avant-garde researchers now terrorizing Rolf and Tina. We viewers begin to realize, too, that the answer to Glas's cryptic question ('Fischinger or Eggeling?') posed prior to the compulsory screening was, in fact, the former. Through a conversion process facilitated by Anger's 1953 short, Tina now begins to think and presumably dream in a pure filmic language exemplified by the abstract visual poetry of Fischinger's *Komposition in Blau*. From then on, the unsuspecting spectators' fate goes down hill. Their attempts to extricate themselves from Tunguska fail. An enraged Tina drives Rolf's car off the road in mad pursuit of precious gasoline and sustains a lethal skull fracture in the process. Rolf sprints back to the avant-gardists' compound where Mr Norbert has undergone a conversion similar to Tina's. With Tina and Major Father Help dead, and Mr Norbert under a spell, Rolf, alone now and lonely, wishes to join Glas, Fitzler and Lossowitsch. 'No, Rolf, we're too different. Tina is dead!' explains Glas. 'We make solitudinarians!' decrees Lossowitsch, shortly before he and his collaborators abscond with Rolf's car.

Phantasus, spectatorship, community

'Loneliness', actress Irene Fischer explains in her orgasmic voiceover that begins the nine-minute short *Phantasus Must Be Different: Phantasus Go Home*, 'is nothing other than the recognition of man's inability to preoccupy himself'. Over the course of her erotically charged monologue, we learn that the arts (above all poetry) and sciences (empirical and speculative alike) are especially at fault for this calamity. Concurrently we see an infant accomplishing the exact opposite; entirely unaware of this inability, the child sits alone yet is anything but lonely. Consumed by itself and the immediate world inside and outside the *mise en scène*, the infant represents a point of origin to which self-reflective, enlightened and thus lonely adults yearn to return. This path away from loneliness is not foreclosed, she adds. On the contrary, it is 'wide open', she reassures us, 'but only as wide as we wish it to be'. At the close of *Tunguska*, no such path emerges for Rolf. He chases the avant-gardists to no avail. In *Phantasus*, however, Schlingensief unfurls two possible solutions to the problem of loneliness: the renunciation of all knowledge, and the building of communal experience out of childlike play. As for the first option, Fischer tells us the story of Phantasus, a youngling crowned with tender roses, who repudiates poetry, philosophy, psychology, and—above all—the unconscious. He locks himself in his bedroom with the resolve to never dream again. Suddenly overcome by forces beyond her control, Fischer's boney hands take on a life of their own; the creatures—or is it a single creature reflected in an imaginary mirror?—sniff one another, kiss and then keel over dead. In effect, the actress' body tells us that Phantasus' revolt against loneliness is nothing less than a narcissistic move with a deadly outcome.

The second solution to loneliness and the poverty of modern experience is illustrated by the Holletschek family. In six brief sequences interspersed regularly throughout the short, the eight-member family lovingly performs an assortment of crude acrobatic acts on a theatrical stage. The Holletscheks' routines evince neither skill nor talent. No family member, neither the parents nor any of their six children, stands out as particularly adept or competent. Harbingers of the many eccentrics, outcasts, and 'freaks' who will later populate Schlingensief's cast of characters, the Holletscheks show no power of self-reflection, no inhibition, and no awareness of any discriminating camera or audience. Certainly laughable to the average spectator, their performances achieve exactly that which Phantasus fails miserably to attain. Filmed with a long shot from a static camera, the Holletscheks appear as a close-knit family in which no single member assumes greater importance, an organic community (in Ferdinand Tönnies' sense of community or *Gemeinschaft*) thoroughly preoccupied with itself and capable of sustaining itself, not because of, but in spite of its risible public performances. They are neither lonely nor alone.

If Phantasus is indeed a film about spectatorship as Schlingensief has insisted, neither the rose-crowned Phantasus nor the acrobatic Holletscheks are necessarily the spectator Schlingensief's film addresses. 'Phantasus' he emphasized in an interview from 1985, 'is primarily about the position of the viewer.'[16] Accordingly, *we* are the spectators Schlingensief has in mind; Rolf and Tina are but stand-ins for us. And it is *our* indulgence in the critical distance inscribed in the architecture of cinema that Schlingensief's trilogy holds accountable for 'man's inability to preoccupy himself', his membership to a society of individuals, and ultimately his loneliness. If only, the film implies, you spectators were more like the Holletscheks and less like Phantasus!

'Everything will be different from now on!' screams Schlingensief at the close of his fourth and last hysterical monologue that concludes *Phantasus*. Delivered from inside a glassed-in white cube—certainly a reification of the crate metaphor central to *Tunguska*— the 24-year-old Schlingensief, presumably quoting the hopeless recluse Phantasus, invites us now, in retrospect, to ponder whether everything at stake in his trilogy has indeed changed for the better. Does *Phantasus* and, for that matter, *Magdalena Jung* and *Tunguska* succeed in transforming the terms of engagement we spectators enter into in the movie theatre and, if so, how? Does Lena's jovial renunciation of the institution of experimental film's standard denial of reality—in other words her neurotic rejection of the avant-garde's sense of reality—foreshadow a more mature *désinvolture* aesthetic yet to surface in Schlingensief's subsequent films? Do the allusions to the genre of the morality play underlying *Tunguska* develop into a political didacticism in Schlingensief's later work? Are we spectators not wiser spectators for witnessing Rolf and Tina's ruinous *naiveté* via-à-vis the terror of avant-garde cinema? Are the self-abandoned Holletscheks and their infantile playfulness in *Phantasus* the seeds of a coming community and communal experience that Schlingensief will go on to stage as a viable counter-public sphere? In response to all these enormous questions, Schlingensief, looking back after his turn to performance art and theatre, saw little if any success in his films. 'I look back at my films today', he explained in a 1998 interview:

> and have to admit to myself honestly that not one of my films was really successful. [...] Naturally my films were always supposed to be brilliant and bombastic. [...] in reality though my films are snail movies. They appear full of strength and motion but in reality you don't advance a centimetre.[17]

Whatever the grounds were for Schlingensief's shift away from film at the close of the twentieth century, his beginnings as a film-maker are anything but ineffectual or negligible. In a 2006 interview with comrade Alexander Kluge, Schlingensief confessed on the eve of his third production of *Parsifal* (2004) in Bayreuth, 'I really come out of film-making and the thing I find interesting about film is the fact that the work can be destroyed'. The anecdote that Schlingensief retells to drive home his point takes us back to *Tunguska*.

My first screening of this first film [...] ended in disaster because the projector took on a life of its own and chaffed the celluloid. Somehow the film caught on fire even though I had already filmed [...] the film burning using an animation stand. We had simulated the burning that later really took place.[18]

Art's simulation of disruption sought to fake reality's breakdown but in the end it was art that was destroyed by the contingencies of reality itself. For Schlingensief's first film trilogy, the primary target of *Störfaktor Realität* is a dominant form of experimental film-making bound to a closed and totalizing conceptualization of the medium and its purchase on reality, and intent on terrorizing its spectators in order to substantiate these foregone conclusions. Most pronounced with Magdalena Jung's fantastic decision to fly, but equally at work in the Holletschek's playful self-abandonment, Schlingensief's 'Trilogy on the Critique of Film' seeks out techniques with which to aggravate the conditions of reality, to render lines of flight away from a restricted and alienating reality defined by loneliness and toward an open reality enriched by more intense forms of joyous social experience. As such, reality for Schlingensief is neither inherently ominous nor essentially redemptive. Reality merely is, and—at least since his first trilogy— Schlingensief has been busy trying to make more of it with every means at his disposal. Contrary then to Freud who argues that neurosis diminishes reality, Schlingensief has continued to insist that neurosis is the necessary precondition for augmenting reality, for only by disrupting our relationship to it, can we enhance it.

Endnotes

1.   For an English-language catalogue of the heterogeneity of West German experimental film-making (in which Schlingensief is conspicuously absent), see Brinkmann, C. N. (1997), 'Collective Movements and Solitary Thrusts: German Experimental Film 1920–1990', in M. Hoolboom (ed.), *Millennium Film Journal*, 30:31, pp. 94–117. See pages 110–117 in particular.

2.   Caws, M.A. (2000), 'The Poetics of the Manifesto: Nowness and Newness', in M.A. Caws (ed.), *Manifesto: A Century of Isms*, Lincoln: The University of Nebraska Press, pp. xix–xxxi.

3.   See Jay, M. (2005), *Songs of Experience: Modern American and European Variations on a Universal Theme*, Berkeley: The University of California Press, pp. 312–360.

4.   'The principle of the "disruption factor reality" [*Störfaktor Realität*] already began in my first theatrical works at Berlin's Volksbühne [...]'. Schlingensief, C. (1998), 'Wir sind zwar nicht gut, aber wir sind da', in J. Lochte and W. Schulz (eds.), *Schlingensief! Notruf für Deutschland*, Hamburg: Rotbuch Verlag, p. 25. For an example of this scholarly periodization, see Hoffmann, A. (2000), 'Scheitern als Chance: Zur Dramaturgie von Christoph Schlingensief', in P. Reichel (ed.), *Studien zur Dramaturgie: Kontext, Implikationen, Berufspraxis*, Tübingen: Gunter Narr Verlag, pp. 247–248. Unless otherwise noted, all English translations from the German are those of the author.

5.   For more on Schlingensief's post-cinematic aesthetic politics, see Langston, R. (2008), 'Schlingensief's Peep Show: Post-Cinematic Spectacles and the Public Space of History', in R. Halle and R. Steingröver (eds.), *After the Avant-Garde: Contemporary German and Austrian Experimental Film*, Rochester: Camden House, pp. 204–223.

6.   The entire trilogy is available on DVD: Schlingensief, C. (2006), *Tunguska—Die Kisten sind da/ Tunguska—The Crates Are Here*, Berlin: Filmgalerie 451.

7.   See Freud, S. (2000), 'Neurose und Psychose' and 'Der Realitätsverlust bei Neurose und Psychose', in A. Mitscherlich, A. Richards and J. Strachey (eds.), *Studienausgabe*, vol. 3, Frankfurt am Main: Fischer Taschenbuch Verlag, pp. 333–337 and 357–361.

8.   The distinction of awareness is central here. On the difference between himself and the luminaries of New German Cinema, Schlingensief remarked in a 1984 interview that the director invested in social criticism is 'a neurotic director who does not admit to his neurosis. I'm not saying that I am not neurotic'. See Benman, D. (1984), 'Zeitgeist in Kisten: Oberhausener Filmemacher vollendet seine Trilogie', *Ortszeit Ruhr*, 7 September. This newspaper review, along with all other subsequent reviews, is included in the Filmgalerie 451 release of *Tunguska*.

9.   'Loosely adapted from a short story by Ernst Jünger', reads the opening credits in *What Happened to Magdalena Jung?* This story in question is certainly the second 'post-political' edition of Ernst Jünger's *The Adventurous Heart* (1960). See in particular 'Zur Désinvolture', in *Das abenteuerliche Herz: Figuren und Capriccios*, 2nd ed., *Werke*, vol. 7, Stuttgart: Ernst Klett Verlag, 1960, pp. 264–266. Jünger appropriates the original Spanish term *desemboltura* in Francis Bacon's essay 'Of Fortune' (1601).

10. For an example of this dismissal, see Huyssen, A. (1995), 'Fortifying the Heart–Totally: Ernst Jünger's Armored Texts', *Twilight Memories: Marking Time in a Culture of Amnesia*, New York: Routledge, pp. 127–144.

11. Cf. Sloterdijk, P. (1987), *Critique of Cynical Reason* (trans. Michael Eldred), Minneapolis: University of Minnesota Press, pp. 101–107. Although Sloterdijk is quick to label Jünger as 'one of the master thinkers of modern cynicism', he nevertheless stops short of dismissing him as a fascist, adding that Jünger's 'hunger for experience' (cf. *Erfahrungshunger* (Michael Rutschky, 1960)) is in keeping with New Left 'openness' and 'liberality' (pp. 462–463).

12. Cf. Jünger, p. 200, 'Jede stereoskopische Wahrnehmung ruft in uns ein Gefühl des Schwindels hervor'. See also Figal, G. (1998), 'Stereoscopic Experience: Ernst Jünger's Poetics of *The Adventurous Heart*', in *For a Philosophy of Freedom and Strife: Politics, Aesthetics, Metaphysics* (trans. Wayne Klein), Albany: State University of New York Press, pp. 91–107.

13. Schlaich, F. (2005), 'Christoph Schlingensief und seine Filme', *Christoph Schingensief und seine Filme—Interview und frühe Kurzfilme*, Berlin: Filmgalerie 451.

14. See, for example, Nekes, W. (1988), 'What Really Happens between the Frames', in E. Rentschler (ed.), *West German Filmmakers on Film: Visions and Voices*, New York: Holmes & Meier, pp 66–70. It is worth noting how the interdiegetic film *Tunguska*, presumably the handiwork of Glas, can be read as a sarcastic reference to Nekes's breakthrough film *jüm-jüm* (1967), released in the same year the former fictional work, Glas's *Tunguska* mentioned in the scrolled back-story, is first screened.

15. See the publicity packet that accompanies the Filmgalerie 451 release of *Tunguska* (2006).

16. Inge Freitag and Wolf Schwartz (1985), 'Heut' würde ich eine solche Ausbildung nicht mehr machen', *Filmfaust* 45, no pagination.

17. Schlingensief, C. (1998), 'Wir sind zwar nicht gut, aber wir sind da', in J. Lochte and W. Schulz (eds.), *Schlingensief! Notruf für Deutschland*, Hamburg: Rotbuch Verlag, p. 27.

18. Kluge, A. (2007), 'In erster Linie bin ich Filmemacher: Begegnung mit Christoph Schlingensief', in S. Huber and C. Philipp (eds.), *Magazin des Glücks*, Vienna:

Springer-Verlag, p. 109 and 113. Cf. Schlingensief, C. (1998), 'Wir sind zwar nicht gut, aber wir sind da', in J. Lochte and W. Schulz (eds.), *Schlingensief! Notruf für Deutschland*, Hamburg: Rotbuch Verlag, pp. 35–36.

AN OBSCENE RECKONING: HISTORY AND MEMORY IN SCHLINGENSIEF'S *DEUTSCHLANDTRILOGIE*

Kristin T. Vander Lugt

> The response of today's generation to the past will not be a response to history, but rather a response to the findings of the present and the present's image of the past that has arisen from rituals of dishonesty vis-à-vis that history. (Hans Jürgen Syberberg[1])

If Visconti's German Trilogy linked nineteenth century decadence, romantic idealism, and everyday fascism with the thwarted desires of male egos in crisis, and Fassbinder's BRD Trilogy mapped the historical amnesia of post-war Germany onto the female body, Schlingensief's *Deutschlandtrilogie/German Trilogy* (1989–92) is indiscriminate in situating the will to madness and the capacity for violence in the populace at large.[2] Beginning with a faux documentary of Hitler's downfall that draws parallels between the Nazi aestheticization of politics and the revolutionary promises of New German Cinema (*100 Years of Adolf Hitler: The Last Hour in the Führer's Bunker*, 1989), proceeding to a twisted spoof of a horror classic that depicts the literal cannibalization of East Germans by West Germans in the hours following the fall of the Wall (*The German Chainsaw Massacre: The First Hour of Reunification*, 1990), and ending with a bizarre detective flick that lays the blame for xenophobia and right-wing violence at the feet of not only the local neo-Nazi gang, but also the media, the police, and the local townspeople (*Terror 2000— Intensive Care Unit Germany*, 1992), the trilogy offers no spaces 'outside' or 'beyond' the politics of exclusion, no critical position that is not itself implicated in the system.

If there is any aesthetic unity between the three films in the *Deutschlandtrilogie*, it is in what George Seeßlen has called 'an aesthetics of destruction', related no doubt to what Schlingensief himself has described as one of the primary functions of art: 'the creation of fear'.[3] In the wake of the Left's largely failed attempts to prevent the folding-over of enlightenment into barbarism through the prohibition of violence, a process that became all too evident in the early 1990s when Germany witnessed a return of repressed right-wing violence and nationalist sentiment, Schlingensief's sexually deviant Nazis, chainsaw-wielding cannibals, and psychotic kidnappers—'people who haven't succeeded in dying'—consistently re-emerge, and violently so, in the post-fascist world to remind us of the past that will not pass away.[4] Appropriately, then, he begins his trilogy with the most insistent revenant of post-war Germany: Adolf Hitler.

100 Years of Adolf Hitler: The eternal return of the same

The first film in the *Deutschlandtrilogie*, *100 Years of Adolf Hitler* was filmed on a shoestring budget in sixteen hours from the morning of 28 November to the wee hours of 29 November in a dilapidated World War II bunker in the German town of Mühlheim, with a hand camera and a handheld spotlight.[5] The conditions of production therefore mimic the ostensible conditions of the historical bunker in the eleventh hour: the ground is shaking, provisions are minimal, figures move between brightly lit spots and total darkness in a kind of unintended chiaroscuro.[6]

The '100 Years' of the title—phrased like the title of a celebratory anniversary video—refer to the years between Hitler's birth in 1889 and the 1989 reunification of the two German states.[7] From the outset, then, the film suggests that Hitler is still 'with us', and—as Susan Sontag might have it—still fascinating us.[8] This 'mock centennial' title is a clever riff, not simply on the continued presence of Germany's fascist past but, more significantly, on the ceremonialization of 'Hitler' as image and idea in popular culture.[9] The title delegitimizes the image of Hitler as a monster, as a singular embodiment of evil whose extinction simultaneously marks the extinction of fascism.

The film is not motivated by plot, but by character. As David Hughes synopsises, 'There is […] no plot as such […], just nine utterly dehumanized characters maniacally awaiting their end'.[10] While the characters do correspond to the key figures of Hitler's entourage, there is certainly no pretence of historical accuracy—Göring and Fegelein are both here in the Führer's last hour, despite the fact that the former had already left and the latter had already been executed. Hitler himself is in fact the least maniacal of the characters—he is depressed to the point of despondency and on the verge of suicide throughout. Fegelein's main function appears to be running around exclaiming, 'Fuck! Fuck!', here quoting the mentally challenged character in Fassbinder's dark farce *Satan's Brew* (1976), a role also played by Volker Spengler. Goebbels (Dietrich Kuhlbrodt) is here as an incestuous father; Magda Goebbels (Margit Carstensen) is a hysterical murderess who, after marrying Eva Braun (who by the film's end has replaced the suicidal Hitler by giving herself a charcoal moustache) in a wedding ceremony presided over by Göring (Alfred Edel), gives birth to a cloth doll and dies during labour. Frau Goebbels is replaced by Fegelein, who adopts the cloth doll and, together with Eva Braun/Hitler, sends it down river in a metal tub, while the bunker TV broadcasts post-war conservative politician Franz Josef Strauss extolling—'from a politically non-judgemental standpoint'—the 'achievement' of the Germans during and after wartime. By interposing the image of a Nazi-lineage Moses figure (the cloth doll on its way to the promised land) with Strauss' words of praise (a conveniently elliptical act of remembrance), the film not only intimates that post-war Germany was born of perversion and destined to deny its true roots, but it also suggests that the post-war culture of amnesia went hand in hand with an illicit continuation of Hitler's new world order.

Though the film brazenly distorts historical fact and violates the laws of physics through its fusion of anachronistic times and places, it starts off with all the signs of rigorous authenticity. During the first 21 seconds, the viewer is confronted with a pitch-black screen and the sound of bombs exploding in the distance. The sound is crackly, with the telltale pops and clicks of an old recording. The handwritten credits shake, as if from the reverberations of the explosions. We are in the Führer's bunker and the Allies are approaching. But wait: at 22 seconds, we see a clapperboard, on which is written 'Udo Kier, Take 1, Date 28.11'. The stick claps down, we hear 'Take 1, go ahead', and on screen in medium shot, throwing a heavy shadow across the map of Germany behind him, is the actor Udo Kier, with a prototypical Hitler moustache and trench coat, smoking a cigarette and holding an AGFA videotape box. Kier/Hitler stares directly at the viewer and nonchalantly recites a list: 'Schnapps, Wim, Trotta, Nico, et cetera'. Military drums begin to roll and, after extinguishing his cigarette, Kier/Hitler peers down at what appears to be a script and slowly stands up to approach the map, caressing it lovingly as he presses his entire body against it and purrs: 'All of Germany is my homeland'. This same line is repeated by an announcer off-screen, and we hear a voice talking about the 40th Cannes Film Festival. As the iconic 'Thus Spake Zarathustra' theme begins—conjuring images of Strauss, Nietzsche, and *2001: A Space Odyssey* the announcer introduces director Wim Wenders, who appears on a small, fuzzy TV screen, intoning, 'We can improve the world's images, and in this manner, we can improve the world'.[11] A clapperboard appears again, a one-frame non-diegetic insert from an outdoor pond, then another clapperboard, and we see a boy in pyjamas standing before the poorly lit backdrop of the bunker, singing a children's song. The title credit appears, and suddenly we hear ragtime music as the actors' credits begin to appear.

These first two minutes of the film, tying together reality and representation, past and present, history and historiography, present the film's central thesis *in nuce*: despite all attempts to exorcise fascism—through liberal gestures toward improving the world through film or song—Hitler continues to reappear, to be re-staged and re-enacted. As Schlingensief later put it in an interview: 'Hitler hasn't been worn out since 1945'.[12] The film's main purpose, then, is to deconstruct the 'Hitler myth', to address the irrationality and pornographic violence of Nazism—and its continued presence—head-on, that is: irrationally and pornographically. Working strictly against the kind of historical realism that characterizes, for example, Oliver Hirschbiegel's detailed portrayal of the Führer's last days in his film *Downfall* (2004), Schlingensief suggests that there is more truth in the over-the-top: 'In the exaggerated situation, [there is] more truth to be found than in this compulsion to make something realistic. And hyperbole [...] is in the end more real than the real one is trying to reconstruct'.[13] That is, only by making visible the conditions of its own production, through hyperbole and self-reflexivity, can film represent reality in a way that is true and honest.

Accordingly, *100 Jahre Adolf Hitler* announces itself within the first 23 seconds as being a film about film, both by highlighting its own constructedness and unreality and also by engaging the legacy of New German Cinema on multiple levels. In addition to the references to Wenders and von Trotta, the film also uses actors who are readily recognizable from the most well known films of New German Cinema (as from many of Schlingensief's films) and who bear little to no resemblance to their historical referents. Although Schlingensief sees himself as following in the footsteps of Fassbinder & Co., by situating Wenders' famous desire to 'improve the world through pictures' against the backdrop of a regime that similarly engaged images in an attempt to found a new world order, the film suggests that New German Cinema proved inadequate in addressing the legacy of fascism precisely *because* it sought to bring the world 'better pictures'.[14] More than a self-reflexive discourse on cinema, however, *100 Years* is concerned primarily with the ways in which post-war German society has remembered (or mis-remembered) the Third Reich and subsequently perpetuated its spirit.

100 Years was shot, as Hughes recalls, 'at the end of a decade of solemn commemorations of national socialism in West Germany', commemorations that conjured the spectre of fascism in service of ritualistic exorcism, but did little to directly address the lingering traces of fascism.[15] These commemorations also emerged in the context of the so-called Historian's Debate (*Historikerstreit*), which several years earlier had sparked concerns over the 'normalization' of the Nazi past. By conflating past and present and—as his detractors might have it—relativizing mass murder through implicit comparison with aesthetic manipulation, the film enters directly into that debate. Indeed, *100 Years of Adolf Hitler* suggests that liberal democracy participates in the repression of historical memory and in the relativization of the Holocaust, by sublimating the fascination with Hitler into made-for-TV documentaries and 'pedagogical exorcisms'.[16] As Schlingensief relates in an interview included on the DVD version of the film:

> That's also the problem with this whole Neo-Nazi scene and all those things [...]. We haven't said 'Dig the shit up, wear it out, use it,' then it'll spin itself into nothingness and become tattered and no one will have any interest in putting on this old jacket. That doesn't happen, because of course high society always comes in and says 'No, for God's sake, cover it up, build a temple, madness, careful, beware, not one wrong word,' and so on.[17]

By rooting the existence of Neo-Nazism in high society's refusal to engage directly with the continued fascination with Hitler, and by subsequently making a film about fascism in the mode of trash horror mockumentary, Schlingensief suggests that coming to terms with the past (*Vergangenheitsbewältigung*) is not only a matter of politics, but a matter of taste as well. In an exasperated review of the film, Christa Thelen described the 'vibe' of *100 Years* as 'somewhere between performance theatre and beer tent', and derided what she saw as a formulaic approach to taboo-breaking where the only difference between one film and another lies in the order in which we see the dramatis personae 'puking, shitting, and fucking'.[18] To be sure, the focus on bodily functions and the interrogation of taste mark *100 Years* as not only a radical experiment in abjection, but also as a successor of the neo-avant-garde tradition. The scene in which Hitler dips his derriere into a container of brown fluid—presumably excrement—and smears it on the wall 'would', according to Bernd Maubach, 'hardly be conceivable without the work of the Vienna Actionists'.[19] In this sense then, Schlingensief is recycling—and further, re-staging and re-situating—established images of experimental art. This seriality—the multiple parodies of artistic traditions and popular genres, together with the circular nature of plots that never seem to be resolved—works to support a larger argument about history that keeps repeating itself. And so it makes sense that Schlingensief's next film should take advantage of the genre best known for formulaic reproductions and sequels: the slasher film.[20]

The German Chainsaw Massacre: Reunification as horror

> They came as friends and were turned into sausage.
> (Tagline for *The German Chainsaw Massacre*)

The second film in the *Deutschlandtrilogie*, *The German Chainsaw Massacre: The First Hour of Reunification* (1990) begins abruptly in the midst of history in action, with grainy archive footage of the 3 October reunification celebration already underway.[21] A German flag is raised in the foreground, fireworks, cheers, and whistles pierce the air over the sounds of a ringing bell, which appears superimposed against the backdrop of a jubilant crowd gathered at the Brandenburg Gate. Cut to the Reichstag lawn: as President Richard Weizsäcker closes his patriotic speech, he turns to Chancellor Helmut Kohl and, still miked, whispers 'Now the national anthem should start'. As Harald Mühlbeyer describes this scene, Weizsäcker's accidental stage direction unmasks the pathos of this pivotal moment in German history 'as contrived, as false, as completely artificial. An entire nation in delirium, flags, the Brandenburg Gate, the national anthem: A case for Schlingensief. And Schlingensief steps into action'.[22]

In fact, Schlingensief wrote the script in a matter of days following the 3 October celebration and the film was completed within a few weeks. As he recalls in the documentary *Christoph Schlingensief und seine Filme*:

> It was a Spiegel-TV show in the evening, I think, [...] and I suddenly saw Trabis [East German cars] driving around, with women waving their hands and men holding bananas in their hand, and then yelling something like 'We are the people'. And I thought, what's going on now? [...] I didn't think it was right, I thought it was wrong. Somehow this image seemed like crap to me, it was just rubbish.[23]

It was at this moment, he explains, that he first conceived of the *German Chainsaw Massacre*.[24] He had recently seen bootlegged versions of the original Tobe Hooper classics (*Texas Chainsaw Massacre*, 1974 and its sequel *Texas Chainsaw Massacre 2*, 1986, which is officially banned in Germany), and he found the latter 'superb' for the richness of its imagery and double entendres. Then as he watched the reunification unfold on the nightly news, something clicked:

> When I saw those apes with their bananas, with their '*Deutschland über alles*' and 'We are the people' and then 'Now the national anthem has to come', as Weizsäcker or whoever said after his important Reichstag speech [....] All the dissembling of this hypocrisy machine, there, in that moment, I thought, 'The German Chainsaw Massacre', that's what's actually got to come now: Germans, West Germans, hunt down East Germans and turn them into sausages. 'They came as friends and were turned into sausage'.[25]

Following the archival footage of the reunification celebration from the film's introduction, the national anthem trails off and we hear deep moans and synthesized minor chords over the low buzz of a chainsaw. The screen turns black for several seconds, and the first scene opens on a deserted roadway. We see a pickup truck speed across the screen, and the camera pans down to a woman lying on the ground who has been cut in half, her intestines splayed out unceremoniously beneath her, singing '*Die Gedanken sind frei*', a well-known German folk song about the importance of freethinking. An intertitle in bold yellow letters relates: 'It happened on the 3rd of October...' We later discover, however, that this scene is a flash-forward of the film's final sequence, and the narrative proper begins with a large painted 'GDR' sign being knocked down as a red Trabi comes into view. Its passengers, a middle-aged East German couple, are singing jovially, the woman with a Coca-Cola can in her hand (a not-so-subtle commentary on the irresistible seductions of western capitalism). At this point, another intertitle relates:

'Since the opening of the borders on November 9, 1989, hundreds of thousands of GDR citizens have left their old home. Many of them live among us to this day, unrecognized. Four percent never arrived.'

The film thus sets the stage for what we can only assume—based on the sinister music and tabloid-headline-style narration, not to mention the severed body—will be a bloody reckoning. This beginning also stays true to the basic formula for a horror film, more precisely, a slasher. As in Tobe Hooper's original *The Texas Chainsaw Massacre*, Schlingensief's tale begins with a journey to a strange location, what Carol Clover, in her famous study of the Hooper film, terms 'the terrible place' (here, West Germany), where all manner of brutality will ensue.[26] The viewer acquainted with the formula can thus predict most of what will happen next: the protagonist will encounter a family of psychotic killers, including maniacal blood-lusting children and a poorly preserved patriarch (the 'marginally alive' Grandpa in the American version and, in the German

Figure 1: Schlingensief and Udo Kier work a scene from *The German Chainsaw Massacre*. Photo: Filmgalerie 451.

version: a corpse with a helmet and a Nazi uniform). The family, having come on hard economic times (occasioned by new machinery in Texas/new cheap labour in West Germany), will have turned to human butchery and cannibalism as a way of life (chilli for the original Sawyer family/sausages for the Germans), and there will be a plucky female heroine (Sally/Clara) who will confront the killers and eventually overpower them, becoming the last girl standing (Clover's 'final girl') who will live to enact a final scene that hints at the upcoming sequel.[27]

Reunification is conceived in retrospect, then, as a process whereby not only land, but also bodies were colonized. As Maubach argues, *The German Chainsaw Massacre* is an act of visualization, a mapping-onto-the-body, of a history that has not yet been made visible, of the hidden negotiations and behind-door bargains that took place between the fall of the Wall on 9 November 1989 and the official reunification on 3 October 1990.[28] Following the film's premiere on 27 October 1990, reception was mixed. While one reviewer has since identified *The German Chainsaw Massacre* as 'one of the key cinematic works of German history', the Berlin movie theatre Babylon was forced to withdraw it from its program in 1990 after charges of 'glorification of violence' (a crime according to § 131 of the Criminal Code [Strafgesetzbuch, StGB]) were levied against the film.[29] As it travelled the festival circuit, the film was confiscated at airports and seized by authorities in Munich. Repeatedly, it became the subject of talk show discussions about the role of violence in contemporary society. The NDR and WDR television studios, which co-produced the film, would not air it in Germany and, according to Schlingensief, one producer even 'vowed to do everything he could to prevent it' from being screened in the future.[30] For Schlingensief, however, violence is located not in its representation, but in its reception. 'The problems with violence always begin when people are […] denied the chance to think about it, and it's turned into a taboo'.[31] Indeed, the real violence, as Schlingensief saw it, was in what actually transpired after 1989: 'Wessis capture Ossis, turn them into sausage—There's some truth to that. When you look at what's happened to the East, it's worse than sausage, it's mincemeat'.[32]

Fascism, anti-fascism, and *Terror 2000*

Terror 2000—Intensive Care Unit Germany (1992), the final film in Schlingensief's *Deutschlandtrilogie*, has been described as fascist, homophobic, xenophobic, anti-police, anti-media, misogynist, and an assault on human dignity.[33] Following a screening of the film at Sputnik, a small arthouse cinema in the leftist Kreuzberg neighbourhood of Berlin, protesters stormed the projection room and destroyed the film reels with butyric acid, leaving behind a note disparaging the film as 'sexist and racist'.[34] Schlingensief describes this incident as follows:

> To be honest, I couldn't quite get my head around that, because I thought, but the film can also be funny [*Spaß machen*]. Not in the sense of laughing one's head off, but funny in the sense of making you feel unsettled [*verunsichert*], that what you're seeing in an exaggerated form might in fact be true.[35]

As with *100 Years of Adolf Hitler*, Schlingensief is not interested in portraying history 'as it really happened', nor is he concerned with making history 'make sense'. What the butyric acid incident reveals, more than anything else, is that *Terror 2000*, despite the leftist leanings of its director, does not fit easily into the established categories of leftist, anti-fascist critique. It lambasts anti-fascism just as much as fascism. Indeed, the film's signature style is almost schizophrenic. As Stephen Holden noted in his review of the film:

> If a Keystone Cops film were written by William S. Burroughs, peopled with characters from George Grosz by way of Russ Meyer, and directed in a style that suggests Jean-Luc Godard on speed, you would have a movie with the style and mood of *Terror 2000*.[36]

In other words, *Terror 2000* is slapstick-meets-beat-meets-expressionism qua sexploitation-meets-psychostimulated French New Wave! Neither its style nor the targets of its critique are easily pinpointed.

In keeping with the mock historicity of the trilogy, the film purports to portray 'an authentic case from the year 1992'. Private detective Peter Körn (played by Peter Kern) and his assistant Margret (played by Margit Carstensen) are investigating the disappearance of social worker Peter Fricke (American writer Gary Indiana), who has vanished, together with the family of refugees he was accompanying from Poland to the small town of Rassau in former East Germany. On the opposite side of the law is a gang of misfits whom Körn had failed to capture in 1988: a kidnapper-turned-priest named Jablonski (Udo Kier) and his accomplice-turned-furniture salesman Bössler (Alfred Edel) who, together with Bössler's son Boessi and nephew Klausi, cavort throughout town assaulting foreigners. Somewhere in between are the residents of a hostel for asylum-seekers, run by a commandeering woman (who introduces the detectives to her 'enclosure' by reciting 'Poland, Dachau, Treblinka') and her two slightly odd sons. Later in the film we meet renowned neo-Nazi leader Michael Kühnen (played with flamboyantly queer overtones by Schlingensief himself), a 'miracle healer' named Pupilla (a lightly veiled parody of Uriella, the leader of the New Age group 'Fiat Lux') who leads the search to find the kidnapped Poles when the detectives prove incapable, and the Minister of the Interior, a conspicuously disabled, anti-immigration conservative who admits to being the secretly proud owner of Goebbels' famed cyanide ring.[37] As the search for the Poles

Figure 2: From left to right: Christoph Schlingensief as Michael Kühnen, Kai Blanke as an unnamed transvestite, Udo Kier as Jablonski, Alfred Edel as Bössler, Dietrich Kuhlbrodt as Nazi leader Ratz (credited as Reisz), Kalle Mews as Bössi (credited as Rösi), Artur Albrecht as Klausi at the Nazi rally in *Terror 2000*. Photo: Filmgalerie 451.

proceeds, it becomes more and more difficult to distinguish between the law-keepers and the law-breakers. Körn turns out to be as violent and perverse as the criminals he is pursuing.

As mentioned earlier, the film is set up as a quasi-documentary. As it begins, the camera zooms in on a bright yellow road sign identifying the town of Gladbeck—the site of a famous hostage crisis from 1988—followed by a shot of a quiet street corner in the town, then a tracking shot down a long narrow hallway inside a building, shot in black and white on poor film stock with a handheld camera and uneven light, the shadow of the cameraman projected on the wall to his left. We see some ramshackle furniture and a couple of trash cans, a dark-skinned woman in a simple cotton dress, several other dark-skinned people sitting against the wall on stools, a doorway covered with a makeshift curtain, and a little girl running toward us in bare feet. A deep-voiced male narrates:

'The following film depicts an authentic case from 1992'. The camera cuts to a small living room with a dark-skinned, dark-haired family cramped onto a couch covered with a cheap, patterned bed sheet, staring expressionlessly toward us. 'Germany has changed', the voiceover continues. 'The refugee hostels are overflowing'. As the camera continues to pan across sparsely furnished rooms with tightly packed cots and more dark-skinned people sitting around doing nothing, the voiceover explains the increasingly dire state of affairs:

> The government is retreating. The local police are left on their own. A large portion of the populace is out of control and is now openly resisting. Only the experts are looking for a solution to the situation, but to this point in vain. Ladies and gentlemen, girls and boys, enjoy with us during the next minutes a world full of love, fear, sexuality, and death. [Here, a close-up of a black man's face] Enjoy with us the world in which we live. [Here, a shot of a jeep filled with four middle-aged men, one in a Ku Klux Klan hood, singing boisterously] Enjoy yourselves. [Here, in bright yellow, jagged-edged lettering, the title 'TERROR 2000'].

As with the first two films of the trilogy, the first few minutes set up the main target of the film's critique, here: the hysterical public sphere. The media—called immediately to mind by the mention of 'Gladbeck'—are set up as the enabling actors behind spectacularized violence.[38] The official disciplinary channels of the government and the police are rendered impotent. As consumers of terror as 'entertainment', we ourselves are implicated in the hyperbolic treatment of the foreign body.

Terror 2000 borrows the imagery, style, and characters of the Gladbeck hostage crisis—insatiable journalists, ineffectual police, a brutal kidnapper with a penchant for sticking a gun in his own mouth, the fetishized body of a blonde-haired nubile female hostage (Silke/Wibke), a zombified, image-addicted public—and transfers these to the year 1992, a time when Germany was experiencing increased violence against foreigners (or those perceived to be foreigners).[39] While the link between the 1988 Gladbeck crisis and early 90s xenophobia is not immediately crystal clear, the role of the media is common to both. As Maubach notes, images in the media of 'criminal foreigners' and 'illegals' abounded around this time in Germany. Maubach cites a number of exemplary sensationalist newspaper headlines from *Bild*—Germany's most widely circulated tabloid newspaper—that appeared around the time of the production of *Terror 2000*, such as: 'Refugees. Who are the fake ones, who are the real ones? How much are they costing us? Why do they live in hotels? Will the Army have to protect the border?' (14 August 1991), 'This Russian drinks blood' (5 August 1992), and 'Asylum: Terror across the country' (7 September 1992).

In this light, the absurd episodes that constitute the main storyline of *Terror 2000* seem to be ripped straight from the rabble-rousing headlines. The film consists of seven such episodes, announced throughout with yellow capital letters superimposed over an establishing shot, in the style of a TV detective series: 'Germany Out of Control', 'The Inspector Arrives', 'Rassau Hostel for Asylum-Seekers', 'The Nazis Arrive', 'The Miracle Healer Arrives', 'The Minister Arrives', and 'Back to the Roots' (this last title in English). The final scene takes us back to Gladbeck as Körn, in the midst of a nervous breakdown, flashes back to the botched capture of Bössler and Jablonski and finally recalls that he himself was responsible for the death of the beautiful hostage Wibke. A mob chases him out of town with shouts of 'Körn get out!' (substituting one target of hate for another). The film concludes with the gang of misfits speeding down the highway, en route to the next crime presumably, as one of the hostel workers responds to a television interviewer with 'Germany must get tough again'. As the misfits escape, an immigrant family smiles passively into the camera. And so it begins again.

From Hitler to Kühnen, and back again: The *Deutschlandtrilogie* in retrospect

From the first grainy images of the Führer in *100 Years of Adolf Hitler* to the skeletal remains of an SS officer in *The German Chainsaw Massacre* to the inevitable return of Nazism in the xenophobic antics of *Terror 2000*, the *Deutschlandtrilogie* is insistent in confronting us not only with the German past that (still) will not pass away, but also with the German present. The trilogy is an irreverent and thoroughly distasteful assault on the very foundations of post-war German democratic tradition; contrary to the originating words of the Republic, human dignity *is* violable. Schlingensief seeks to unmask the violations of dignity that occur not only in the realm of right-wing extremism but also in the representational practices of the Left, and he does so in ways that are themselves often violent, shocking, offensive and obscene. For Schlingensief, then, the only 'proper' way of coming to terms with the past is one that refuses the hypocrisies of tasteful political correctness and the self-contradictory rhetoric of universal tolerance by calling attention, instead, to the necessary inadequacy of any attempt to render violence visually digestible.

Endnotes

1. Syberberg, H. (1999), *Vom Unglück und Glück der Kunst in Deutschland nach dem letzten Kriege*, in M. Stiglegger, *Sadiconazista: Faschismus und Sexualität im Film*, St. Augustin: Gardez! Verlag, p. 9. All translations from the German are my own unless otherwise noted.

2. I have left *Deutschlandtrilogie* in the original German to distinguish it from Visconti's 'German Trilogy' (*Trilogia Tedesca*, 1969–1973) and Fassbinder's 'BRD Trilogy' (*BRD Trilogie*, 1979–1982).

3. Seeßlen, G. (1998), 'Vom barbarischen Film zur nomadischen Politik', in J. Lochte and W. Schulz (eds.), *Schlingensief: Notruf für Deutschland. Über die Mission, das Theater und die Welt des Christoph Schlingensief*, Hamburg: Rotbuch Verlag, p. 52. On Schlingensief's comment on the objective of art as 'the creation of fear' (*Angsterzeugung*), see *Christoph Schlingensief und seine Filme* (2005), Berlin: Filmgalerie 451.

4. The phrase 'people who haven't succeeded in dying' (*Menschen, denen das Sterben misslungen ist*) stems from an interview with Schlingensief by Hans-Christian Dany. See Dany, H-C., 'Psycho für Arme', 16.9.90. http://ftp.fortunaty.net/com/textz/textz/schlingensief_christoph_psycho_fuer_arme.txt. Accessed 21 February 2009. The phrase 'the past that won't pass away' is slightly modified from the title of a speech by historian Ernst Nolte that sparked the Historian's Debate (*Historikerstreit*). See Nolte, E. (1986), 'Die Vergangenheit, die nicht vergehen will'/The Past that Doesn't Want to Pass Away', *Frankfurter Allgemeine Zeitung*, 6 June. With respect to Schlingensief's use of violence, David Hughes makes a similar argument, summarizing the message of the trilogy as such: 'Confront the return of nation and, at least, be honest about the violent processes underlying it'. See Hughes, D. (2006), 'Everything in Excess: Christoph Schlingensief and the Crisis of the German Left', *The Germanic Review*, 81:4, pp. 317–339, here p. 323. Hughes also interprets Schlingensief's portrayals of violence as attempts to answer both the Left's 'refusal to treat the nation as a political category with violent implications', and the increasingly diffuse nature of violence in the global public sphere (pp. 322–323). See also Bernd Maubach's discussion of the relationship between Schlingensief's use of violence and the historical avant-garde (most notably, Dada) and the neo avant-garde (most notably, Viennese Actionism) in Maubach, B., (2005) *Christoph Schlingensiefs Deutschlandtrilogie - Geschichts- und Gesellschaftsdiagnose im Film*, Norderstedt: Grin Verlag.

5. Christoph Schlingensief, *100 Jahre Adolf Hitler: Die letzte Stunde im Führerbunker* (Filmgalerie 451, 2004).

6. As Martin Brady and Helen Hughes write, 'Schlingensief's film is almost an exercise in *cinéma vérité*, documenting the location, performances and conditions under which it was made'. See Brady, M. and H. Hughes (2006), 'Downfall and Beyond: Hitler Films from Germany', *gfl-journal*, 3, http://www.gfl-journal.de/3-2006/brady_hughes.pdf, p. 108. With respect to the film's use of stark light

and dark contrast, several critics have interpreted the chiaroscuro effect as part of an overall 'expressionist' aesthetic, according to which one can see *100 Years* as an attempt to bridge the gap created by the Third Reich between the classic expressionist cinema of Weimar and the post-war return to artistic innovation with New German Cinema. Along these lines, see Maubach, p. 55; and Kuhlbrodt, D., 'Portrait: Christoph Schlingensief', *Filmzentrale: Gesammelte Filmkritiken*, http://www.filmzentrale.com/rezis/schlingensiefdk.htm, 1989. Accessed 28 March 2005.

7. On the film's title, see also Maubach, p. 40.

8. See Sontag, S. (1980), 'Fascinating Fascism', in *Under the Sign of Saturn*, New York: Farrar, Straus and Giroux, pp. 73–105.

9. 'Mock centennial' is a formulation I borrow from David Hughes. See Hughes, D. (2006), 'Everything in Excess', p. 325.

10. Hughes, D. (2006), 'Radical Destruction: The Films of Christoph Schlingensief', in *Reinventing the Left: Radical Responses to German Reunification*, Ph.D. dissertation, Durham, North Carolina: Duke University, p. 110.

11. This is a famous line from Wim Wenders' acceptance speech at the fortieth annual Cannes Film Festival, where he received the Best Director Award for *Der Himmel über Berlin* (1987).

12. From the interview with Schlingensief in *Christoph Schlingensief und seine Filme* (2005).

13. *Christoph Schlingensief und seine Filme* (2005).

14. With respect to Schlingensief's relationship to New German Cinema, he is often quoted as saying that he sees himself in the tradition of New German Cinema, though distances himself from its later devolvement into what he regards as self-pity ('It started with the idea of making innovative films, but then it got very whiny'). See Seeßlen (1998), p. 42. The frequency with which Schlingensief's initial allegiance to New German Cinema is referenced points to the importance attached to locating him within an avant-garde tradition that he alternatively admires and lampoons.

15. Hughes, D. (2006), 'Everything in Excess', p. 325.

16. Anonymous review from the *Frankfurter Allgemeine Zeitung*, excerpted from '100 Jahre Adolf Hitler (1988/89)', http://www.schlingensief.com/projekt.php?id=f035. Accessed 29 April 2009.

17. *Christoph Schlingensief und seine Filme* (2005).

18. Thelen, C. (1989), 'Darf's noch ein Tabubruch sein?', *die tageszeitung*, 19 August, p. 32.

19. Maubach, p. 24. The Actionists famously incorporated blood, urine, faeces, semen, animal entrails, and more into their art.

20. Consider also Hughes' discussion of Schlingensief's self-stylization as a 'serial artist.' Hughes, D. (2006), 'Everything in Excess', pp. 324–325.

21. Christoph Schlingensief, *Das deutsche Kettensägenmassaker* (Berlin: Filmgalerie 451, 2004).

22. Mühlbeyer, H. (2008), 'Das deutsche Kettensägenmassaker', *Screenshot Online— Texte zum Film*, April, http://screenshot-online.blogspot.com/2008/04/christoph-schlingensief-edition-7-das.html. Accessed 21 February 2009.

23. Bananas, not commonly available in East Germany under socialism, became an iconic symbol of western free-market consumerism after the fall of the Wall. See, *Christoph Schlingensief und seine Filme*, (2005) Filmgalerie 451 dvd.

24. It is somewhat unclear from the interview whether Schlingensief first conceived of the film following the fall of the Berlin Wall on 9 November 1989 or after the official ceremony on 3 October 1990. He seems to conflate the two events, noting that a friend had phoned him and exclaimed 'The wall's gone!' while he was watching the TV report (which seems to date the story to 1989), but then he also mentions seeing Weizsäcker's speech (which dates it to 1990).

25. *Christoph Schlingensief und seine Filme* (2005).

26. See Clover, C. (1993), 'Her Body, Himself', in *Men, Women, and Chainsaws: Gender in the Modern Horror Film*, Princeton: Princeton University Press, pp. 21–64.

27. Ibid., pp. 35–64.

28. Maubach, pp. 79–80.

29. Thomas, A., 'Das Deutsche Kettensägenmassaker: Blut und Boden und Schleim', *Filmzentrale*, http://www.filmzentrale.com/rezis/deutschekettensaegenmassakerat. htm. Accessed 21 April 2009. On allegations of 'glorification of violence', see Löser, C. (2007), 'DDR Revisited: Mediale Umcodierungen', *Recherche Film und Fernsehen*, 1, www.school-scout.de/extracts/p-6637/2-Leseprobe.pdf, p. 8.

30. *Christoph Schlingensief und seine Filme* (2005).

31. Schlingensief, C. (1995), 'Heulkrampf im Busch' (interview with Joachim Kronsbein and Peter Stolle), *Der Spiegel* 8, 20 February, p. 209a, available at: http://wissen. spiegel.de/wissen/dokument/dokument.html?id=9159268. Accessed 21 February 2009.

32. *Christoph Schlingensief und seine Filme* (2005). Schlingensief's commentary here foreshadows critiques later advanced by political and social scientists—critiques that surfaced frequently and sometimes sensationally in the media—that reunification and the concomitant transition to a market-based economy was marred by (and indeed perhaps effected by) rising unemployment and increased right-wing violence in the East. Further, some argued that reunification was less a peaceful merger of two nations and more a hostile takeover or economic colonization in the mode of disaster capitalism. These critiques reappear in the final entry in the trilogy, *Terror 2000*. On the growing incidence of right-wing extremism in former East Germany and an analysis of its possible causes, see Krueger, A.B. and Pischke, J.S. (1996), 'A Statistical Analysis of Crime Against Foreigners in Unified Germany', National Bureau of Economic Research Working Paper No. W5485, March, available at: http://ssrn.com/abstract=225518. Accessed 25 June, 2009. On the metaphor of colonization as applied to German reunification, see Dümcke, W. and Vilmar, F. (eds.) (1996), *Kolonisierung der DDR. Kritische Analysen und Alternativen des Einigungsprozess*, Münster: Agenda Verlag, cited in Maubach, pp. 77–81.

33. Christoph Schlingensief, *Terror 2000: Intensivstation Deutschland* (Water Bearer Films, 1999). On contemporary reactions to the film, see *Christoph Schlingensief und seine Filme* (2005); Katsiaficas, G. (2006), 'The Autonomen in Unified Germany', in *The Subversion of Politics: European Autonomous Social Movements and the Decolonization of Everyday Life*, Oakland, CA: AK Press, p. 237; and Thelen, p. 32.

34. See Katsiaficas, p. 237.

35. *Christoph Schlingensief und seine Filme* (2005).

36. Holden, S. (1994), '*Terror 2000* (1992) Absurdist Spoof of Nazism', *New York Times*, 18 November, available at: http://movies.nytimes.com/movie/review?res=9A04EE DD1031F93BA25752C1A962958260. Accessed 23 May 2009.

37. The conservative, partly physically disabled Minister of the Interior in the film may be based on the then-current Federal Minister of the Interior, conservative politician Wolfgang Schäuble, who was confined to a wheelchair after a 1990 assassination attempt; it may instead or also refer to the then-current Minister of the Interior for the state of Saxony, Rudolf Krause, as Maubach suggests. Krause was criticized for not having intervened earlier to protect asylum-seekers who became the target of right-wing violence in Hoyerswerda in 1991, shortly before *Terror 2000* was filmed. See Maubach, p. 105.

38. The reference to 'Gladbeck' refers to a hostage crisis in August 1988 that became emblematic of media sensationalism and botched police work. After robbing a bank in Gladbeck, Dieter Degowski and Hans-Jürgen Rösner (in the film, they become Jablonski and Bössler) went on the run for several days, taking several hostages along the way, one of whom was killed by the kidnappers during negotiations and another during the final shootout with police (18-year-old hostage Silke Bischoff, who becomes the fetishized, blonde-wigged 'Wibke' in the film). Both the police and the media were heavily criticized for their actions during the crisis. Journalists followed the chase closely and intervened directly at times. On the Gladbeck crisis, see for example *Focus* (2008), '54 Stunden Angst', 14 August, p. 6, available at: http://www.focus.de/panorama/welt/tid-11465/gladbeck-54-stunden-angst_aid_324612.html. Accessed 20 February 2009.

39. As Maubach notes, the case of Rostock—where, during August 1992, one of the worst xenophobic riots in postwar Germany history took place—is an important reference point for *Terror 2000*. Although the riots occurred after filming for *Terror 2000* was already complete, they were 'an important point of reference in the media reviews and feuilleton discussions about the last part of the German Trilogy'. Maubach, p. 90. At the same time, Rostock was also not entirely unpredictable: attacks on refugees had begun escalating in the mid-eighties. The right-wing extremist attacks in Hoyerswerda in 1991 are a prime example.

THEATRE OF SELF-QUESTIONING: *ROCKY DUTSCHKE, '68*, OR THE CHILDREN OF THE REVOLUTION

Sandra Umathum

Prologue

As so often it all began much earlier. *Rocky Dutschke, '68* was the first theatre production I saw by Christoph Schlingensief. That was in June 1996 at the Volksbühne on Rosa-Luxemburg-Platz in Berlin. But my first encounter with some of the basic parameters of the Schlingensief cosmos had taken place a few years previously, in March 1993 during the screening of Schingensief's film *Terror 2000—Intensive Care Unit Germany.*

After *100 Years of Adolf Hitler* and *The German Chainsaw Massacre, Terror 2000* was the last part of the Germany trilogy Schlingensief filmed between 1989 and 1992. At that time the director was barely known to a wider audience. His work was primarily enjoyed by a select community of underground-film fans, and the attention that *Terror 2000* attracted after its release was less due to audience success than to an occurrence in February 1993 at a cinema in Berlin-Kreuzberg. According to press reports, after the first screening an attack occurred during which several hooded assailants doused the film with acid and sprayed the projectionist with teargas. The fleeing attackers—members of the autonomist scene, said the police—left behind a letter describing the film as racist and sexist.[1]

A month after I read about this event, *Terror 2000* was on the programme of the Acud cinema and I went along with two friends. In those days the cinema was a medium-sized room. The audience sat on ordinary wooden chairs; the large windows were hung with heavy black curtains. That evening the cinema was full to bursting and, from the conversations we could overhear before the screening, it was clear that nobody really knew who Schlingensief was. Only a few of those present would have heard his name prior to the events a month before. Most of the audience wasn't there out of interest in his latest work, but rather because of the film's apparent potential for scandal.

Terror 2000 began with an address to the audience:

> The following film portrays a true story from the year 1992. Germany has changed. The homes for asylum seekers are overcrowded. The government is in retreat. The police are on their own. A large part of the population is out of control and in open resistance. [...] Ladies and gentlemen, boys and girls, enjoy with us now a world full of love, fear, sexuality and death. Enjoy with us the world we live in. Have a good time.

What the audience was then treated to was the consolidation of an ugly reality in trash-aesthetic guise. Schlingensief combined references to the hostage drama of Gladbeck[2] with the rampant xenophobia that emerged in the former East Germany during the early 1990s. In a remorseless portrayal of insurgent asylum seekers and brawling Hitler Youth, overburdened local authorities, unsuccessful police officers and the sensation-hungry media, he presented the image of a battle on screen that allowed us to peer into the deepest chasms of reunited Germany.

After only half an hour the screen suddenly went black. The lights went up, and a young woman came out of the projection room. Addressing the audience, she apologised for the interruption, saying something about a tear in the film. If we would please be patient, the projectionist was trying to repair the damage as quickly as possible. Up to this moment we might have assumed that this was one of those things that do sometimes happen when you go to the cinema. But once the woman began distributing sweets to people in the front row who were prepared to recite a poem or sing a song, it became clear that something was wrong here. In the back rows, the first disgruntled voices could be heard when a second gentleman stood up to recite a poem. The woman abruptly ceased being friendly. Her tone became authoritarian as she announced that those who were looking for trouble could certainly have it. She ran like a mad thing to the back of the room, pulled a key from her bag and locked the exit door. The audience became fitful. Several people protested. 'You wanted Terror 2000?' she screamed. 'You can have terror! Your own personal terror.' Then she tore some books from a cupboard and set them on fire. She stamped on the floor, performing a kind of witches' dance, and hurled wild criticism at the audience for the base motives of its interest in Schlingensief's film. She created such an atmosphere of insecurity and tension that finally a few people intervened and asked her to unlock the door. For this favour, however, she also required a quid pro quo, informing us that those who wanted to leave had to come up front and explain exactly why they wanted to go. A woman in the third row got up and said that she had to get back to relieve her babysitter. The door was unlocked. She was allowed to leave. Then the door was relocked and the game repeated itself several times until one of my friends lost his patience. As the door was being opened for the fourth or fifth time, he charged up to the exit, seized the door and held it open until everyone who had had enough of the spectacle was able to leave.

Outside on the street we talked to other viewers about the events in the cinema. We were still talking about it on the way home. And even weeks and months later we would come back to it. We had been strongly affected by the occurrence: by the way in which the woman had terrified the audience; by the viewers who had followed her demands without resistance; and not least by the apparent tear in the film. Had it really existed? Had the woman taken advantage of it for a spontaneous performance? Or had it been faked? Had it been planned from the very beginning, along with the woman's performance?

Some time passed before I attended my first stage production by Schlingensief. The events at the Acud had left their mark, and although Schlingensief himself hadn't even been there, for me his name had become associated with crisis and vexation. In retrospect you could even say that the evening had become something of a portent because, long before my first encounter with his stage work, I had already been confronted by experiences that would occupy me for many years in relation to Schlingensief's theatrical aesthetics.

A director on stage

When the Volksbühne reopened under the new directorship of Frank Castorf in 1992, Schlingensief was brought into the circle of those who had made it their task in post-socialist East Berlin 'to observe meticulously, to make—as malignantly as possible—the disease in the national body of Germany the subject matter of theatre and to create feelings of uncertainty.'[3] In his luggage, the Catholic son of a pharmacist from the West German town of Oberhausen brought with him much exploitable material from his own biography and post-war German history.

His first production, *100 Years of the Christian Democratic Union: Game Without Limits,*[4] (premiere April 1993) showed, according to its flyer, the 'vision of a fascistic madhouse Germany.' In an attempt to recreate the state of chaos in which Germany found itself after the fall of the Berlin Wall, Schlingensief put it all on stage and, in doing so, transformed the stage into a madhouse as well. Faster than any professional television junkie could have done, he and his protagonists zapped through the German TV landscape. There were quotations from game and talk shows, news programmes, calls for donations and religious broadcasts, until the absurdly distorted stage figures overlapped with the various television formats, representatives and content. The former German president Richard von Weizsäcker—kitted out with high boots, epaulettes and an Alsatian dog—sang a song about the lovely Bellevue Palace[5] and stupid Berlin; a UN officer bet that he would be able to paint a Star of David on the window of a Turkish grocery and be back in the studio in ten minutes; Leo and Pitty, victims of a neo-Nazi attack, warbled the famous pop song of a children's charity. A number of media celebrities also took part in this revue-like event including Cicciolina,[6] representatives of the Protestant and Catholic Church, and the jurors who had recently turned down *Terror 2000* for the Berlin Film Festival. Schlingensief served up a mixed bag from which the grimacing visage of the media-generated fun society stared back at the audience.

The critics panned the production. It was described as a 'politically adolescent gaffe.'[7] Its director was certified as having 'no talent'[8] and lacking a concept.[9] Schlingensief felt he hadn't been taken seriously. During the sixth performance he sat in the canteen wondering how the thing could be salvaged. Having got up some Dutch courage, he stormed onto the stage, rammed a syringe into the blood-bag under his shirt, bit on a blood capsule and screamed, 'Lights down!' Then he continued, 'I am the pharmacist's son from Oberhausen, and now you've got me. You wanted it.'[10] Schlingensief looked bad. He was covered in fake blood from head to foot. A sad victim of his own trash. With tears in his eyes he began to talk about the death of his grandmother. You could have heard a pin drop in the auditorium. The director's appearance had apparently unleashed consternation and confusion.

Directors are figures rarely seen on stage. They usually only come to the premiere to take their applause before an enthusiastic or dissatisfied audience. But Schlingensief had his say—and an enigmatic one at that—in his own piece. Was his appearance on stage really a part of the production? Was his emotional outburst real or was he only acting? And was the story about his grandmother's death true or invented? Schlingensief had set a situation in motion that held the answers to these questions in abeyance. It could all have been simulated. But the possibility that everything was genuine, and that reality had indeed sneaked into the theatre, provoked the audience into abandoning its aesthetic distance. Schlingensief's entrance threw everything into confusion. Regardless of whether you were prepared to give credence to his emotions or not, you couldn't really be sure if he was being sincere.

Today, over a decade later, audiences have long become accustomed to such ambiguous situations, which are a characteristic of postdramatic theatre, as Hans-Thies Lehmann has shown in his eponymously titled work.[11] Lehmann was one of the first to talk about the 'aesthetics of undecidability', in order to give a name to the ambiguity of reality and fiction with which the theatre of the 1990s had been so preoccupied[12]. This ambiguity has been much discussed, and it has been internalized as a stylistic device of contemporary theatre. But back then it was a challenge, and frequently an overwhelming one, for many theatregoers. The incursion of reality into the theatre was an affront, and it was often possible to listen to conversations during or after a performance that were about little other than whether something had been staged or was the result of chance, mishap or a spontaneous decision. Schlingensief has explored the generation of undecidable situations and the play with them like no one else. But it wasn't only that the planned and the unplanned, the invented and the true sometimes became so inextricable that you scarcely knew what to think or how to respond; with Schlingensief, even categories like right and wrong, good and bad were put to the test in such a way that you seemed to lose track of your own system of values.

Schlingensief's tearful, bloodstained appearance on stage was the result of a spur-of-the-moment decision. But with his next production *Kühnen '94: Bring Me the Head of Adolf Hitler,* (premiere New Year's Eve, 1993) his presence on stage became a significant feature of his theatre work. As a film director Schlingensief was initially unsure about what to do with theatre. But he soon realized that it offered him possibilities that were unavailable to him as a filmmaker. With film there comes a point in the editing room when you have to tie yourself down. Theatre, on the other hand, allowed Schlingensief to intervene even after the premiere and to go on reorganizing, altering or supplementing scenes that had been set during rehearsal. But it wasn't enough for him to adjust his productions only before or after a performance, so he put himself on stage—as director and actor in one—where he could respond as needed to everyone and everything, and be able to take up and spontaneously deal with anything from the critics to the audience to the activities of his fellow actors, or even his own aimlessness.[13] But this also meant that what had been developed in rehearsal or during a performance was in danger of being thrown out the next moment. All of a sudden, no one was sure of his or her role, neither Schlingensief himself, nor his actors or audience.

In Schlingensief, a director came to the theatre and onto the stage who refused to deliver productions as exactly simulated reproductions. He was instead interested in the possibility of situational resetting, of variation, of the surprise effect and the revelation of what is usually concealed: the gaps, the mistakes, the perplexities, or the moments of failure. During the 1990s, playing with variables became a trademark of Schlingensief's theatre, and with it he revealed what few directors had explicitly dealt with until then: that performances are not only unpredictable, but also singular events, unrepeatable in the sense that the actors are not in the same physical and mental condition each evening and that the audience is always different. Because Schlingensief had abandoned the assumption of exact repetition in favour of difference and uniqueness, it was not uncommon to tell someone about a particularly impressive scene that this person, who had seen the production on another night, hadn't experienced. And he or she might tell you about an incident that hadn't occurred, or not in that way, the night you had seen it.

The audience as a part of the picture

June 1996: a little more than twenty years after the death of Ulrike Meinhof, and only a few days after the premiere of *Rocky Dutschke, '68*. In contrast to 1993, when Terror 2000 had screened at the Acud, Schlingensief was no longer an unknown quantity in Berlin. Several of my friends told me I shouldn't miss the production. At last, quite a different kind of theatre. You could sit on the floor and even actively take part.

When we arrived at the forecourt of the Volksbühne, the participatory theatre had already begun. Some of those present, easily recognizable as the Volksbühne's then typical audience, were sitting on the steps up to the foyer drinking beer and smoking cigarettes, while the others had gathered around a brass band that was marching behind a banner bearing the words 'No Power for Anyone!', conducted by a young woman with a red flag in her hand. Actors dressed as police were calling out various orders into the crowd and busily checking out the area when Schlingensief turned up to present two of the evening's main protagonists in a kind of twin pack: Rudi Dutschke (1940-1979), spokesman of the West German and particularly West Berlin student movement of the 1960s, and himself, master of ceremonies and spokesman of the performance. In an ill-fitting wig, and with a beaten-up megaphone in his hand, he evoked Dutschke without quite disappearing behind him. 1968 and 1996 were already curiously brought together in this double role.

'To the party headquarters!' yelled Schlingensief, alias Dutschke, into the megaphone and led the audience, now turning into a demonstration, towards the PDS[14] building at the end of the street, where a banner with the slogan 'Have no Fear!' was hanging from one of the first-floor windows. The theatre police wanted to stop him, but already a few of the demonstrators were trying to storm the PDS headquarters. The rest of the crowd looked amused. The theatre police refused entry and ensured order. Schlingensief/Dutschke fired two shots, then everyone went back to the main entrance of the Volksbühne.

A second Rudi Dutschke, this time embodied by the actress Sophie Rois, was riding around on a bicycle. Schlingensief bawled into the microphone, 'Who wants to shoot Rudi Dutschke this evening? Volunteers come forward!' Then three shots rang out—just like in 1968 on the Kurfürstendamm in Berlin-Charlottenburg, where Joseph Bachmann struck down the eloquent thinker of the political protest movement and the SDS (*Sozialistischer Deutscher Studentenbund*/Socialist German Student Union). Rois/Dutschke fell off her bicycle. Theatre nurses hurried over, along with the theatre police, in order to carry the wounded person away. Then the demonstrators were asked to take their seats in the auditorium.

Everyone who had come for an evening in the theatre had been transformed into actors in a street scene that revived the late 1960s—with its political campaigns, demonstrations and revolutionary gestures and slogans—while simultaneously emphasizing how much these features belonged to the past. The students of 1996, who were now entering the theatre in jeans and T-shirts, were putting themselves on display as the heirs to those events whose news-at-a-glance comeback had just been made possible through their participation. Whether you wanted to be or not, you were already part of the picture.

Schlingensief had shifted the opening of this production to outside the front doors of the Volksbühne. But that wasn't all. He had also used this opening for the instantiation of his altered concept of the audience. After *100 Years CDU* and his second production *Kühnen '94*, he had begun to include the audience as active participants in his productions.

Figure 1: Christoph Schlingensief, alias Dutschke, in front of the PDS building. Photo: David Baltzer.

This integration of the audience—from which other productions, such as *Passion Impossible—7 Day Emergency Call for Germany* (1997), *Chance 2000* (1998), and *Please Love Austria!* (2000) drew their essential life—began with *Rocky Dutschke, '68*. In this respect, *Rocky Dutschke, '68* was not simply a turning point. In view of Schlingensief's attempt to challenge the conventionalized receptive patterns of the audience, it was also a first test run.

In the foyer leading into the auditorium, we went past grey, blurred photographs of the rehearsals and the actors. The photos were countered by various quotations: 'There are no utopias any more, there is no meaning any more, there is no significance any more, there is only this vacuum, this empty space. We don't know where we are going in this empty space, how we should move, which direction makes sense. So we act. The play emerges from this.' Or: 'There is no accommodation with this world any more; we only belong in it to the extent to which we rebel against it.' These and other quotes from Rudi Dutschke, Heiner Müller, Theodor W. Adorno, Wolf Biermann, Georges Bataille and others ushered the audience through to the corridor around the auditorium itself. Naked men and women cavorted about on mattresses on the floor—an echo of Kommune 2[15]—while theatre police carried out occasional identity checks. At the entrance stood a young woman who stamped people's wrists with the word *Einreise* (entry).

'Who the fuck is Rudi Dutschke?'

The stage designer Bert Neumann had removed all the seating, replacing it with a stand in the middle of the stalls upon which stood a tent and a banner explaining that this somewhat ramshackle installation represented Luckenwalde, the small town in East Germany where the real Dutschke had grown up and gone to school during the 1950s. At the back of the auditorium there was a lectern. The theatregoers could find themselves a place somewhere in between on the wide steps of the floor, which had been affixed with narrow yellow-and-black tape bearing the phrase 'More emotion!' While the audience was filling up the space, on stage the Workers and Veterans Choir of Berlin-Neukölln sang Ernst Busch's version of *Spaniens Himmel* (The Spanish Sky)[16], which was one of the political songs taught in East German schools and sung in the NVA.[17] From the circle hung a large banner upon which the central question of the evening was written in large letters: 'Who the fuck is Rudi Dutschke?'

Gradually, the performance itself began. The audience was divided up into different classes: music, geography and politics. We ended up in the music class and huddled with our fellow pupils on the left of the auditorium, while at the lectern Schlingensief/ Dutschke and his ensemble of disabled, amateur and a few professional actors re-enacted the run-up to and opening of the exhibition in Luckenwalde that shortly before—on 11 April 1996, exactly twenty-eight years after the attack on the town's famous son— had been initiated in remembrance of Dutschke by some dedicated school students. The Volksbühne became Luckenwalde, and the audience everything in one: pupils, visitors to the exhibition, and witnesses to a play located somewhere between plan and improvisation that so relentlessly put its amateurishness on display that its distanced stance could hardly be misunderstood.

Rocky Dutschke, '68, it now at least became clear, was not aligning itself with the pupils in Luckenwalde. Unlike them, Schlingensief and his ensemble were clearly not interested in producing a glorifying homage to Dutschke. The homage they paid was to make him the pivotal figure of a revue with political content in the good old Volksbühne tradition from

Erwin Piscator to Benno Besson —an act which was neither apotheosis nor genuflection. Instead they used this icon of the left—both then and now—his life and its significance for 1968 primarily as the supplier of images from an era that, as Schlingensief once said, 'still had something holy about it.'[18] In *Rocky Dutschke, '68* these images, lodged in the collective memory, served as the pattern for scenes in which the events of the time were re-enacted and played out, events which Schlingensief and his ensemble, and large sections of the audience, had not experienced themselves. But this re-enactment and playing out had nothing at all to do with realistic imitation. It was much more of an extreme struggle with both the past and, by entering the past, its repercussions in the present: As Schlingensief points out, 'The protestors of 1968 still had ideals and utopias and an initial spark, qualities that have been lost to my generation. But I'm hard on them, because what has become of them? Today they laze around in Tuscany drinking fine eco-wines and reading the *taz*. How can this be?'[19] In the permanent oscillation between resignation, plaintiveness, irony and anger, Rudi—and with him 1968 and its heirs—was put through the ringer in a manner that could perhaps only be undertaken by a younger generation.

What happened during the performance can hardly be described in sequence. Sometimes up to three Dutschkes rampaged through the auditorium: portrayed by Rois in a tight, striped T-shirt and open fly button as a hysterical pill popper, by Schlingensief armed with either megaphone or microphone and/or the actor Bernhard Schütz, who fired sentimental revolutionary compound sentences into the audience in the student leader's circuitously academic style. At other times, Rois appeared as 'Norma' and Schütz in a dress. Dutschke's mother (Rosemarie Bärhold) complained about how her son had preferred to go to the West instead of into the NVA, and on stage the journey to West Berlin was played out with the participation of the audience. Theatregoers voluntarily or involuntarily placed in the limelight mingled with the ensemble, and suddenly Dutschke's transit to the West was grotesquely interwoven with 1989 and the fall of the Berlin Wall. The journey came to an end before the audience really knew what exactly was expected of them. The lights went up; ugly close-ups from an operating theatre appeared on a screen above the stage, followed later in the evening by images from a concentration camp. Mario Garzaner, one of Schlingensief's disabled performers, appeared as Wolf Biermann and endlessly strummed a guitar. Rois/Dutschke hammered on a blackboard. Now and then actors yelled 'Ho! Ho! Ho Chi Minh!' through the auditorium, while a woman explained how every year she went with her family to Bergen-Belsen, where her husband recited the names of the six million murdered Jews. In the interval, the audience was invited to have sex with the members of Kommune 2. Seriousness and slapstick combined in an uneasy symbiosis. A corny joke mingled with an image of torture, the stuttering Dutschke—who after the attack was limited in his ability to articulate himself—was immersed in sentimental television falsity and the intellectual dramatist Heiner Müller met Germany's gentleman boxer Henry Maske.

From the flotsam and jetsam of German history, Schlingensief and his team mounted a synaesthetic frontal attack on the senses. Sometimes one scarcely knew where to look, and whenever it seemed as if it was going to get really funny, embarrassment put a brake on the laughter. From time to time Schlingensief interrupted the performance and explained, with the help of chalk diagrams on a blackboard, what had happened up to that point. 'I'll give you a summary,' he shouted before recapitulating. But instead of providing an answer to the question of how all this material was related and what it had to do with Rudi Dutschke, he explicitly invited the audience not to make connections between the images. In an impassioned attempt to defy arbitrariness and loss of meaning, Schlingensief confronted his audience with both of them. He produced disorientation, with the result that his viewers were left to themselves, to their perception, bewilderment, ethics, doubts and reactions, and not least to their understanding of theatre itself. Yet Schlingensief never simply delegated this self-questioning to the audience. He also conducted and demonstrated it himself.

Figure 2: Unromanticizing the past: two Dutschkes (Christoph Schlingensief and Sophie Rois) with Kerstin Grassmann. Photo: David Baltzer.

The critics accused this production of all kinds of things. Schlingensief had turned Dutschke into a 'halfwit',[20] had 'screwed [...] everything that couldn't get out of his way'[21] and produced 'ballsy shallowness'.[22] Only a few reviewers took the trouble to look more closely, and only some recognized that, with *Rocky Dutschke, '68*, Schlingensief—defiantly, angrily, but also with tongue-in-cheek zestfulness—was lamenting both the fact that the revolution had taken place without him, and that since 1968 a know-it-all paralysis has become widespread. Using theatrical means and a theatrical setting, Schlingensief worked off both circumstances: he re-enacted the revolution and, in doing so, produced exercises in de-paralysation. It was no surprise that such exercises also affected the traditional role of the audience. 'The images alone aren't enough,' said Schlingensief, 'so we include the audience physically in the action. Because they have to feel things, understand them physically [...].'[23] The time of undisturbed, distanced enjoyment of art was gone. No one asked if you wanted to take part. When the first gentleman was required to drop his trousers in order to bath his bottom in milk in the style of an African ritual (and actually did so), it soon became clear that things could become uncomfortable. Or worse: really embarrassing.

Following this scene, two of my friends went to sit at the edge of the auditorium in order to be on the safe side. They were well advised. Only ten minutes later Bernhard Schütz stormed up to my boyfriend, of all people, and before he knew what was happening, Schütz had taped his ankles and was dragging him by the arms to the stage. 'You're coming with me!' he screamed. The situation was anything but enjoyable. Neither my boyfriend nor I knew how to respond. We weren't used to being bulldozed in such a way in the theatre, a space where events usually only take place in an 'as if' mode. But here this convention was being circumvented. Here the game was suddenly becoming serious. Here someone was really being tied up and couldn't tell how far things would go. What should we do? Start a discussion? Wave our arms? Scream? Out of the question. We didn't want to make a bad situation worse. As I was trying to undo the tape as quickly as possible, another actor (Astrid Meyerfeldt) came running up. She yelled at my boyfriend, 'Why are you putting up with this? Why aren't you defending yourself?' And while she got involved in a scuffle with Bernhard Schütz to prevent him from dragging my boyfriend away, she shouted at the audience, 'And you lot? You'd rather gawk than intervene?' The situation then calmed down, but it left a stale aftertaste, and not only because of the shock created by Schütz's aggressive behaviour. It was perhaps primarily to do with the fact that both actors had unmasked the audience as compliant spectators.

Epilogue

We left the theatre towards the end of the performance when Schlingensief was standing in a boxing ring, surrounded by portraits of socialist heroes from Karl Marx to Ché Guevara, and inviting the audience up on stage for a free beer. The evening had been strenuous. And it had hurt a little too. Schlingensief's banquet had been difficult to digest and had plunged us into a whirl of contradictory emotions, attitudes and opinions. *Rocky Dutschke, '68* had been wonderful and enervating, tiring and exhilarating, profound and banal, ugly and beautiful, grotesque and ingenious at once. Schlingensief had not only confronted us—at a rapid pace—with all the clichéd tableau images from 1968, Dutschke's biography and East Germany, but also with various chapters from the history of avant-garde theatre. It had been an encounter with the past, somewhere between a whale of a time and harassment, which showed that through theory alone, and from a distance, much can become romanticized.

We sat for a long time on the steps outside and felt similarly affected as when, three years previously, we had attended the screening of *Terror 2000*. It wasn't easy to grasp what we had experienced, and this was certainly one of the reasons why *Rocky Dutschke, '68* attracted only cursory interest at the time from both critics and theatre scholars. How can one talk, in a helpfully interpretive way, about a work that can't be dealt with through conventional explanatory models? And how can such a work be integrated into theatrical discourse when it has thrown all known conceptual or categorial access possibilities overboard? During the mid 1990s, being a critic or a theatre scholar still meant reading the theatrical signs that constituted a particular performance, and asking how directors interpret plays and actors their roles. But *Rocky Dutschke, '68* was not only a celebratory departure from literary theatre. It had also radically put the permeability of the fourth wall to the test, along with the rules of role-playing and the standard 'as if' mode characteristic of institutionalized theatre. It hassled and accosted its audience, some of whom were treated to unpleasant experiences. Schlingensief may have remained silent on the question of who Rudi Dutschke really was, but by approaching the insurgent leader of 1968 using all theatrical means he became an insurgent himself: a director who has explored the possibilities of theatre in multiple directions and who, by thwarting every convention, has contributed to both the establishment of a new aesthetics of the theatre and to an altered approach to discursive theatre criticism and scholarship.

– Translated by Michael Turnbull

Endnotes

1. See, for example, Anon. (1993), 'Anschlag auf Berliner Kino', in *Hamburger Abendblatt*, 25 February.

2. Three people were killed during this incident. On the morning of 16 August 1988, two bank robbers took hostages after raiding a bank in Gladbeck, and fled with them for two days through Germany and the Netherlands. The behaviour of the journalists involved—who granted the perpetrators live interviews on the radio and television, went along in the getaway vehicle, and obstructed the police through their proximity to the events—sparked off a vigorous public debate about the limits and responsibilities of journalism.

3. Castorf, F., quoted in H.-D. Schütt (1996), *Die Erotik des Verrats. Gespräche mit Frank Castorf*, 1st edition, Berlin: Dietz Berlin, p. 17.

4. The following description is based on a video recording of one of the performances of *100 Jahre CDU*.

5. The Bellevue Palace in Berlin is the residence of the German president.

6. Cicciolina is a Hungarian-Italian former porn star who, after leaving the pornography business, became active for the Italian Partito Radicale, which she represented in the Rome parliament from 1987 to 1992.

7. Schödel, H. (1993), 'Der Abend der Zerstörung', in *Die Zeit*, 30 April.

8. Stadelmaier, G. (1993), 'Gelaber satt', in *Tagesspiegel*, 4 May.

9. Rochwoh, C. and Schalk A. (1993), 'Metaphern stinken', in *Zitty*, October.

10. See Schlingensief, C. (1998), 'Wir sind zwar nicht gut, aber wir sind da', in J. Lochte and W. Schulz (eds.), *Schlingensief! Notruf für Deutschland. Über die Mission, das Theater und die Welt des Christoph Schlingensief*, Hamburg: Rotbuch Verlag, pp. 12–39, here p. 26.

11. Lehmann H.-T. (1999), *Postdramatisches Theater*, 1st edition, Frankfurt am Main: Verlag der Autoren.

12. On the aesthetics of undecidability, see ibid. p. 170ff.

13. See also Schlingensief's own remarks in J. Lochte and W. Schulz (eds.) (1998), p. 36f.

14. The PDS emerged from *the Sozialistische Einheitspartei Deutschlands* (SED—Socialist Unity Party of Germany), which renamed itself in February 1990. From July 2005 onwards it was known *as Die Linkspartei.PDS* (*Die Linke.PDS*—The Left Party.PDS) until it fused with a new left-wing party, the WASG, on 16 June 2007 to become *Die Linke* (The Left).

15. Kommune 2 (1967–68) was a commune in Berlin-Charlottenburg that attempted to combine collective living with political activity. Its name was a reference to the recently founded Kommune 1, in contrast to which it was also known as the political commune.

16. Ernst Busch (1900–1980) was a German singer, cabaret performer, actor and director.

17. *The Nationale Volksarmee* (NVA—National People's Army) was the army of the German Democratic Republic from 1956 to 1990.

18. Quoted from 'Ich bin lieber wieder pubertär' (1996), interview with Christoph Schlingensief, in *Zitty*, November. *Die Tageszeitung* (abbreviation *taz*) is a national newspaper that was founded in West Berlin in 1978 as a left-wing, independent newspaper project.

19. Quoted from ibid.

20. Arend, I. (1996), 'Emotions-Grusical', in Freitag, 24 May.

21. Lehmann, A. (1996), 'Hosen runter!', in Wochenpost, 23 May.

22. Oesterreich, V. (1996), 'Die Zuschauer bleiben nicht verschont', in *Berliner Morgenpost*, 19 May.

23. Quoted from 'Ich bin lieber wieder pubertär' (2006), interview with Christoph Schlingensief.

PASSION IMPOSSIBLE OR MAN WITH A MISSION:
A GOFFMANESQUE INTERVENTION

Anna Teresa Scheer

Passion Impossible: 7 Day Emergency Call for Germany (1997) took place in diverse public spaces in Hamburg over seven days during October 1997. The title is a pun on the action film *Mission Impossible*[1], which follows the activities of an undercover agent on a dangerous foreign mission, and meshes it with an allusion to the Christian concept of Christ's 'passion'; the term used to describe the physical, mental and emotional sufferings he endured prior to his crucifixion. The compounding of these narratives in the title *Passion Impossible* implies both a dangerous undercover mission, (in this case performed by Christoph Schlingensief) and a notion of Christian martyrdom, wedded to the task of opening a mission for the socially underprivileged: an act of charity that may well prove to be 'impossible'. Undeniably, the task at hand—Schlingensief's efforts to aid the homeless, sick, and socially destitute—had Christian overtones of charity, sacrifice and redemption along with a certain messianic zeal. However, as I shall discuss in this chapter, the strategies employed to undertake such a mission did not have much in common with a more conventional missionary approach.

Schlingensief's intervention into the everyday experiences of a destitute sub-strata of Hamburg's population, whose situation he viewed as a 'staging' or production, recalls the theories of Erving Goffman, in particular his influential work *The Presentation of Self in Everyday Life* (1959).[2] In this book, Goffman sets out theatrical principles that can be applied to the social sphere in order to construe daily behaviour from a theatrical standpoint. He posits that social interaction is a 'performance', which he defines as: 'all the activity of a given participant on a given occasion which serves to influence in any way any of the other participants'.[3] Using the metaphor of social life as theatrical performance, he developed concepts such as 'front' and 'back regions'[4] that can be read as parallel to the front and backstage of a theatre.

In order to relate Goffman's theories to Schlingensief's project, I will first briefly describe the events in Hamburg and their consequences. Secondly, following Goffman, I will consider the idea of everyday life as a staged reality in which roles are allocated to us by social circumstance and political policy. I will argue that by rejecting a theatre venue in favour of a series of events staged in public places, Schlingensief was—in line with Goffman's ideas—attempting to re-stage reality for socially critical purposes.

Producing social embarrassment to effect social change

In 1997, The Deutsches Schauspielhaus in Hamburg (one of Germany's leading theatres), had invited Schlingensief as guest director to stage a production with its ensemble but, after only two days in the theatre, he broke off rehearsals announcing his intention to 'get out of this shack and into life!'[5] For Schlingensief, apparently, it had become clear that the real theatre was across the road in Hamburg's central railway station. This was a meeting point for the city's homeless people, heroin addicts and prostitutes who, in the absence of other facilities, used the station as a shelter, surviving ever more deteriorating conditions amidst police violence, public hostility and political apathy. In the preceding months, conditions had worsened for these station dwellers because the state had attempted to evict them through the use of harassment and strong-arm police tactics in order to remove this 'eyesore' from one of the main gates to the city.[6]

In view of the dire situation opposite the prestigious Schauspielhaus, Schlingensief suggested that the facade of the theatre be torn down and the seats turned around to face the miserable scene across the road—a plan rejected by the theatre for 'technical reasons'.[7] He then conceived another plan whereby the theatre would be utilized as a venue for the opening event and then function in name only as the main sponsor of the action. Thus *Passion Impossible* began with a 'benefit gala', held in the theatre's plush interior. Here, actors and 'VIPs' were invited to auction off designer clothing and props to raise funds for a prototype mission that Schlingensief planned to inaugurate for the destitute people at the station. The mission would also be open to the public and, for a period of seven days, would offer a programme of art events as well as tea, coffee, warm meals and a place to sleep.[8]

Typical aspects of the benefit gala genre, such as appeals for donations made by earnest VIPs past their prime, were juxtaposed with rather more unusual elements. Schlingensief, wearing a white, seventies-style entertainer suit, played the master of ceremonies in an impromptu oratorical style and attempted to encourage audience donations by exhorting 'Let's just be human!' and 'You simply have to believe in yourselves again. You simply have to say, yes, we can do it if we want to'.[9] The clichéd sentiment behind these phrases was, it seems, intentionally echoed by a film projection of a German politician calling for compassion and understanding as part of a fundraising appeal for AIDS patients.

The appeal was drowned out by loud music and interjections from performers onstage, apparently ignoring the politician's pre-rehearsed 'performance' of pathos.

Over the course of the evening, an auctioneer encouraged the audience to bid for clothing worn by the guests, a Japanese pop singer performed a song, and Schlingensief and his ensemble danced around the stage in a haphazard fashion chanting: 'We want to help! Help, help, help!' Actor Bernhard Schutz repeatedly interrupted the proceedings by posing questions to the audience, such as: 'What sort of a world do we live in where someone has to ask for donations so that a young girl doesn't have to prostitute herself? What is going on?'[10] The uncertainty created by his interjections was trumped when—following speeches made by Salvation Army representatives—an emaciated chicken in a cage was brought onstage for which three thousand marks was demanded as a donation to save it from execution. Schlingensief commented to the audience:

> I want to see how much money will be donated to save the life of a chicken. We are all addicted. We are all hooked on a needle. That is the centrepiece of this evening and of this action.[11]

'Everything can be bought', he added, while the audience loudly expressed their displeasure after he insisted it was a battery hen, something they all ate, which would have been killed anyway.

An actress from the theatre came onstage and announced that she found the gala event shameful, that people were being exploited and that she was distancing herself from her colleagues and the whole dilettantism of the event. Whether this scenario had been pre-planned or was a genuine expression of outrage remained uncertain. Further discomfort was produced when the audience was encouraged to silently applaud following an embarrassingly pedagogical interview with deaf people. The evening finally drew to a close as the gala participants sang 'Let it be' with a black gospel choir, before joining in a freestyle dance to the Bee Gees song 'Staying Alive' (1977).[12]

This 'gala' kick-started the proceedings of the following day when Schlingensief and his ensemble—a mixture of actors from the theatre, disabled lay performers, friends and colleagues—occupied an empty police station, some one hundred metres from the Schauspielhaus. The station had achieved notoriety in 1994 due to a scandal involving the Hamburg police and their targeted victimization and maltreatment of foreigners, homeless people and junkies in the St. Georg area.[13] The former police station now became the centre for Schlingensief's theatre of operations, which extended beyond the confines of the station walls into public thoroughfares and streets. On day one, the building was turned into a mission comprising a soup kitchen, hostel, open forum, and art area for the neighbourhood's needy, audience members and assembled media representatives. Schlingensief and his mission team were variously costumed as United Nations peacekeepers, paramedics, Salvation Army volunteers and police. The mission slowly filled up as word spread amongst the station dwellers and food and drinks were served as the Salvation Army band played the hymn 'Praise the Lord'. Audience members who had paid for tickets to the event at the Schauspielhaus were met outside its doors by Schlingensief who encouraged them to 'Come away from this ugly bunker of art and culture, tonight we want to show you real life [...] many people are waiting to meet you [at the mission], people excluded from places like this.'[14]

At the mission, some performance elements of the gala evening, such as an actor's recitation of a text and the Japanese pop song, were repeated but were loudly contested by one visitor who complained that they were 'commercial and crap'.[15] This led to the implementation of the 'open microphone' principle, with the destitute and heroin addicts—normally found at the main station—talking instead to the audience about their experiences in the former police station. Many had been held there and beaten by police, refused medical treatment or left in their cells without food and water for 48 hours for their non-observance of a ban from the station.[16]

In light-hearted contrast to the personal testimonies, various songs punctuated the activities at the mission and helped to create a sense of collective presence for the diverse group in the public interventions they conducted over the following days. The mission dwellers and attendees were encouraged to join Schlingensief's ensemble in singing the chorus to a corny American pop song, which had been rewritten in German as: 'We want to grieve, grieve, grieve until the world understands us, cos we are alone, so alone'.[17] But the main refrain of the event—repeated at very opportunity—was lifted from Bertolt Brecht's 'Rosa Luxemburg Fragment': 'To look into the face of someone who has been helped, is to look into a lovely place, friend, friend, friend!'[18], which was cheerfully sung to the Al Jolson melody, 'Let Me Sing and I am Happy'. These songs became the anthems of the new congregation with Schlingensief, who functioned as its ministrant, wryly commenting in an interview after the event:

> The constant repetition of the songs was a straw we could hold onto when things threatened to sink into chaos. [...] it functions the same way with every family at Christmas time, after the presents are unwrapped and no one knows what to do next, everyone can sing "Oh Christmas tree" together.[19]

Today we will help Jill Sander's customers carry their bags!

On the second day, Schlingensief and Schutz dressed as policemen, marched to one of Hamburg's main shopping thoroughfares with mission inhabitants and supporters carrying banners which read 'Hallo You!', 'We Want to Help' and 'Transparency'. Employing a megaphone, Schlingensief proclaimed to passers-by: 'This is the Hamburg police, we are overwhelmed, we are exhausted, we are giving up'—a point which he underscored by saying: 'If you do not help the homeless and the junkies it will cost you your lives, we cannot guarantee your safety any longer.'[20] A policewoman approached the group to question whether permission had been given for the march, which had drawn near to the 'off-limits zone' in front of the town hall. After a brief exchange with Schlingensief, she returned to the patrol car to request backup and he announced to the onlookers that, after ten years of service, 'Frau Müller's' nerves were raw and that she could not cope anymore with the whole 'exhausting, emotionally loaded business'.[21] Two policemen then arrived to enquire about the activities taking place and to ask if Schlingensief was a 'real' policeman. Schlingensief answered affirmatively, asking the policeman if *he* was real and explaining that he wanted to find out who was responsible for the 'staging' of the Mönckeberger Street. A discussion then ensued as to whether the action was a demonstration, an advertisement or an artwork.[22] Permission finally arrived for the group to proceed after Schlingensief maintained that the march was an art action and that all participants were, in fact, artists.[23] Schutz encircled the group with red and white police tape declaring: 'Come inside the protection of your own artwork: the off-limits zone of art!'[24] Two protagonists dressed as police handcuffed themselves to the town hall doors where one of them had a nervous collapse and had to be taken to hospital by the real police observing the scene.[25]

On day three a mock church service was celebrated in the station forecourt, advertised by Schlingensief as 'High Mass and a Feeding of the Five Thousand'. Church bells rang out from a ghetto-blaster and Schlingensief—in a Cardinal's robe and a policeman's cap—addressed the crowd, inviting everyone to come forward and speak about 'your wishes, your doubts and your fears [...] fear connects us in the same way as addiction'.[26] A woman read aloud a poem she had written, a Polish man recited the Hail Mary in his language and a young homeless man with a punk haircut commented that the state was not there to help those like him, concluding: 'first, we have to kick ourselves up the arse'. Everyone sang the mission songs and the mood became euphoric as the crowd danced to 'Staying Alive' and Schlingensief began a call and response chant in an ever increasing tempo: 'Life/For everyone!'[27]

That night the group respectfully attended a local church service and at the end, Schlingensief addressed the congregation and invited members of the mission to the pulpit to speak about the desperate conditions they faced. On this occasion a young woman spoke at length about her catastrophic history and circumstances (an account that included being raped by her stepfather, prostitution, pregnancy and heroin addiction). Her story shocked many in the congregation who were motivated to make a collection for her and, according to the theatre, she was later offered practical support in leaving the squalor of life at the station.[28] The emotional speeches made in the church prompted the group to head back to the theatre where they disturbed a performance of *Peer Gynt* (Henrik Ibsen, 1867) in order to inform the audience of their complicity in the misery that lurked outside the theatre doors. This action resulted in the promise of a serious discussion about the mission's future by the theatre manager.[29]

Figure 1: *Passion Impossible*: High Mass at the main station. © Matthias Horn

Finally on the evening of day six, a large group of mission participants holding lanterns, led by Schlingensief and accompanied by a marching band with drums, took part in a procession to the town hall demanding that the mission be financially supported by the city and granted permission to remain in the current premises. Public interest and the press corps accompanying the action had grown so large by this point that, under pressure and after hours of waiting, the mayor finally came out to a frenzy of cameras and agreed to visit the mission the following day. Thus, on the final day of the action, the lord mayor of Hamburg took a tour of the mission and—employing the inconclusive language of political rhetoric—made comments such as 'in a democracy one cannot decide alone', and deferred any other decisions with promises of further discussions.[30] Refusing to be dismissed by the lord mayor's 'promises', Schlingensief initiated a symbolic handing over of the baton to the director of the theatre, Frank Bambauer, in front of running cameras to seal *his* commitment to carrying the mission project forward.[31] After the departure of Schlingensief and his group, the Deutsches Schauspielhaus decided, along with other cultural institutions, to support the mission as an 'artistic measure against the cold'.[32] The homeless, with the aid of a non-profit support committee, would run the mission independently, offering 'art and soup' on a daily basis.

The events of *Passion Impossible* garnered much media attention and the press were both courted and encouraged by Schlingensief throughout the duration of the project. On the one hand, this led to a reconsideration of Schlingensief as someone whose name had become synonymous with theatrical chaos and bad taste: someone who sought only to provoke theatre audiences and the broader German public.[33] Schlingensief was, however, also accused (in some cases by actors from the Schauspielhaus who were not involved in the project) of exploiting the marginalized for his show in order to both promote himself and generate a media spectacle.[34] Journalistic responses were mostly skewed in favour of sensationalism—as typified by the following examples—where the work was described as a 'bizarre sort of social pedagogical operetta' or a mixture of 'committed street worker discourse and aesthetic dilettantism spiced up with trash'.[35] As I will make clear in the following section, such cynical responses resisted both the exploratory nature of the work and its unexpected, yet positive, outcome for the marginalized individuals who participated over the seven days of its duration.

The theatre of the self in the theatre of the street

In an effort to provide an alternative reading of the project, I will consider Schlingensief's interest in 'the staging of Mönckeberger Street' (together with the other locations traversed as part of *Passion Impossible),* which has a counterpart in Erving Goffman's microsociological concepts of the self as a performer and social interaction as a collective form of theatrical performance. Goffman's terminology and his 'dramaturgical approach' to social interaction will provide a framework via which to examine Schlingensief's project.[36] In addition, I will argue that Goffman's analysis of stigma can be productively applied to explore the inclusion of marginalized groups in Schlingensief's practice.

In *The Presentation of Self,* Goffman posits that social interaction in daily life is analogous to a staged drama in which individuals participate in a series of performances. That is to say, they actively create themselves in the guise of a character/performer, in an attempt to 'guide and control' the reactions of others toward them.[37] The desire to control our own performance extends to our behaviour in society, encompassing the environments we live and work in, as well as those we encounter as part of our daily routines—such as public transport, shops, schools, churches, and public squares. A central component of Goffman's argument is that the social performances created by individuals possess what he terms a 'front', which functions as a 'setting' with all the necessary 'scenery and stage props'.[38] This idea, in turn, relates to the notion of a 'personal front', which reveals specific qualities of the performer such as social status, age, gender, ethnic and racial characteristics, and approximate earning power through variables such as clothing and accessories.[39] By means of these specific qualities, Goffman's concept of the 'front' is closely connected with the formation of social identity.

Key to Goffman's argument is the distinction he makes between 'front' and 'back regions' that pertain to both the performances of individuals and to those of social institutions.[40] The division of a performance into these regions is predicated upon the variations in behaviour that occur within them and is based upon the performer's goal of effectively controlling the desired performance. The 'front region' is where the performance occurs and is connected to 'decorum' and how one 'comports oneself within the visual and aural range' of others.[41] Accordingly, for Goffman, the 'back region' corresponds to a backstage in the sense that certain elements belonging to the front region can be adjusted or changed by the performer commensurate with the specific requirements of the occasion. In the back region, the performer can behave informally, unobserved by those for whom her/his performance is intended. Keeping the 'back region' hidden from view is a primary technique of 'impression management': the attempt on the part of the performer to convincingly portray an idealized version of oneself to onlookers.[42]

While Goffman's dramaturgical concept of social interaction can be understood more as an extended metaphor rather than a verifiable scientific theory, his conclusions are surprisingly apt in regard to Schlingensief's project in Hamburg. Goffman acknowledges the concerns of the individual as a performer to transmit the right impression and abide by the social standards (not excluding their bewildering diversity) according to which one is judged.[43] Nonetheless, he makes the following harsh assessment:

> Individuals are concerned not with the moral issue of realizing these standards, but with the amoral issue of engineering a convincing impression that [they] are being realized. Our activity, then, is largely concerned with moral matters, but as performers we do not have a moral concern with them [...] the very obligation and profitability of appearing always in a steady moral light [...] forces one to be the sort of person who is practiced in the ways of the stage.[44]

Goffman's observation goes to the heart of Schlingensief's attempt to intervene in the scene at the station in Hamburg and to question the role of the theatre and its audience in participating in the staging of the scene. The 'convincing impression' one hopes to leave—wedded to the 'profitability' of appearing in a steady moral light—is exactly the sort of 'concern' that motivates people to attend benefit galas in order to confirm the feeling that 'one has done one's bit'. From the gala onwards, such dubious motivation was one of the socially approved routines Schlingensief's project attempted to question.

In keeping with Goffman's analogy, it can be argued that Schlingensief's comment to the theatre audience, 'we are all addicts', questioned their unwillingness—as socially privileged individuals—to concede their own complicity in the unjust processes of daily life. For him, the vested interest in believing in one's innate innocence (or, at least one's performance of it) is at the root of social injustice. What is addictive, in this context, is the desire to permanently position oneself as being beyond reproach. During the gala event, Schlingensief critiqued the ethos of needing to be entertained before taking any kind of ethical action to help others. This critique was demonstrated by the verbal ambiguity intended by platitudes such as 'you have to become soft and open your hearts', juxtaposed with both the threatened decapitation of a chicken and a combination of tacky guest performances.

Furthermore, the idea of including the audience as part of an event staged in a world of destitution and hopelessness—a parallel world which the marginalized had forcibly become accustomed to—was heightened by having them pay for tickets to participate in the various activities inside and outside the mission. As spectators, they were normally excluded from such scenes of deprivation by means of status, money and, perhaps, disinterest. Paying to be included was, in addition, an ironic comment on the socially destitute who can participate in penury for free. Nonetheless, the uncertainty, or disagreement, generated by the gala event, remained unresolved in terms of whether it was a 'serious' fundraising event for the destitute, or a complete mockery of the do-gooder posturing characteristic of such spectacles. The disagreement itself—in regard to Schlingensief's motivation—was, quite possibly, both part of the project's meaning and responsible for the media attention it attracted.

A theatrical renegotiation of public spaces

The interest generated by the project as it unfolded in public squares and streets was due, in part, to Schlingensief's reflexive utilization of his persona. Here, 'reflexive' refers to the way in which Schlingensief, (as director of, and actor in, his own production) maintains complete control over which aspect or 'front' of his character will be revealed to the audience. Schlingensief's self-reflexivity informed both his orchestration of the daily activities and motivated his alternating roles throughout the event from benefit gala host, to policeman, priest and agitator. The effect of changing roles according to the situation enabled Schlingensief to playfully facilitate a renegotiation of public spaces in order to make space for socially underprivileged groups that are usually rendered invisible within the city's infra-structural 'staging'. By appropriating the clothing and props of various authority figures, Schlingensief was able to interrogate their functions and, when worn together in public, they created a semiotic slippage that implied that authority figures were—in essence—characters in costume, therefore less threatening and more approachable as a result.

Figure 2: March on the town hall: Schlingensief and Bernhard Schutz with the brass band. © Matthias Horn

The intention to forcibly generate visibility for the socially marginalized was further demonstrated by Schlingensief's deliberate disruption of the classical play *Peer Gynt*. The unexpected appearance onstage—in the 'front' area of the theatre—of people from the 'back region' of the station constituted both a breach in the staging of 'everyday' life and a disruption of the business-as-usual activities of the theatre. The discomfort occasioned by the disturbance, as noted previously, prompted a quick response from the theatre management. Baz Kershaw has argued elsewhere that theatre has increasingly become 'a social institution from which equality and mutual exchange [...] is all but banished'[45], thus revealing its function as 'a kind of social engine that helps to drive an unfair system of privilege'.[46] Schlingensief's direct intervention into what constitutes conventionally mainstream theatre practice underscores his confrontational relationship with this particular 'social institution'. He recognizes theatre as a 'social engine' that ensures the automatic accessibility of theatrical events for those privileged enough to afford entry which does not extend its invitations to those on the economic margins, or those with potentially disruptive voices unless—as happened at the Schauspielhaus—they arrive uninvited.

The unpredictable nature of the visit to the theatre, together with other mission events, proved to be one of the project's strengths. *Passion Impossible* was intentionally carried out in experimental fashion without a pre-planned or fixed dramaturgical structure. Events were planned on a daily basis and impromptu suggestions made by participants were also integrated, allowing space for the unpredictable to occur. The open method of working, with opportunities for loopholes, new risks, and possible failure, is what drove the action and allowed it to build an authentic momentum without pre-planned goals having to be met. The disparate groups at the mission forged a connection through songs, shared rituals, and the collective transgression of social boundaries, which in turn allowed the 'performance' of 'any given participant on any given occasion' to influence the behaviour of others.[47] The informal atmosphere established within the mission—which functioned both as an assembly point and a sanctuary to retreat into after the euphoria of the day's activities—encouraged free expression and spontaneity. As a result of this, the marginalized became bolder in their participation in the public incursions and less fearful of authoritarian backlash due to Schlingensief's ability to theatricalize potentially risky situations by reframing them as art. Through observing the flexible way in which Schlingensief and his team operated in public, the marginalized members of the collective became politically empowered and grew more confident in their ability to demand solutions to their abject circumstances.

While it was Goffman's contention that social interaction is constituted by individuals projecting a desired image of themselves and participating in self-directed scenes, he saw the 'means for producing and maintaining selves' as being 'bolted down in social establishments'.[48] The impersonation of police officers, the speeches before the town hall, and the celebration of an anarchic public mass all transgressed allocated social roles and eluded conflict—although not contact—with those in positions of formalized power. Taken together, the activities of *Passion Impossible* reversed the normal front and back divisions of 'social establishments', thus refusing to be kept hidden in the back regions of charity—in the case of the church—or relegated to the fringes of political discourse.

The provocative stance intended by this reversal elicited a response from at least one very irritated passer-by who yelled at Schlingensief in an altercation: 'What have the homeless got to do with me? Only the tax-payer is a human being!'[49]As astounding as this comment is, it may not be far-removed from attitudes held by people overexposed to capitalism's gospel of the free-market, or new-age philosophies that preach that we all create our own reality; the point being that we only have ourselves to blame if we end up on the street. The social disenfranchisement experienced by the homeless and destitute, amongst other groups, was itself the focus of a further study by Goffman to which I shall now turn to discuss his concept of the stigmatized self in relation both to his concept of regions and Schlingensief's project.

Confronting stigma and questioning the normative

To summarize briefly, we have seen that social spaces can be categorized according to regions, and I have argued that Schlingensief's project was, in part, an attempt to get behind the 'front regions' of the institutions with which *Passion Impossible* engaged. In doing so, he sought to question the legitimacy of the criteria for inclusion in normative (non-marginalized) society and to challenge what, in fact, constitutes a socially normative identity. The subtle insistence upon idealized modes of conduct by those who can successfully operate within its frameworks inevitably produces individuals who fall short of the ideal, and who, consequently, are viewed as somehow deficient. Goffman's study of stigma posits that marginalized people are, based on the type of stigma they carry, forced into 'discredited' or 'discreditable' groups, by socially accepted definitions of normality.[50] In an attempt to justify the exclusion of people alleged to be deficient, Goffman claims:

> We construct a stigma-theory, an ideology to explain his inferiority and account for the danger he represents, sometimes rationalizing an animosity based on other differences such as those of social class.[51]

The socialized adherence to 'stigma theory' on the part of the non-marginalized mission visitors began to unravel as they had the opportunity to listen first-hand to the stories of those stigmatized by misfortune. Through the sharing of food, drink, music, activism and performance the audience/participants could engage with people who had experienced life differently from them. As a result, generic stigmatized terms (such as vagrant, junkie and prostitute) dissolved, as the people behind the terms became known.

However, Schlingensief's visit to the church with the mission group functioned in quite a different fashion. The interruption of the congregation's usual behaviour at the end of the church service inverted the established 'front' and 'back' positions. The marginalized, marked by their shabby clothing and worn physical features, had entered through the main doors to attend the service. At its end, they faced the assembled church goers who—in their own frontal performances of 'socialized beings' (or 'normals' to use Goffman's terminology)—could not retreat to a back area to adjust themselves to their accustomed mode of dealing with homeless people, prostitutes and addicts. Instead of 'seeing through them', or hurrying past, the congregation was forced to listen to their stories of suffering in a place where the consideration of suffering more commonly occurs at some distance.

In the context of the Church, the telling of 'private stories' that belong to those people who make up society's back regions not only presented the stigmatized, but also reversed the telling of stories of suffering attributed to biblical personages who are, in their biblical context, reified and given special meaning. The decision of the congregation to make a collection was necessary in order to maintain their idea of themselves as socialized beings and to cope with the unexpected arrival of those who—although a cause for social concern and prayer—are expected to receive their charity away from the church service and its members.

In his exploration of human interaction between the socialized and the marginalized, Goffman points out a significant discrepancy in the behaviour of the former:

> The nature of a 'good adjustment' is now apparent. [...] It means that the unfairness and pain of having to carry a stigma will never be presented to them; it means that *normals* will not have to admit to themselves how limited their tactfulness and tolerance is [...] and can remain relatively unthreatened in their identity beliefs.[52]

The visible contrast the stigmatized group presented to the churchgoers—unmarked by hardship or addiction—was, on this occasion, utilized to the advantage of the marginalized. The church in its social 'front' aspect would have been perceived as callous and authoritarian had it refused them entry. In addition, access to 'back regions' for members of the congregation to conceal, change, or adjust their social performances was prevented as a result of the unexpected nature of the mission group's visit. For those living with visible stigmas, the experience of belonging to a larger group engaged in social activism encouraged them, in turn, to participate and to protest, in the knowledge that (a certain) protection from retribution was guaranteed due to the project being financed by the theatre as 'art'. Schlingensief's focus on a fluid form of activism meant that - at times - the anarchic energy of the event was focussed solely on political and social work with art silently framing the situation in the background.

Literalizing Goffman's metaphor and re-staging reality

Having examined the connections of Schlingensief's activities in relation to Goffman's theatrical metaphor it can be argued that the core concerns of *Passion Impossible* bear little resemblance to either social work or traditional theatre. Instead, its concerns were driven by a desire to question the social order by employing the theatre as a metaphor and frame to investigate social issues by means of playful guerrilla-style tactics. In doing so, social groups normally divided by class and status were brought together. Schlingensief's attempt to re-direct the 'staged reality' of the scene at the station in Hamburg was an enquiry into how the situation there had been created and did not, at its inception, have the goal of establishing a long-term social welfare scheme. It was also not his intention to produce an interesting theatrical experience for an audience. *Passion Impossible* challenged the ostensible neutrality of public spaces such as shopping areas, the theatre and the station, forcing them to reveal their hypocrisies and covert exclusionary processes. Although not identified with a particular political or social philosophy, Schlingensief's action was a direct enquiry into the cultural life of a city and its institutions, questioning who was permitted to be included in cultural events and under which conditions. The rediscovery of a public voice and some political clout led the mission inhabitants, removed from their roles as isolated examples of abjection, to call for the institutionalization of this 'new form of social culture' and its headquarters in the mission.[53] The positive repercussions of *Passion Impossible*, although not planned by Schlingensief, exemplify the potential of innovative modes of performance to intervene in the production and consumption of culture. In this instance a significant outcome and increased agency for people marked by stigma was achieved.

Endnotes

1. Brian de Palma (1996), *Mission Impossible,* USA: Paramount Pictures.

2. Goffman, E. (1959), *The Presentation of Self in Everyday Life,* New York: Anchor Books.

3. Ibid., p. 15.

4. Ibid., pp. 107–112.

5. ('Raus aus dieser Bude - rein ins Leben!'), Schmitter, E. (1997), 'Christoph Schlingensiefs "Bahnhofsmission -7 Tage Notruf für Deutschland" im Deutschen Schauspielhaus Hamburg', *Die Zeit*, http://www.zeit.de/1997/44/schlinge. txt.19971024.xml. Accessed 5 May 2009.

6. Briegleb, T. (1998), '7 Tage Notruf für Deutschland: Ein Bahnhofs Mission', in J. Lochte and W. Schulz (eds.), *Schlingensief! Notruf für Deutschland. Über die Mission, das Theater und die Welt des Christoph Schlingensief,* Hamburg: Rotbuch Verlag, p. 114.

7. Ibid., pp. 100–101.

8. My description of the performance, the mission and the events are based on the book cited above and the documentary film, Alexander Grasseck and Stefan Corinth (1998), *Freund, Freund, Freund!*, Germany: ZDF/arte. Unless otherwise stated, all translations are my own.

9. *Freund, Freund, Freund!* (1998).

10. Briegleb, T. (1998), p. 108.

11. Ibid., p. 107.

12. Ibid., p. 108.

13. Mahr, M., (1997) 'Polizeiübergriffe als "Strafe vor Ort", Grundrechte-Report Zur Lage der Bürger- und Menschenrechte in Deutschland', http://www.grundrechtereport.de/1997/inhalt/details/back/inhalt-1997/article/polizeiuebergriffe-als-strafe-vor-ort-1/. Accessed 21 March 2009. In the first eight months of 1995 the police conducted over 30,595 evictions *(Platzverweise)* in and around St. Georg. Following numerous charges of police racism and misconduct, Werner Hackman, the Interior Minister, stepped down.

14. *Freund, Freund, Freund!* (1998).

15. Briegleb, T. (1998), p. 117.

16. Ibid., p. 117.

17. The original song and its melody were from 'I don't want to live my life without you' by Toni Braxton (Arista Records Inc., 1996).

18. 'Der Blick in das Gesicht eines Menschen, dem geholfen ist, ist der Blick in eine schöne Gegend, Freund!' See, Mittenzwei, W. and Müller, K.D. (eds.) (1997), *Bertolt Brecht Werke Stücke 10*, Frankfurt am Main: Suhrkamp Verlag, p. 981.

19. Schlingensief, C., 'Wir sind zwar nicht gut aber wir sind da', in Lochte and Schulz (1998), p. 14.

20. *Freund, Freund, Freund!* (1998). The title of this section was the motto of the day's activities.

21. *Freund, Freund, Freund!* (1998).

22. Briegleb, T. (1998), p. 124.

23. This is a clear reference to artist Joseph Beuys' famous statement, 'Everyone is an artist', revealing the links between Schlingensief's project and Beuys's concept of 'social sculpture', defined by him as: '[...] how we mould and shape the world in

which we live'. Beuys cited in Kuoni, C. (1993), *Energy Plan for the Western man— Joseph Beuys in America*, New York: Four Walls Eight Windows, p. 19.

24. *Freund, Freund, Freund!* (1998)

25. Briegleb, T. (1998), p. 126.

26. Ibid., p. 119.

27. *Freund, Freund, Freund!* (1998)

28. Briegleb, T. (1998), p. 121.

29. Ibid., p. 121.

30. Ibid., p. 135.

31. Ibid., pp. 134–135.

32. Mix, I. and Bäurle, P. (1998), 'Neue Räume für die "Mission"', http://www.hamburg.de/Behoerden/Pressestelle/Meldungen/ tagesmeldungen/1998/okt/w44/fr/news.htm. Accessed 12 April 2007.

33. Schmitter, E. (1997) '[…] ist er nicht eigentlich ein Synonym für Chaos und Geschmacksverirrung?' Accessed 5 May 2009.

34. Briegleb, T. (1998), p. 106. Schlingensief's response to these accusations was to graffiti the phrase 'Ensemble, where are you?' onto the freshly painted facade of the theatre.

35. Briegleb, T. (1998), p. 98.

36. Goffman E. (1959), p. 240.

37. Ibid., p. 3.

38. Ibid., p. 22.

39. Ibid., p. 24.

40.   Ibid., pp. 107–112.

41.   Ibid., p. 107.

42.   Ibid., p. 208.

43.   Ibid., p. 251.

44.   Ibid., p. 244.

45.   Kershaw, B. (1999), *The Radical in Performance: Between Brecht and Baudrillard*, London and New York: Routledge, p. 32.

46.   Ibid., p. 31.

47.   Ibid., p. 12.

48.   Goffman E. (1959), p. 253.

49.   Briegleb, T. (1998), p. 120.

50.   Goffman, E. (1959), 'Stigma', p. 42.

51.   Lemert, C. and Branaman, A. (eds.) (1997), *The Goffman Reader*, Cambridge, Massachusetts: Blackwell, p. 73.

52.   Ibid., p. 75.

53.   Briegleb, T. (1998), p. 118.

PUTTING THE PUBLIC SPHERE TO THE TEST: ON PUBLICS AND COUNTER-PUBLICS IN *CHANCE 2000*

Solveig Gade

Art ought to be more political and politics more artful.
(Christoph Schlingensief)[1]

The desire to challenge and interrogate the limits of art and politics has been a *leitmotif* of Christoph Schlingensief's work throughout his career, be it in the form of his work as an action artist, theatre director, or talk show host. This interrogation did, however, reach a temporary climax with his project *Chance 2000* (1998), in which he sought, quite literally, to make a spectacle out of the theatricalized character of politics in the current society of the spectacle. In the following chapter, I want to pursue this interplay of art and politics, or art and non-art, by focusing on Schlingensief's manner of testing both the limits and the possibilities of the public sphere.

Chance 2000 took place in 1998 as a parallel action to the then raging German federal election campaign. Schlingensief—in cooperation with the Volksbühne in Berlin—established a political party offering marginalized minority groups a chance to voice their concerns.[2] The party was dubbed *Chance 2000—Partei der letzten Chance/ Chance 2000—The Party of The Last Chance,* and in addressing the unemployed and mentally ill, as well as physically disabled citizens in particular, it encouraged people to become candidates in the upcoming election. Thus, under *Chance 2000's* motto, 'Vote for yourself!', citizens were given the chance to speak for themselves instead of voting for candidates belonging to the established political parties.

The project spanned several months and was divided into various phases. The union *Chance 2000* (which later became the political party of the same title) was founded during the first phase of the project within the framework of the 'Election Campaign Circus' that took place in a circus tent in Berlin's Prater Garden. The show was directed by Schlingensief and included the 'Circus Family Sperlich' and a number of actors from the Volksbühne's ensemble. In the next phase, 'Election Campaign in Germany', Schlingensief and the *Chance* candidates undertook a (performance) tour of Germany in an attempt to collect enough signatures from various regional districts to be allowed to run in the national election. The candidates *did* manage to garner the requisite number of signatures and, in the third phase of the project, they moved on to the election campaign tour (the so-called 'Tour of Crime'). The fourth phase of the project took place at the Volksbühne on election night (27 September 1998), where it was announced that *Chance 2000—The Party of The Last Chance* had received the unexpectedly high number of 28,500 votes. Shortly after election night, the so-called 'political remains' of *Chance 2000* were transferred to the political organizations of the German federal states, while the so-called 'utopian remains' were transferred to the independent, so-called 'State of Chance', founded by Schlingensief at the Haus der Kulturen der Welt in Berlin in October 1998. Later, the newly founded state organized an action for homeless people at the Graz festival for contemporary art, *Steirischer Herbst,* followed by the establishment of embassies of the State of Chance in Sarajevo, Johannesburg and Namibia.[3]

Figure 1: *Chance 2000* on the '98 election campaign trail. Photo: Katrin Schoof.

As is probably clear by now, it is rather difficult to determine exactly where *Chance 2000* began and ended and how it is to be distinguished from the rest of Schlingensief's oeuvre. Furthermore, due to its hybrid character, the project obscured any easy attempt to pin it down as either an art or a political project. Constructed out of a diverse range of elements (from the circus, the theatre, and the freak show, to television, action art, political rally, learning lab, think tank and revivalist meeting), the project generated uncertainty and confusion wherever it went.[4] The parameters for decoding the project seemed open to negotiation, and the public was never offered a clear answer as to whether the project was intended seriously or was just an arty gag. As Schlingensief declared on the founding night of the union *Chance 2000*, whilst riding a pony around the ring of the 'Election Campaign Circus': 'This night is more political than it seems [...] It contains theatrical parts, and it contains political parts. Now, the question is where the former begins and where the latter ends!'[5]

After having briefly sketched the events of *Chance 2000* and some of the questions the project raises concerning the relationship between art and politics, I will now explore how Schlingensief addressed the question of the public sphere within the framework of the project.

Public scenes of 'Dissensus'

According to Schlingensief, one of his central concerns is 'to put public spaces to the test'.[6] Within his body of work, this 'testing procedure' often articulates itself as an interrogation and foregrounding of the exclusionary mechanisms governing the seemingly democratic and inclusive public sphere. In this respect, Schlingensief appears to draw inspiration from Oskar Negt and Alexander Kluge's critique of the notion of the public sphere as a unitary and inclusive entity and, more specifically, their insistence that the public sphere is in fact constituted by a multitude of publics that relate to each other in more or less conflictual ways.[7] In their book, *Öffentlichkeit und Erfahrung/Public Sphere and Experience* (1972), Negt and Kluge criticise the seminal concept offered by the early Jürgen Habermas of a universal public sphere populated by free and equal citizens who, bracketing their own socially determined interests and relying on universal and abstract norms, discuss matters of public relevance, whilst striving to reach a generally agreed-upon consensus.[8] According to Negt and Kluge, the strict distinction between public and private contained within this definition does, in fact, lead to an exclusion of important aspects of social reality and thereby also numerous groups of people. Therefore, rather than relying on abstract norms, Negt and Kluge seek to widen the notion of the public sphere in such a way as to secure its constitutive relationship to the very possibility of social and individual experience in general. Furthermore, they argue that a collective organization of aspects of the social and individual experiences excluded from the dominant public sphere will help pave the way for the rise of a proletarian public or, perhaps better, a potentially infinite number of *counter-publics* able to contest the dominant public sphere and the norms and values associated with it.[9]

Returning to *Chance 2000*, the interrogation of the exclusionary mechanisms of the public sphere, as we shall see, proved crucial to the effort to articulate and organize the social and individual experience of the *Chance* members. Schlingensief's attempt to tease out the exclusionary character of the public sphere was structured around three different types of public spaces. These were the cultural public sphere, the market sphere, and the semi-intimate sphere of leisure. More specifically, many of *Chance 2000*'s performances and actions took place at: (1) public art institutions such as the Volksbühne in Berlin, Theaterhaus Hannover and Hamburg Schauspielhaus; (2) fashionable shopping malls such as Kaufhaus des Westens (KaDeWe) in Berlin; and (3) the posh holiday location Lake Wolfgang in St. Gilgen, Austria, where German chancellor Helmut Kohl spent his summer holidays. In spite of their clear differences, these public places had one thing in common, namely, the unlikelihood that the unemployed and mentally and physically disabled members of *Chance 2000* would frequent them under normal circumstances. That is, even though the *Chance* members were not excluded from these places in any formal or legislative sense of the word, various factors, such as cultural and monetary capital, would prevent, or at least decrease the likelihood of them visiting such locations. However, by using these places as the public stages of *Chance 2000,* and by orchestrating and inviting the sensation-seeking media to document the public performances of the *Chance* members, Schlingensief was able to shed light on the complex relation between the 'excluded' and the implicitly exclusionary mechanisms of certain public places. This relation can be further explained by reference to the so-called 'System Theory' that Schlingensief developed for the *Chance 2000* project.

In his home-grown theory, Schlingensief distinguishes between System 1—the discourses created by, among others, the media, political parties and the art system—and System 2, which is populated by those who find themselves excluded from the discourses of System 1, such as the mentally and physically disabled, the unemployed and asylum seekers. The aim of Schlingensief's project is to catapult the 'invisible' citizens of System 2 into a third system where, without being appropriated by System 1, they would be able to relate critically or even subversively to the various discourses governing the dominant system.[10]

Jacques Rancière's definition of the relation between police (*la police)* and politics (*la politique)* can be used to support and develop the claim that certain sectors of the public are excluded from, and made invisible within, the ruling public discourse, but that it is nonetheless possible to render visible that which is excluded in a form that exceeds the dominant public discourse. Roughly put, according to Rancière, *the police* designate the general law that determines the so-called 'distribution of the sensible'. The latter can be understood as a system of coordinates defining modes of 'being', 'doing' and 'making' that establishes the borders between the visible and the invisible, the audible and the inaudible, the sayable and the unsayable within the social order. In that respect, the given distribution of the sensible refers both to forms of inclusion and to forms of exclusion, while *the police* can be seen as a practice of organizing 'bodies', placing them on either side of the border and thereby determining those who partake in and those who have no part in the societal community. However, according to Rancière, any social order and political practice presupposes a basic equality, and it is in the name of this equality that *politics* intervenes in and contests the ruling consensus that defines who and what is considered visible, audible and sayable. Rancière terms the political interventions as 'scenes of dissensus' and claims that by juxtaposing and publicly displaying the heterogeneous logics and processes of *la police* and *la politique* respectively, they aim at reconfiguring the ruling distribution of the sensible. He writes:

> Political activity is always a mode of expression that undoes the perceptible divisions of the police order by implementing a basically heterogeneous assumption, that of a part of those who have no part, an assumption that, at the end of the day, itself demonstrates the sheer contingency of the order, the equality of any speaking being with any other speaking being.[11]

In the case of *Chance 2000,* one could define the (overwhelmingly well-documented) performances of the 'invisible' *Chance* members in public spaces such as art institutions, fashionable shopping malls and upper class holiday areas, as examples of the above-mentioned 'scenes of dissensus'. By bringing those who have 'no part in the societal community' into both these spaces, and the consciousness of the 'dominant public', the various actions caused different forms and 'logics of visibility' to clash. For instance, by invading public art institutions throughout the country and forcing the art public to not only acknowledge their existence, but also to relate to them as political beings by asking for their signatures in support of the election, the *Chance* members insisted upon their right to be visible within the public sphere. In that respect, the actions disturbed the ruling, exclusionary discourse of the social order in order to assert the basic equality upon which not only politics but the social order itself is founded, as per Rancière. However, the fact that the actions were disrupted and prevented in different ways bears witness to the difficulties of verifying and practicing this logic of equality. For example, the *Chance* members were expelled from KaDeWe due to the fact that their presence—they were all dressed in white T-shirts that read *Chance 2000*—'disturbed' the other customers, as the press agent of KaDeWe put it.[12] Likewise, in order to avoid breaking the law, Schlingensief, who was told he was not allowed to organize a public action in St. Gilgen, had to change the planned public swim in Lake Wolfgang—where the participation of six million unemployed Germans was supposed to 'make the lake rise and flood the summer cottage of Chancellor Kohl'—into a 'private swim'. Furthermore, after the

Austrian tabloid newspaper *Kronen Zeitung* had proclaimed the *Chance* members to be left-wing extremists, the mayor of Salzburg, Josef Dechant, ordered the leader of the Salzburger Festspiele to exclude Schlingensief's planned *Chance 2000* performance from the festival programme under threat of retracting the 500.000 DM subsidy the festival had received. Despite much protest, the leader of the festival was forced to obey.[13]

Summing up, we can say that by making different forms of logic clash in the manner described above, the *Chance 2000* project displayed not only the plural and heterogeneous character of the public sphere; it also sought to reconfigure the ruling distribution of the sensible by disturbing the logic of the exclusionary mechanisms underlying that sphere. Just as important, however, the project encouraged the *Chance* members to come together as a (counter) public and to articulate and organize their experiences, needs and wishes in political party programmes that were not planned or articulated beforehand.

Self-organizing networks and programmatic lack of party programmes

The motto of *Chance 2000*, 'Vote for yourself!' was pursued throughout the project and Schlingensief did not decide on the general political guidelines of either the union or the party. Instead the *Chance* members themselves decided what their particular programme(s) should look like and on which particular experiences they should be based. The project was thus conceived as a self-organizing, non-hierarchical network rather than as a sealed off work of art controlled by the artist. More specifically, the *rhizome*—conceived by Gilles Deleuze and Felix Guattari[14] as an open, constantly proliferating and acentric system with a potentially infinite number of entries and exits—served as the model for the project.[15] As Schlingensief put it: '*Chance 2000* is a network that anyone is free to enter with his own name. It is the most autarkic system that one could imagine.'[16] In accordance with this idea, the situations that the project generated were not regarded as reactions delimited by the project itself. On the contrary, unplanned and unforeseeable events, such as the near bankruptcy of the party—a scenario that was avoided thanks to the capital of wealthy fashion designer Wolfgang Joop—were actively integrated into the project and seen as incidents that helped fuel and shape the further development of *Chance 2000*.

The fact that Schlingensief did not pretend to speak on behalf of the 'disenfranchised' in the *Chance 2000* project, but instead encouraged them to speak for themselves, was reflected in yet another of the project's statements, namely the motto 'I am one people'. On the one hand, the motto that was printed on posters with photographs of the *Chance* candidates could be read as an ironic inversion of the slogan of a reunited Germany: 'We are one people'. Thus, while insisting on the visibility of marginalized minorities—represented by disabled *Chance* candidates such as Werner Brecht and Achim von Paczensky, who both made it to the national election—the motto implicitly

Figure 2: The *Chance 2000* official election campaign flyer, 1998.

raised the question as to whether such citizens were actually acknowledged and included in the official 'We' of the then recently re-unified German people. At the same time, however, the motto could, together with the slogan 'Vote for yourself!', be read as a form of encouragement to not only the *Chance* candidates, but to anyone else who would like to stand up for him/herself and claim his/her rights as a citizen.

Within the framework of *Chance 2000*, this encouragement manifested itself in various performative events where the participants experimented with coming together as a (counter)public by articulating and attempting to organize their particular experiences. The establishment of the so-called *Hotel Prora* (1998) is a good example of one of these events.

In May 1998, a nonstop ten-day live-in performance titled *Hotel Prora* was organized in Prater. Here, the public was invited to check in as guests and to discuss the politics and possible actions and strategies of *Chance 2000* on a 24-hours-a-day basis. Moreover, they were encouraged to join the *Chance* candidates on their daily visit to Alexanderplatz, where they collected signatures in support of the party. However, the hotel did not only provide the framework for political discussions, it also demarcated the ground for a social experiment and a place for living together. The hotel itself looked rather like a scout camp, designed with tents scattered across the stage of the theatre with a campfire in the middle. In the best scouting spirit, a stay at the hotel also included cooking and various sing-along sessions around the campfire at night. Schlingensief, however, ensured that the social interaction and the political discussions at *Hotel Prora* did not coagulate into a feel-good consensus or the development of a common ideology. By constantly twisting his own statements, tirelessly testing the arguments of others, and checking that the hotel did not admit just one social group, but instead a broad spectrum of citizens ranging from the unemployed and homeless to the aforementioned Wolfgang Joop, Schlingensief sought to unearth the implicit antagonisms of the group in order to prevent a homogenizing consensus. In the words of Sandra Umathum:

> *Chance 2000* seeks to avoid consensus in any way possible [...] The only guideline given is: 'Vote for yourself!' or 'Prove that you exist'. While doing his outmost to prevent any kind of unambiguous statement or delegate objectives ('everybody constitutes his own party programme'), he [Schlingensief] creates a disorganized movement.[17]

Thus, although Schlingensief invited the participants of *Chance 2000* to organize their experiences and to come together as an emerging (counter)public, he was very careful not to let this public coming-together be overshadowed by an all-encompassing ideology.[18] This concern was further reflected in the very general formulations of the party programme of the *Partei der letzten Chance*, which read:

> PLC encourages the population, especially all marginalized minorities, to represent themselves in order to be able to be someone. As an alternative to the common marginalization practiced by the political parties, PLC initiates the cultivation and politicization of diversity. Everybody should be granted the role that suits him. Each constitutes the smallest unit of the people [...]. Everyone can be his own talk show host. According to the will of our constitution, everybody should be able to elect himself.[19]

This insistence that everybody should speak up instead of subscribing to some dictated common political agenda can be illuminated further by the concept of 'political subjectivization' as conceived by Rancière. As Rancière puts it, political subjects appear as singular *effects* of the aforementioned 'scenes of dissensus', challenging the identities imposed on their bodies in society by *the police*. This means that political subjectivization is *not* about subscribing to a common identity politics, but instead about *disidentifying* with the identities proposed within the ruling distribution of the sensible. As Rancière writes:

> Political subjectivization is the enactment of equality—or the handling of a wrong—by people who are together to the extent that they are between. It is a crossing of identities, relying on a crossing of names: names that link the name of a group or class to the name of no group or no class, a being to a nonbeing or a not-yet-being.[20]

Viewed from this perspective, what united the *Chance* members most of all was not so much their so-called common identity as 'minorities', but their heterogeneous and multiple acts of *disidentifying* with the excluded identities they had been assigned to in society. In line with this, the project—not least due to its open-ended and processual structure—seemed to incorporate the notion that neither (counter)publics nor political subjects are ontological givens, but instead have to be acted out in a never-ending chain of singular events.

As if a universal public sphere existed…

While *Chance 2000* emphasized the plural character of the public sphere and the importance of singular political events, rather than the development of a uniform ideology, the project also encouraged the respective publics to temporarily bracket their own more or less socially determined interests and biased perspectives in order to engage in a collective imagining of a common public sphere. Pursuing this question further, I will now—following Schlingensief's aforementioned tongue-in-cheek distinction between the 'political remains' and the 'utopian remains' of *Chance 2000*—turn to the utopian aspects of the project. More specifically, drawing on aspects of the modern ideals of aesthetics and the public sphere championed by Immanuel Kant and Habermas, I will address the notion of a *universal* public sphere indirectly evoked in the project.

In *The Critique of Judgement* ([1790] 1987), Immanuel Kant proposes the idea of a *sensus communis,* which is the ideal of an aesthetic sensibility common to all. Ideally, this sensibility goes beyond social differences and relates the individual to a universal aesthetic community, thereby enabling the viewer to overcome self-interest and to judge 'not just for himself but for everyone'.[21] Even though it is widely acknowledged that the notion of common sense is a postulate in Kant's philosophy rather than a truthful description of existing human relations[22], by bracketing our personal interests and opening ourselves up to the other, we might nevertheless strive to behave *as if* such common sense existed. Turning to the Kantian inspired ideal of the bourgeois public sphere of Jürgen Habermas, a similar relation is at stake. Even though Habermas can, to a certain extent, be said to conflate the descriptive and the prescriptive levels in his analysis of the rise of the bourgeois public sphere[23], he is very careful to point out that the full utopian potential of the idea of bourgeois public sphere has never been fully realized. Differently put, like Kant's *sensus communis,* the Habermasian conception of a universal public sphere for discursive interaction between free and equal human beings does not constitute a historical fact, but functions instead as a regulating ideal or, perhaps, as a fantasy. As pointed out by Miwon Kwon, however, this fantasy seems more important than ever in contemporary society, where the idea of a democratic and non-biased public sphere has increasingly come under pressure due to the dominance of mass media and the advance of neoliberalism and global capitalism.[24]

In the case of *Chance 2000*, I would contend that the fantasy of such a utopian universal public sphere was indirectly evoked. This aspect of the project is closely related to the subsequent attempts to prevent the participants from relying on, and identifying 'safely' with, one singular and biased perspective. The disturbance of perspectives was, for its part, closely related to the uncertainty of the project's framework; it mutated from theatre, to freak show, to political rally, etc., and throughout, Schlingensief attempted to confuse the distinction between whether *Chance 2000* was 'art' or 'politics'. This instability, and the unsettling effects of the discursive framing of the project, caused the participants to establish a self-reflexive view of their own positions within the project. A good example of this is the ambiguous framing of the aforementioned *Hotel Prora*. On closer examination, it turns out that the hotel not only evoked the image of a scout camp, it could also be likened to a kind of human zoo. At the end of the camp scenario, the set designer Nina Wetzel had installed bars through which people could goggle at the hotel guests carrying out their daily tasks. And every night audiences would buy tickets to come and watch the social experiments taking place at the spectacular hotel. It was, however, not really possible for the audience to lean back and enjoy the show without being confronted with their own voyeurism and, perhaps also, their own pleasure in observing the physically and mentally disabled people participating in *Chance 2000*.

Schlingensief's actions have been described as 'training programmes for self-observation and behaviorism'.[25] Differently put, they can be seen as aesthetic laboratories, where the recipients are encouraged to observe and reflect upon not only the behaviour of the other participants, but also their own perceptions and actions. As for *Chance 2000*, the different levels of observation were contained within each other like a series of

Chinese Boxes, where not only the *Chance* members and candidates, but also the regular politicians and other members of the population were placed in a laboratory for mutual observation. How far were Schlingensief and the *Chance* candidates willing to go? Would the regular politicians accept the candidates in the event that they received enough votes to officially enter the parliament? And what impact would their election have on the public's confidence in the elected politicians and the political process in general? The project was thus not just about provoking 'scenes of dissensus' or forming (counter) publics based on the experiences of particular social groups. Rather, one of the project's key aims seemed to be to encourage the various participants to transcend their habitual perspectives of the world and to question their own socially and culturally determined ways of acting within the project.

Furthermore, even though at first glance it might seem as if the project addressed only specific publics such as the unemployed, the disabled and asylum seekers, *Chance 2000* did, in fact, project the utopian ideal of a universal public. As pointed out in relation to the (lacking) party programme and the 'check-in policy' of *Hotel Prora*, Schlingensief insisted on *Chance 2000* being a radically open project that *anyone* could enter and contribute to in whatever way he saw fit. Thus, as Matthias Wulff points out in the introduction to *Die Dokumentation—Chance 2000*, the project did not let itself be monopolized by the interests of a single group:

> Some tried to use the party as the voice of the unemployed only. Others took part in the intellectual discussions that characterized *Chance 2000*. In ThinkTank, the internet forum for discussion, and in real-life discussions, thoughts, intellectual structures and analyses became apparent that would not have emerged without *Chance 2000*. On the other hand, however, *Chance 2000* would not have emerged the way it did without them. [26]

However, rather than consolidating the project's various participating publics in their possible self-containment, *Chance 2000,* due to its all-inclusive formal structure, constituted an arena for discursive and phenomenological *interaction* between these publics. That is, within the framework of art institutions such as the Volksbühne, *Chance 2000* established temporary public spaces where people could meet in spite of social, political and cultural differences, to exchange and come into contact with views other than their own, and to work towards the possibility of a politics based on equality and heterogeneity. In that respect, *Chance 2000* could be said to produce zones that— discursively demarcated as art—addressed the participants *as if* they were free and equal citizens, who, bound by a common feeling of belonging to a universal aesthetic community, were able to renounce self-interest and open themselves to the other. Consequently, I would claim that the project cannot be reduced to its 'political remains'. It cannot be reduced to the 'actual' political statements or the 'actual' events it spurred, since a crucial aspect of the project was its utopian urge to establish self-determined universal public spaces, free for anyone to enter. In line with this, Schlingensief often referred to the project as a 'parallel election' to the German federal election.[27] Therefore, rather than developing a political praxis that could readily be translated into regular politics, the project functioned as a space for a common *imagining* of politics. Differently put, within the discursive framework of the institution of art, the project constituted a public space for imagination and for experimenting with forms of thinking and interaction that followed rules other than the ones governing the political spectacle of the then raging German election campaign.

Closing remarks

Having now examined the 'political' and the 'utopian' aspects of *Chance 2000,* I posit that the project proposed a rather complex notion of the public sphere. That is to say that whilst orchestrating the plural character of the public sphere, the project nevertheless evoked a utopian image of a universal public sphere, inviting the participants of *Chance 2000* to come together and discuss matters of public interest as free and equal citizens. In this regard, I would argue that in *Chance 2000,* the very different concepts of the public sphere offered by Habermas and Negt and Kluge, respectively, do not exclude one another; rather, various elements from both interrelated in the project. Taking as its point of departure the acknowledgement of the plural and heterogeneous reality of the public sphere, *Chance 2000* aimed to establish, within the discursive framework of the art institution, an inclusive utopian public space for not only discursive but also phenomenological and experience-based interaction. By indirectly referring to the ideals of equality and freedom associated with the modern project of liberation—ideals championed by thinkers as different as Rancière, Habermas and Negt and Kluge— *Chance 2000* also set out to examine the state of these ideals in contemporary society. More specifically, by rendering the mentally and physically disabled *Chance* members visible in public spaces they would normally be excluded from, Schlingensief invited not only the project's participants but also the general public to discuss and reflect upon the possible betrayal of these ideals within contemporary society. To conclude, bearing in mind the aforementioned claim that the notion of a democratic public sphere has increasingly come under pressure in contemporary society, I posit that artistic practices such as Schlingensief's constitute some of the remaining spaces left for us to experiment with reconfiguring the distribution of the sensible and for coming together momentarily as a critical public.

Endnotes

1. See Alexander Grasseck and Stefan Corinth's documentary on *Chance 2000*: *Scheitern als Chance* (1999).

2. As noted in the regulations for the union Chance 2000: 'The purpose of the union is to support the minorities of our society in terms of their integration into and appearance in the public sphere. In this context, the term minorities refers to the unemployed and the disabled in particular, but also to a lot of other people, be they from here or from abroad, who live amongst us, but are nonetheless excluded from the public sphere'. Hegemann, C. (1998), 'Chance 2000—Vereinssatzung', in C. Schlingensief and C. Hegemann (eds.), *CHANCE 2OOO, Wähle dich selbst*, Köln: Kiepenheuer & Witsch, pp. 19–20. All translations from German to English are my own unless otherwise noted.

3. For a detailed account of the further life of *Chance 2000*, see Strehler, S. (1999), 'Das Mysterium vom Wolfgangsee', in J. Finke and M. Wulff (eds.), *Die Dokumentation— Chance 2000*, Berlin: Lautsprecher Verlag, pp. 88–89 and the chronological overview of the life of the project in the same book, pp. 305–308.

4. As pointed out by Sandra Umathum, the journalists covering the project seemed to have difficulties deciding in which section of the paper the vast number of articles generated by *Chance 2000* should be located. See Umathum, S. (2003), 'Christoph Schlingensief: Regisseur der schnellen Reaktion', in A. Dürrschmidt and B. Engelhardt (eds.), *Werk-Stück. Regisseure im Porträt*, Berlin: Theater der Zeit, p. 145.

5. See Albers, I. (1999), 'Scheitern als Chance—Die Kunst des Krisenexperiments', in J. Finke and M. Wulff (eds.), *Die Dokumentation—Chance 2000*, Berlin: Lautsprecher Verlag, p. 44.

6. Ibid., p. 57.

7. See Negt, O. and Kluge, A. (1972), *Öffentlichkeit und Erfahrung*, Frankfurt am Main: Suhrkamp. Negt and Kluge's definition of the public sphere has been highly influential within public sphere theory, and today there is more or less a consensus that the public sphere should be addressed in plural terms. See, for instance, Robbins, B. (ed.) (1993), *The Phantom Public Sphere*, Minneapolis: University of Minnesota Press, and Warner, M. (2002), *Publics and Counterpublics*, New York: Zone Books.

8. See Habermas, J. (1990), *Strukturwandel der Öffentlichkeit*, Frankfurt am Main: Suhrkamp.

9. See Negt, O. and Kluge, A. (1972), p. 17–18.

10. See Albers, I. (1999), p. 54.

11. Rancière, J. (1999), *Disagreement*, Minneapolis and London: University of Minnesota Press, p. 30.

12. See Albers, I. (1999), p. 59.

13. Strehler, S. (1999), p. 75.

14. See Deleuze, G. and Guattari, F. (2005), *A Thousand Plateaus*, Minneapolis: University of Minnesota Press, pp. 3–25.

15. See Schlingensief, C. (1998), '"Pilzgeflecht" (Rhizom)', in C. Schlingensief and C. Hegemann (eds.), *CHANCE 2OOO, Wähle dich selbst*, Köln: Kiepenheuer & Witsch, p. 84.

16. Schlingensief, C. (1998), p. 28.

17. Umathum, S. (2003), p. 147.

18. As Schlingensief writes in the foreword to *CHANCE 2OOO, Wähle dich selbst* (1998: 3): 'This book does not contain any new ideology, it contains no consumer offers and no fantasy of rescue'.

19. Schlingensief, C. (1998: 80), 'Parteiprogramm—Chance 2000 PLC'.

20. Rancière, J. (1992), 'Politics, Identification, and Subjectivization', *October*, 61, p. 61.

21. Kant, I. (1987), *The Critique of Judgement*, Indianapolis: Hackett Publishing, p. 62.

22. See, for instance, Kester, H.G. (2004), *Conversation Pieces*, Berkeley: University of California Press, p. 28.

23. Habermas himself later agreed with this criticism. See Calhoun, C.J. (1992), 'Concluding Remarks', in C.J. Calhoun (ed.), *Habermas and the Public Sphere*, Cambridge, Massachusetts: The MIT Press, pp. 462–463.

24. See Kwon, M. (2005), 'Public Art and Publicity', in S. Sheikh (ed.), *In the Place of the Public Sphere*, Berlin: B-books, pp. 29–31.

25. See Umathum, S. (2000), 'Der Theatermacher', in *Theaterwissenschaftliche Beiträge*, Berlin: Theater der Zeit, p. 38.

26. Wulff, M. (1999), 'Einleitung', in J. Finke and M. Wulff (eds.), *Die Dokumentation— Chance 2000*, Berlin: Lautsprecher Verlag, p. 15.

27. See Schlingensief, C. (1998), 'Chance 2000—Zirkus der lustigste Wahlkampf der Welt', p. 27.

'Right now Austria looks ridiculous': Please Love Austria! — Reforging the Interaction Between Art and Politics

Denise Varney

Please Love Austria: First Austrian Coalition Week (June 2000)

In writing about the week-long installation and performance *Please Love Austria: First Austrian Coalition Week* (2000)[1] for this first edited collection of English-language essays on Christoph Schlingensief, I am mindful of the ten years that have passed since it occupied Vienna's Herbert von Karajan-Platz. A brief description of this radical, postmodern, interactive and politically-motivated performance event, that was devised and directed by Schlingensief and his creative team, will set the scene for readers before I elaborate more fully on key aspects of the political and aesthetic features of the work.

Please Love Austria was staged as part of the 2000 'Vienna Arts Festival'. Devised as a critique of the rise of the anti-foreigner far right Austrian Freedom Party (FPÖ), the performance took place over six days in June. In February that year, the FPÖ had become a coalition partner with Wolfgang Schüssel's conservative Austrian People's Party (ÖVP) in a controversial new government that was sworn in the midst of opposition from home and abroad. By mid-2000, Austria had become the 'pariah state' of Europe.[2] Fourteen member states of the European Union had imposed sanctions against the inclusion of a far right party in a governing coalition. Other western democracies, including the United States, recalled their ambassadors, temporarily, in protest. US Secretary of State, Madeleine Albright, announced that:

> We are deeply concerned about the Freedom Party's entry into the Austrian government. [...] There is clearly no place inside the governments who make up the Euro-Atlantic community—and a healthy democracy—for

a party that does not clearly distance itself from the atrocities of the Nazi era and the politics of hate.[3]

In stark contrast to the gravitas of diplomatic discourse, Schlingensief devised a richly parodic conceit for his week-long protest. The parody took the form of an adaptation of the hugely popular *Big Brother* television format that it recast as a competition for immigrants and asylum seekers. Twelve chosen 'contestants' lived in a compound of

Figure 1: Animated and agitated crowds gather to discuss the installation and performance while the blue flag of the FPÖ flaps in the breeze above the '*Ausländer Raus*' (Foreigners Out) sign. Photo: Paul Poet.

disused shipping containers that were installed in the square for the duration of the event. Above the containers a large sign with the words 'Foreigners Out' (*Ausländer Raus*) was visible. Alongside the sign, the blue flags of the FPÖ flapped in the summer breeze while the logo of the right-wing tabloid newspaper, *Die Kronen Zeitung,* was also prominently displayed.

Austrians were invited to evict two asylum seekers a day from their country. A website was set up for voting and for providing information about each foreigner's 'name', age, country of origin and skills.[4] The analogy between *Big Brother* housemates and asylum seekers continued through the use of a 35,000 Austrian schilling prize for the one who remained 'un-evicted' at the end of the week. On eviction, the asylum seekers were escorted by men in black T-shirts and pants, with the word 'Security' printed on their backs, to a waiting black Mercedes, with the Austrian Coat of Arms on its driver door, to be 'deported' to an unknown destination. The link made between Security and the National Coat of Arms underscored the performance's critical point that the coalition partner, the FPÖ, considered foreigners to be a threat to national security.

The asylum seekers, like the housemates in the *Big Brother* series, were under constant camera surveillance and could be observed through peepholes in the containers, on CCTV and through live web streaming. The cameras trained on the containers quoted both *Big Brother's* mode of surveillance and the FPÖ's view of foreigners as a security threat. This double coding of signification continued throughout the performance. Using a megaphone, Schlingensief as director and media host played a prominent leading role in the event. Throughout the week, he addressed the public that gathered around the container compound, announced the daily evictions and criticized Austria's coalition government. A persistent target of the performance's critique was FPÖ leader and populist Nazi-apologist Jörg Haider, whose anti-immigration rhetoric included the revival of Nazi-era slogans such as 'Stop the *Überfremdung*' (stop over-foreignization).[5] His image was visible on the walls of the containers and his speeches, including the exhortation that 'there must be a stop to immigration', were broadcast each morning for the duration of the performance.[6]

The performance took place in real time during which the asylum seekers ate, showered, slept, and relaxed in the container compound. They waited for deportation, were observed by the public and were protected by security guards. They undertook structured activities, took exercise and German lessons, and performed a short piece of puppet theatre they devised with playwright and novelist Elfriede Jelinek. A final notable feature of the installation and performance that should be mentioned in this brief introduction was that the mode of performance positioned the public as participants rather than spectators. The website invited people to experience the event (*'Sie werden es erleben'*).[7]

Taking the incidents and events that transpired during the week as a whole, it is possible to perceive a narrative, as in an imagined scenario or fable, that concerned a suspicious and fearful people who, under the influence of the malevolent Haider, evicted outsiders and foreigners from their community. Played out with the public as participants, this negative scenario presented a deplorable situation that demanded action, lest the country succumb (once again) to malevolent forces. In this way, the performance, as I will argue later in my analysis, displayed the qualities of Brecht's dialectical, epic theatre without being simply reducible to it.

To summarize briefly: the performance was a multi-media event, performed live in real time, simulcast on webfreetv.com and filmed for a documentary. It can be viewed, along with most of Schlingensief's subsequent work, as 'a hybrid theatre of transmediality' that Johannes Birringer has recently identified as theatre that 'moves between forms drawing from diverse popular cultures and the digital media which drive them and distribute them globally'.[8] I have indicated that this mode of performance is deployed here for political purposes. The location and 'liveness' of the event and the primacy of its only partially scripted format, ensured that *Please Love Austria* was a site-specific, interactive performance and a disruptive intervention in contemporary politics. It disrupted, in particular, the smooth running of the political-juridical process whereby, despite winning only 27 per cent of the national vote, a far right political party became a coalition partner in a democratic government. This chapter argues that Schlingensief and his team devised a radical performance in the tradition of German political theatre that revitalized, transformed, and brought new techniques to bear on the interaction between art and politics.

Documenting the performance: *Foreigners Out!: Schlingensief's Container*

The enduring appeal of *Please Love Austria* has far exceeded the essentially ephemeral nature of live performance. This is because the performance can be accessed via Paul Poet's documentary, *Foreigners Out!: Schlingensief's Container* (2002).[9] The documentary has screened on global television networks and is widely available in university and private collections. The dissemination of the documentary, along with its authoritative voiceover that describes and contextualizes the performance, has contributed, in no small part, to *Please Love Austria*'s continuing circulation. It has contributed to the artist's reputation as not only a radical theatre artist and an astute commentator on current affairs, but also an artist who managed to re-ignite political debate in the space of late-capitalist consumer culture. I draw on Poet's documentary for my analysis of the visual, aural, and moving images that constituted *Please Love Austria*. For this reason, a brief account of the documentary's format, including its discursive construction of the performance, is provided below.

Poet's documentary

Poet's 90-minute documentary, that combined footage with commentary, emphasized the debates that spread out from the epicentre of the performance. It featured an extensive interview with Schlingensief, filmed after the event, which foregrounded the artist's position as the linchpin of the performance. Adding emphasis to the discursive elements of the live performance, Poet also interviewed selected commentators. These included German philosopher, Burghart Schmidt, editor of the left-wing Austrian weekly *Falter*, Armin Thurnher and Volksbühne dramaturgs, Carl Hegemann and Matthias Lilienthal, who were favourable towards the work, and Helene Partik-Pablé and Heidemarie Unterreiner of the FPÖ, who were at pains to appear reasonable in their opposition. The interviews were intercut, so that Schlingensief was often responding to others' views and commenting on the ongoing debate about the performance. The interviews were further intercut with an introductory sequence explaining the political events that gave rise to the performance. A bar graph was shown that demonstrated that each of the coalition partners had polled 27 per cent of the vote in the October 1999 elections, behind the centre left Social Democrats (SPÖ) that polled 33 per cent. The narrative voice explained that the alliance was forged 'despite election promises and presidential opposition' after talks between and the ÖVP and the SPÖ broke down.[10] This sequence was followed by extensive footage of the six-day performance, with special attention given to debates among Austrians in the square.

The documentary also constructed a narrative for the performance telling us how Schlingensief's invitation to the 2000 Vienna Arts Festival was a political statement by festival director, Luc Bondy, in response to the election outcome. His decision to use the festival as a means of opposing the coalition brought together the critical possibilities of aesthetics and politics. The strategic use of the *Big Brother* television format, described by project manager Claudia Kaloff as an 'inspired choice'[11], was explained in the documentary by Schlingensief in the following way:

> A process of elimination is at the heart of the program [...] Once the focus is shifted onto the process of elimination itself (and not the winners), it gets interesting because you see how society becomes involved and takes part in the creation of losers.[12]

Schlingensief spent a considerable part of each day standing with a megaphone on a platform above the containers playing the role of the artist as *provocateur,* challenging the coalition to remove the sign and claiming he could see swastikas in bystanders' eyes. Failing to provoke a crackdown, he then called on tourists to take photographs and told Austrians they had elected a 'super-stupid government'.[13] The documentary segmented the event into seven days building the drama to key points of conflict and confrontation.

Christoph Schlingensief, with the container as his stage, plays the role of artist as *provocateur* within the bourgeois precinct of Herbert von Karajan-Platz. Photo: David Baltzer.

It captured how each day, the megaphone-wielding Schlingensief, live in the square and online, invited Austrians to evict the two asylum seekers they hated the most. By 'Day Three', Schlingensief announced that a pattern of elimination had formed: 'It's another black today.' Irate Austrians squirmed under the tough love of Schlingensief's pronouncements, that 'Right now Austria looks ridiculous'.[14]

The documentary's cameras tracked the installation, the signage and the people, framed by the elegant Viennese buildings, including the Opera House and the Hotel Sacher. The impression given was that the containers, the signs, the logos and flags, as well as the daily broadcasts of Haider's xenophobic speeches, confronted Vienna's elegant bourgeois precinct with its distilled enactments—exemplified by the disembodied voice of Jörg Haider—of ugly racism and incipient neo-fascist tendencies.

The documentary has contributed, it must be said, to the marketing and promotion of not only Schlingensief but of multi-modal, transmedial performance, of which *Please Love Austria* is a prime example. Poet, who worked for the European Internet-TV broadcaster, webfreetv.com, the company that provided the technical infrastructure for the event and whose logo was clearly visible in the documentary, contends that 'The classic neutral documentary never ever existed and the idea of it is a bold lie'.[15] Nonetheless, by recording and documenting *Please Love Austria,* the film continues the life of the project, promotes its modus operandi and self-reflexively documents its practice.

Critical response

In addition to the documentary, scholarly essays in German and English have since generated further debate around the means and efficacy of the performance as a form of political intervention and contribute to what is now a substantial body of literature on the event. The German language literature is extensive but of these Matthias Lilienthal and Claus Philipp's 'pocketbook'—an edited collection of essays, interviews, and letters of protest entitled *Schlingensiefs Ausländer raus. Bitte liebt Österreich* (2000)—must be mentioned as a valuable primary source. [16]

Reading *Please Love Austria* as a mode of interactive 'reality theatre' that generated public debate, Tara Forrest has argued that 'meaningful political engagement' is not generated by a 'pre-packaged, well-argued position' on an issue but by the debate that is 'sparked, but not foreclosed' by the mode of performance.[17] Forrest showed how vastly different audiences— from the Mayor of Austria, Michael Häupl, to anti-FPÖ activists, to individual members of the public—were drawn to the event and ascribed contrasting meanings to it. Citing the evidence in Poet's documentary of the high levels of audience participation in the event, Forrest found that Schlingensief's 'publically accessible performance practice' was integral to the interactivity of the performance.[18] The open-ended form—in so far as no one knew how the event would unfold—together with the multiple ambiguities—were the asylum seekers real of fake?—proved, she argued, to be 'highly effective' in mobilizing public participation in the event. In Forrest's view, the accessibility of the popular *Big Brother* format first drew the public into the square and then into debate about the meaning of the event. Her argument in favour of popular culture as a means of mobilizing public debate puts her among those, like Schlingensief but also Johannes Birringer, who argue for the continued political efficacy of performance in the media age.

Silvija Jestrovic raised the crucial question about agency that adhered to the asylum seekers in the performance.[19] Focusing on the use of real refugees, immigrants and asylum seekers in artistic events, Jestrovic compared Schlingensief's use of the twelve asylum seekers in *Please Love Austria* with Catalan couturier Antonio Miro's use of illegal Senegalese immigrants as models in fashion shows. Jestrovic argued that in Schlingensief's case, when, for example, the asylum seekers in wigs danced to a racist song (that included lyrics such as 'Oh, a Congo Negro has got it good'[20]), the key ethical question revolved around whether they understood the racist German lyrics of the song to which they 'cheerfully' danced.[21] The difference between the beat of the music and the lyrics of the song, the one innocuous and rhythmic, the other verbal and offensive, is critical here. She pointed out that not one of the asylum seekers was interviewed or asked to comment on the performance for Poet's documentary. Nor have any of the participants, to date, spoken in public about their experience.

Jestrovic is correct to question the extent to which the asylum seekers were fully aware, given the open-ended form of the event, of how the performance might unfold, whether they felt free to withdraw at any point and whether, subsequently, they shared in any remuneration. The maintenance of the ambiguity about the identities of the asylum seekers, that Forrest rightly claimed was a key component of the performance, leads Jestrovic to leave open the question of whether the asylum seekers were manipulated. I suggest, however, that the asylum seekers can be productively viewed as historical subjects rather than individuals. As I will shortly discuss the performance in terms of the Brechtian *Gestus,* I will only note here that the political point of the performance was not to galvanize sympathy for individual asylum seekers but to target Haider, the FPÖ and the historic re-emergence of the far right. In this way, the asylum seekers were necessarily 'typical' subjects. As Fredric Jameson has commented:

> What is 'typical' in the Brechtian *gestus* is, rather, the action itself, and even, as we have seen already, the various henceforth unrecognisable components or building blocks of an action: here the stable and recognizable subject is gone from the outset.[22]

Hence, the question of the asylum seekers' individual identities is subordinate to the action in which they become exemplary figures.

In a further study, Richard Langston argued that while *Please Love Austria* 'fluctuated between cinema and television, as well as theatre and performance' it was 'above all' the 'explicit incorporation of reality television' that 'mesmerized a majority of spectators and commentators alike'.[23] Yet, the paradox was that spectators remained 'fully aware of the constructed nature of the reality on display'.[24] Furthermore, the promised access to the real was circumscribed by the complex modes of seeing that Schlingensief deployed. There were, Langston explained, three access points to the containers for spectators: a low-lying, narrow slit in the outlying wooden fence (Poet's documentary shows spectators bending down to see through this slit); a live video feed of round the clock footage from eight surveillance cameras accessible on site via CCTV; and video streaming through a web browser.[25] By utilizing past and present modes of spectatorship, the peep show and the electronic spectacle, Langston argued that Schlingensief 'rehabilitated the conscious exhibitionism and voyeurism typical of early cinema and theatre' and in so doing 'disrupted' postmodern modes of passive reception. Hence, he concluded, the efficacy of *Please Love Austria* was in the mode of production of the event's 'insistence' that the past, with its 'potential legacies from Austria's fascist past', could return.[26] Langston's discussion of the scopic aspects of the event is more complex than this brief reading can convey, however, I offer a glimpse of his approach, along with Forrest's and Jestrovic's, in order to make the point that the work has opened up subtle and intriguing lines of enquiry.

In my own previous writing on *Please Love Austria,* I drew links between key aspects of its mode of performance and Brecht's epic theatre, including the techniques of *Verfremdungseffekt* (estrangement or defamiliarization), the basic model of the street scene and *Gestus* (the deployment of socially-attitudinal markers).[27] In evoking Brecht, I made the case that *Please Love Austria* bore traces of theatrical modernism that have been overlooked in the performance's more obvious placement within the postmodern 'turn to performance' whose partners include avant-garde performance art, Alan Kaprow's happenings and the paradigm shift from drama to performance.[28] *Please Love Austria* fits Baz Kershaw's model of the radical in performance in so far as it 'participates in the most vital cultural, social and political tensions of its time'.[29] Yet, as Kershaw also observed, Brechtian modernity has continued to make an important contribution to contemporary performance and, as I argue here, *Please Love Austria* exemplifies the kind of 'cultural hybrid' that borrows from many sources including theatrical modernity.[30] I now return to that aspect of Schlingensief's work for the remainder of my discussion.

The parallels between Brecht's and Schlingensief's times, crudely sketched, see both devising theatrical techniques to counter the rise of the far right, the National Socialists in Germany, and the FPÖ in Austria, although the economies of scale and the levels of violence are markedly different with incomparable consequences. I am not suggesting that Brecht's view of his times applies to twenty-first century Europe. However, Brecht's best-known anti-Hitler plays, *Fear and Misery of the Third Reich* and *The Resistible Rise of Arturo Ui,* both deployed the kind of ironic, negative scenarios that critiqued not only the rise of Nazism, but also the inability of liberals, intellectuals and artists to mount an effective opposition. Jameson has said that Brecht's plays exposed the 'trope of cynicism' that was rife in Weimar culture that, I suggest, enacted defeat in the face of the rise of fascism. Jameson then makes the important distinction that applies equally to Schlingensief as to Brecht, that the plays exposed 'the cynicism, not of the writer, but of reality itself'.[31] Buried within both artists is not cynicism but the kernels of hope, the naïve desire to make a difference, to intervene and achieve some form of transcendence whether it is through full-blown socialism or as the thorn in the side of the far right. Yet hope is tempered by Schlingensief's acute sense of the ironic while his capacity to represent cynical reality is as highly developed as Brecht's. His critique of Austria is also levelled at the failure of 'well-meaning leftie activists' to mount an effective opposition to Haider and the far right.[32]

The historicization of the far right

Expanding on these ideas, Schlingensief's outdoor installation and performance recalled Brecht's proposal that the drama that surrounds a simple traffic accident on the street contains the key elements of epic theatre. As Brecht explained, 'an eyewitness demonstrating to a collection of people how a traffic accident took place' enables those who may or may not have seen the accident to form an opinion about it.[33] The demonstration is not an artistic one and the demonstrator need not be an artist, but this is precisely the point. To 'cast a spell' over the bystanders through a mesmerizing performance would put them in the thrall of the performer and cloud their critical judgement. Brecht stipulated that for theatre to qualify as epic, it must not create the illusion of reality, it must be 'essentially repetitive' and it should have a 'socially practical significance'.[34] That in his last writings Brecht preferred the term dialectical to epic theatre emphasizes the element of debate that this kind of theatre intended to evoke. Applied to *Please Love Austria,* Schlingensief's performance drew its audience like a traffic accident, or a magnet, as the artist himself remarked.[35] Its daily evictions were varied but 'essentially repetitive', people aired their opinions about their country, Germans and art, and it was a performance that had its basis in a real situation, that of the fate of asylum seekers in present-day, anti-foreigner Austria. As Brecht wrote about the basic model of the street scene:

> The performance's origins lie in an incident that can be judged one way or another that may repeat itself in different forms and is not finished but is bound to have consequences, so that this judgement has some significance.[36]

Please Love Austria was a street scene that was judged by its participants in a variety of ways, including directly by those who voted to evict an asylum seeker and those who argued about the value of the event itself. At any rate, people came to the square in response to the demonstration of a series of incidents (the formation of the coalition, the broadcasting of Haider's speeches, the daily evictions) that were presented in a striking, unfamiliar and strange light. Here the term 'demonstration' refers to both a display showing how things are done (here an ironic display of Austria's anti-foreigner sentiments) and a public gathering of people to oppose an issue (Schlingensief and his team's denouncement of the coalition). The critical discussion arose in response to the *Verfremdungseffekt* (estrangement effect) created by the demonstration, that is, the combined strangeness of the containers, the *Big Brother* adaptation, the signage, and the interruption of daily life in the square.

In my introduction, I referred to the use of the *Big Brother* format and the container-compound as a richly parodic conceit. I now propose that the containers are also readable through the Brechtian concept of *Gestus* that will open up further understandings of the radical critique 'contained' in the performance. *Gestus,* as described by Brecht, was a layered and complex device for indicating historical class positions in the present and for showing and criticizing hierarchical relations of power under capitalism. Brecht's famous examples included Richard Gloucester courting his victim's widow and Woyzeck buying a cheap knife in order to do in his wife.[37] John Willett described *Gestus* as 'at once gesture and gist, attitude and point: one aspect of the relation between two people, studied singly, cut to essentials'.[38] Jameson reads Brecht's examples as 'satiric unmaskings' that are 'situated in time and space, and affiliated with specific concrete individuals' that are then 'identified and renamed, associated with a larger and more abstract *type* of action in general, and transformed into something exemplary.'[39] Hence *Gestus* is multi-layered and moves from the specific to the historical and the ideological. *Gestic* incidents contain contradiction and paradox—Woyzeck, for example, commits a crime of passion on a cool assessment of his budget—and in so doing points to the logic of the alternative course of action—he could save his money and his wife. This necessary fluidity of *Gestus*, that is, its point of indeterminacy and discontinuity becomes visible, for instance, when in *The Caucasian Chalk Circle,* Grusha, the servant-girl, hesitates before picking up the abandoned baby. The dialectical operation of *Gestus* thus includes, crucially, its capacity for change. The term has proved amenable to a number of applications, including feminist and postcolonial theatres where the aim is to historicise and de-naturalize the social relations of gender and race as well as class.[40]

The *Big Brother* conceit constituted a complex and paradoxical *Gestus*. Like Mother Courage's wagon, which indicated the character's personal and historical circumstances, the containers pointed to the circumstances of its inhabitants, asylum seekers in present day Austria, as transient and incarcerated. Their presence in the square critically revealed, not only Austria's but also, the West's power over its non-citizen others. The physical movements of the asylum seekers, who arrived on a bus and entered the containers wearing wigs and with their faces hidden from the cameras, were a further building block in the representation of the hierarchical relationship between citizen and outsider. Their social determination as lesser beings with less human rights than Austrian citizens was made clear and readable. The sign, 'Foreigners Out', quoted and exposed the ideology of the FPÖ. The *Gestus* of voting off a housemate in *Big Brother* or an asylum seeker in *Please Love Austria* was shown as amounting to the same thing: the exercise of privilege over the other.

On a broader understanding of *Gestus,* the *Big Brother* conceit represented race ideology 'cut to essentials'. Where Helene Partik-Pablé of the FPÖ claimed that Austria was not a migrant country, *Please Love Austria* showed the mythical basis of the *Gestus* of deportation, that is, how history is distorted and myth becomes party policy. The radical appropriation of the *Big Brother* form gave race ideology a material form and *gest*-ured to the social structures of inclusion and exclusion, and citizen and foreigner that define the modern sovereign state. The FPÖ, as the performance made clear, had disseminated an ideologically-driven narrative that raised people's fears of being overrun by immigrants who were also, as Haider's speeches suggested, linked to crime, drugs and social unrest.

The *Gestus* constituted by the placement of foreign human beings in redundant shipping containers historicized and estranged the regimes of power and the ideology that supported it. The performance enacted the potential of the far right to radically transform dreams of freedom into a living hell. Specifically, the containers materialized what Giorgio Agamben has theorized as the state's 'biopolitical' power, that is, 'its need to redefine the threshold in life that distinguishes and separates what is inside from what is outside'.[41] The containers constituted the *Gestus* of showing the link between inside and outside and the creation of docile bodies based on their determination as citizen or foreigner, winner or loser. The entrance to the container-compound and the 'vote' button on the website were two such *gestic* thresholds estranged and historicized by the performance.

In a further layering of signification and historicization that I am equating here with the Brechtian *Gestus*, late in the week, Schlingensief appeared in a brown farmer's jacket, or *Tracht*, that is worn as the Austrian national costume. The *über*-chic version worn by the artist incorporated the characteristic fern green cuffs, collar and pocket lining set against the brown fabric of the jacket, but it was also festooned with spots so that it took on an appearance halfway between the *Tracht* and a TV compère's jacket. It re-emphasized the nationalist roots of anti-foreigner sentiment and also played up the theatricality of the performance and of Schlingensief's self-referential role as the master of ceremonies. Utilizing a sequence of distancing devices, bearing out Jameson's claim that, '*gestus* is an estrangement-effect in its own right'[42], the German Schlingensief played the Austrian national in a jacket that evoked the pastoral homeland at the same time as he played a sideshow spruiker and a TV host cajoling and exhorting people to vote for their evictee. His image with the megaphone, on TV, online, and in the documentary presented a consummate media personality exuding the confident air of the TV host underpinned by the nationalist imagery on his back. Yet he remained detached and cool throughout. His attitude to the performance in which he was actor and director recalled Brecht's description of *Verfremdungseffekt:* 'in this way his performance becomes a discussion (about social conditions) with the audience he is addressing'.[43] This *gestic* reading finds that the figure of Schlingensief coolly inviting people to expel an asylum seeker, or to do something about racism (for the love of Austria) is a heightened gesture, attitude and point about contemporary society.

The question remains as to the capacity for change that emerged from the epic or dialectical aspects of the performance. In the first instance, Schlingensief's continued provocation to the coalition to tear down the sign, 'Foreigners Out', and its failure to do so, pointed to the path not taken by the authorities. The asylum seekers were defined in the meantime as subjects whose capacity for change was obstructed by state imposed restrictions on their freedom to live in exile. On the website, it was noted that Wole from Nigeria's story was that he could not return to his home country where he was subject to religious persecution.[44] His hopes were in the meantime closed down by his illegality. Hence the various incidents of *Gestus* show the foreclosure of change, the curtailing of agency and the boundaries erected around the narrative of freedom in the West.

Conclusion

Please Love Austria brought together the resources of media, the Internet, modern theatre, and live performance to create a paradigmatic aesthetic representation of contemporary politics. In doing so it expanded the parameters of political theatre by recognizing the shift from print to media in political activism and the rise of interactivity as a dominant mode of public discourse. The container compound can be understood as a contemporary multi-purpose *gestic* space that produced new perspectives on arts practice and criticism and on meaning making and representation. Its utilization of the *Big Brother* format, and its adaptation for live performance, created a powerful critical intervention in a media-saturated cultural sphere.

The website, banners and posters made the point that contemporary asylum seekers are performatively produced through slogans, citations, surveillance and containment. With the sign 'Foreigners Out' clearly visible above the containers, those who stood underneath it became modern versions of the historical outcast; the blue FPÖ flag that flapped in the wind above made it perfectly clear who the perpetrators of the politics of exclusion actually were. In more general terms, the container-compound spoke of the transnational flows of human cargo—immigrants, asylum seekers and refugees—that were but the latest wave of displaced peoples impounded in ships, detention centres and other places of transient life. More disturbingly, many observers read the container-compound as a container-camp ghosted by the spectre of Nazi concentration camps. It was 'as if' Schlingensief's installation and performance made such a camp appear in the square under the noses of the good burghers of Vienna. On this view, the containers bore witness to Giorgio Agamben's thesis that the camp is 'the hidden matrix and nomos of the political space in which we are still living'.[45] In so doing, Schlingensief's containers struck a mighty blow to liberal and patriotic sensibilities. They materialized the link between Haider and Hitler, Austria and Nazi Germany, and modern liberal democracies and totalitarian states in which the processes of elimination, of inclusion and exclusion define the boundaries of modern life. Agamben's point resonates further with *Please Love Austria* when he points out that the first concentration camps in Germany were not established by the Nazi regime but by democratically elected Social Democratic governments that interned East European refugees, including Jews, in the concentration camps for foreigners (*Konzentrationslager für Ausländer*) at Cottbus-Sielow in the 1920s.[46] Located in the city centre, Schlingensief's container-camp makes visible and reminds us of the 80 year-old internment protocols that detention evokes, and it radically estranges the way in which containment and expulsion are naturalized in modern life.

The performance included stunning adaptations of the techniques of Brecht's epic theatre, originally directed against the rise of National Socialism, now revitalized and re-politicized to intervene in Austrian politics. As Philip Auslander has commented in relation to the argument that theatre and performance belong to different paradigms, the former redundant and the latter contemporary, 'theatre is not invalidated, but rather remains "deeply engrained" in both the practice and discourse of western performance".[47] That Brechtian techniques were deeply engrained in *Please Love Austria* tells us that Schlingensief's multimodal, transmedial performance had a history—the German tradition of political theatre—but it was also a transformation of that history.

Finally, I have connected Schlingensief's project with Brecht's theatre, but the connection to George Orwell should also be addressed. Schlingensief can be seen to restore the critical component of Orwell's concept of *Big Brother* that he re-situates within the expanded surveillance culture of the post-Orwellian twenty-first century. In this new location, *Big Brother*, the reality TV show superimposed on Orwell's novel, is the metonym for the state's biopolitical power; its assertion of power over the movement and placement of bodies in space. The game format in Schlingensief's reworked conceit merely exposed the devolution of state power to the people whose proxy votes created winners and losers, but also, by extension, citizens and exiles.

Endnotes

1. Christoph Schlingensief (2000), *Please Love Austria: First Austrian Coalition Week*, Vienna International Festival.

2. *The Independent* (2008), 'Haider is back. Just don't mention the war', 26 September, http://www.independent.co.uk/news/world/europe/haider-is-back-just-dont-mention-the-war-942827.html. Accessed 24 June 2009.

3. *New York Times* (2000), 'U.S. Recalls Ambassador to Vienna, Temporarily', 5 February, http://www.nytimes.com/2000/02/05/world/us-recalls-ambassador-to-vienna-temporarily.html. Accessed 22 June 2009.

4. http://www.schlingensief.com/backup/wienaktion/. Accessed 22 June 2009.

5. For a more detailed discussion of the FPÖ's anti-immigration policies, and for the original citation of the quotation repeated here, see Forrest, T. (2008), 'Mobilizing the Public Sphere: Schlingensief's Reality Theatre', *Contemporary Theatre Review*, 18:1, p. 91.

6. Poet, P. (2002), *Foreigners Out!: Schlingensief's Container*, Austria: Bonus GmbH. All further references will be cited as *Foreigners Out!*

7. http://www.schlingensief.com/backup/wienaktion/. Accessed 24 June 2009.

8. Birringer, J. (2006), 'Interacting 1', *Contemporary Theatre Review*, 16:4, pp. 389–405.

9. *Foreigners Out!* (2002).

10. Ibid.

11. Ibid.

12. Ibid.

13. Ibid.

14. Ibid.

15. Interview with Paul Poet, http://www.theblurb.com.au/Issue32/PaulPoet.htm. Accessed 21 May 2009.

16. Lilienthal, M. and Philipp, C. (eds.) (2000), *Schlingensiefs Ausländer raus: Bitte liebt Österreich*, Frankfurt am Main: Suhrkamp Verlag. Lilienthal was a dramatic advisor on the project.

17. Forrest (2008: 91).

18. Ibid., p. 98.

19. Jestrovic, S. (2008), 'Performing like an asylum seeker: paradoxes of hyper-authenticity', *Research on Drama Education: The Journal of Applied Theatre and Performance*, 13:2, pp. 159–170.

20. *Foreigners Out!* (2002).

21. Ibid.

22. Jameson, F. (1998), *Brecht and Method*, London: Verso, p. 129.

23. Langston, R. (2008), *Visions of Violence: German avant-gardes after fascism*, Evanston Il.: Northwestern University Press, p. 236.

24. Ibid., p. 239.

25. Ibid., p. 239.

26. Ibid., p. 243.

27. See Varney, D. (2006), 'Gestus, affect and the post-semiotic in Contemporary Theatre', *International Journal of the Arts in Society*, vol. 1, http://www.arts-journal. com; '*Transit Heimat*: Translation, Transnational Subjectivity and Mobility in German Theatre', in *Transit* 2:1, Article 61008, http://repositories.cdlib.org/ ucbgerman/transit/vol2/iss1/art61008; and 'Being Political in German Theatre and Performance: Anna Langhoff and Christoph Schlingensief', in *Proceedings of the 2006 Conference of the Australasian Association for Drama, Theatre and Performance Studies*, http://ses.library.usyd.edu.au/bitstream/2123/2484/1/ADSA2006_Varney. pdf. Accessed 24 May 2009.

28. See Carlson, M. (1996), *Performance*, London and New York: Routledge, pp. 100–120; Lehmann, H.-T. (2006), *Postdramatic Theatre* (trans. Karen Jürs-Munby), London and New York: Routledge, p. 4.

29. Kershaw, B. (1999), *The Radical in Performance: Between Brecht and Baudrillard*, London and New York: Routledge, p. 7.

30. Ibid., p. 12.

31. Jameson, F. (1998: 9).

32. I refer here to the failed attempt by activists on day four of the performance to 'free the refugees' and shut down the container-compound, and the guest appearance of American theatre director, Peter Sellars, who claimed there should be containers in New York, in San Francisco, and in Sydney. Schlingensief told Paul Poet that Sellars would say that but not do it.

33. Brecht, B. (1984), *The Theatre of Bertolt Brecht* (trans. John Willett), London: Methuen, p. 121.

34. Ibid., p. 122.

35. *Foreigners Out!* (2002)

36. Brecht, B. (1984: 128).

37. Ibid., p. 200.

38. Willett, J. (1967), *The Theatre of Bertolt Brecht*, London: Methuen & Co., p. 173.

39. Jameson, F. (1998: 100–101).

40. Diamond, E. (1997), *Unmaking Mimesis,* London & New York: Routledge, pp. 43–55.

41. Giorgio Agamben developed this concept from Foucault. Foucault's concept of 'bio-power' referred to the power of the state to administer and create docile controlled bodies. Agamben, G. (1998), *Homo Sacer: Sovereign Power and Bare Life* (trans. Daniel Heller-Roazen), Stanford, California: Stanford University Press.

42. Jameson, F. (1998: 99).

43. Brecht, B. (1984: 139).

44. Lilienthal, M. and Philipp, C. (eds.) (2000: 20–21).

45. Agamben, G. (1998: 107).

46. Ibid., p. 107.

47. Auslander, P. cited in Shepherd, S. and Wallis, M. (2004), *Drama/Theatre/Performance*, London and New York: Routledge, p. 152.

Productive Discord: Schlingensief, Adorno, and *Freakstars 3000*

Tara Forrest

In an interview with Alexander Kluge conducted in 2001, Christoph Schlingensief reflects on the degree to which he is often perceived as a prankster: someone who just likes to have fun and who cannot, as a result, be taken very seriously.[1] In another context, and presumably in reaction to this negative portrait generated by the media, Schlingensief discusses the critical, one-dimensional conception of fun that underpins such criticism of his work:

> When I scramble about for, and in front of, other people, then of course I can't say that I'm not having fun, otherwise I wouldn't do it. But as soon as you say that, you are immediately in the Fun Factory, or in the Fun Parade or about to get an invitation to 'RTL Samstag Nacht' [RTL Saturday Night] where you can tell another joke about Poland or homeless people. When it comes to the word 'fun', everyone listens attentively and says: 'Ah, a bit of fun? Do you like a bit of fun?' No, I don't like this kind of fun. Fun is not the Comedy-Show, but desire and enthusiasm for making associations and rebuilding sentences in order to keep [fun] alive. One has to transform the lack of desire to participate in life into energy for the process of searching for something that affords pleasure.[2]

Schlingensief distinguishes here between two different modes of experiencing what he interchangeably refers to as 'fun' or 'pleasure'. The first mode—which is associated with the idea of the 'fun factory'—is strongly reminiscent of the passive, alienated mode of engagement that Theodor Adorno associates with the mass-produced products of the 'culture industry'. In Adorno's writings on popular music, television, and other forms of mass-produced culture, fun is associated with 'canned' laughter, conformity, standardization, and pre-digested material that reinforces the status quo. As Adorno and Max Horkheimer write in *Dialectic of Enlightenment*: 'Amusement', in this context, 'congeals into boredom, since, to be amusement, it must cost no effort and therefore moves strictly along the well-worn grooves of association. The spectator must need no thoughts of his own: the product prescribes each reaction'.[3]

In his essay 'On Popular Music' (1941), Adorno claims that this non-productive, non-participatory mode of having fun fostered by the entertainment industry is a 'correlate' of alienated forms of mechanized labour which leave workers feeling exhausted, bored and unfulfilled.[4] According to Adorno, because standardized forms of mass entertainment (such as popular music and television) do not require any real effort or concentration, they provide the worker with 'relief from both boredom and effort simultaneously'.[5] The workers, he writes, 'seek novelty, but the strain and boredom associated with actual work leads to avoidance of effort in that leisure-time which offers the only chance for really new experience'.[6]

In stark contrast to this alienated conception of what it means to 'have fun', the second definition touched on by Schlingensief is associated with an active, creative mode of engagement: a mode in which the capacity to draw and make one's own connections and associations is absolutely central to the production and experience of pleasure. The emphasis here is not on the kind of 'canned' pleasures that Adorno associates with the consumption of 'premasticated material'.[7] Rather, the particular experience of pleasure outlined in this context, is bound with the capacity to actively 'participate in life', and to draw on one's own imagination and experience in the process of engaging creatively with the material in question.

In Adorno's writings, a similarly active, creative mode of engagement is explored in his analysis of modernist art practices, and in his essays on the work of Austrian composer Arnold Schönberg in particular, whose atonal compositions result in what Adorno describes as 'the renunciation of the customary crutches of a listening which always knows what to expect'.[8] In contrast to the formulaic, familiar structure of both popular and 'classical' forms of music, Adorno argues that what is important about the discordant form of Schönberg's work is the degree to which it 'fails to provide [the listener with] a safe centre for enjoyment'.[9] Unlike 'easy listening' music, which can be experienced in an absentminded, disengaged state, Adorno claims that the open, fragmentary structure of Schönberg's work prompts the listener to actively participate in the composition process. His music, he writes, 'demands [...] not mere contemplation but praxis'.[10]

In *Composing for the Films* (which Adorno co-wrote with Hanns Eisler in 1947) the role that a discordant music practice could play in actively stimulating audience participation is discussed in some depth. In a statement that echoes his criticism of the formulaic structure of popular music, Adorno and Eisler argue that 'one of the most widespread prejudices in the motion-picture industry is the premise that the spectator should not be conscious of the music'.[11] Instead of reinforcing what is taking place on screen, they argue that music should 'throw its meaning into relief'[12] and, in doing so, encourage the spectator to actively participate in the meaning-making process that is initiated, but not foreclosed, by the film in question. By generating a sense of discord between the music and the image on screen, the audience is not only made conscious of the music, but 'sound is robbed of its static quality and made dynamic by the ever-present factor of the "unresolved"'.[13]

Interestingly, this emphasis on an open, discordant, unresolved musical form is also present in Schlingensief's reflections on the experimental form of his own work, which he compares to a musical composition that generates tension because its direction and meaning cannot easily be anticipated.[14] In a statement that evokes Schönberg's work, Schlingensief claims that he has 'always worked atonally'[15], while in his analysis of *Art and Vegetables, A. Hipler*—a production he staged at the Volksbühne in 2004—Schlingensief goes a step further, stating that Schönberg's music provided him with an important 'point of departure', and that his aim for the production was to develop a theatrical 'counterpart' to Schönberg's work.[16]

While Schlingensief's observation that he has 'always worked atonally' could be explored productively in relation to his work in a range of different fields, the specific aim of this Chapter is to analyze the degree to which the atonal form of Schlingensief's television series *Freakstars 3000* (2002) cultivates the kind of active, creative mode of engagement that he associates with the production and experience of a non-reified form of pleasure. Focusing on the 2003 film documentation of the program (also entitled *Freakstars 3000*), this chapter will explore how (and with what effects) Schlingensief has sought to cultivate an active, critical mode of spectatorship by working firmly within—rather than outside of—the mass-produced, standardized products of the culture industry.

Atonal re-enactment

Since 1997, Schlingensief has produced four television series, three of which are organized around a variety talk show format.[17] The standout of the group, *Freakstars 3000*, was also modelled on a highly popular, mass-produced format: in this case, the casting show model popularized by programs such as *Popstars* and *Deutschland sucht den Superstar* (*Germany seeks a Superstar*). Although the structure, rules, and organization of the program are modelled closely on the casting show format, *Freakstars 3000* differs from other programs in the genre in the sense that it was shot at the Thiele Winkler Home for people with physical and mental disabilities in Lichtenrade, Berlin. The contestants who perform for the panel (consisting of Schlingensief and two other judges) thus differ from the predominantly young, highly commodified types who ordinarily feature on such programs.

In other regards, however, *Freakstars 3000* (which originally aired on the youth oriented popular music channel VIVA) re-enacts the conventions of the format, and charts the experiences and performances of the contestants as they participate in an audition and casting process that includes, among other activities: dance and vocal coaching workshops (the latter of which are conducted by Irm Hermann); studio recording sessions; the formation of the band 'Mutter sucht Schrauben' (Mother seeks Screws); the release of a CD; and a 'free jazz' concert at the Volksbühne in Berlin.

In keeping with the conventions of the format, we are also presented with behind-the-scenes footage of the contestants. Andreas, for example, takes us on a tour through his room that reveals the source of his musical inspiration, while Achim demonstrates how a bath lift functions to lower disabled residents into the water. The program was also supplemented by a web page that included contestant profiles and details about the hobbies and passions of the successful band members. Viewers were also encouraged to vote online for their favourite contestants, while a guestbook provided visitors with the opportunity to reflect on their thoughts about the show.[18]

Figure 1: Members of the band 'Mutter sucht Schrauben' perform with some of the other *Freakstars 3000* contestents. © Thomas Aurin

Throughout his career, Schlingensief has frequently deployed a critical strategy of re-enactment in his attempt to facilitate public discussion and debate about a broad range of topics and issues. This strategy was most famously deployed in his production *Please Love Austria: First Austrian Coalition Week* (2000) in which he staged a version of the then hugely popular *Big Brother* reality television series in an attempt to mobilize debate about the xenophobic, anti-immigration policies of Jörg Haider and the Freedom Party of Austria (FPÖ).[19]

In 2002, Schlingensief also staged *Quiz 3000—You are the Catastrophe* at the Volksbühne and other theatres in Germany and Switzerland. In keeping with his interest in re-enacting and transforming popular formats, *Quiz 3000* was modelled on the highly successful game show *Who Wants to Be a Millionaire?* (the German version of which, hosted by Günther Jauch, has screened on RTL since 1999).[20] However, as revealed below, the questions posed by Schlingensief to the on-stage contestants deal with themes and issues pertaining to subjects that are largely avoided by the German entertainment media:

Question: Order the following concentration camps from north to south!:

A: Auschwitz, **B:** Bergen-Belsen, **C:** Dachau, **D:** Ravensbrück

Answer: DBAC

Question: What percentage of women will be afflicted at least once in their life by thrush?:

A: 25%, **B:** 45%, **C:** 75%, **D:** 90%

Answer: C

Question: The rape of members of which minority group are, according to the German criminal code, less heavily penalized?:

A: Men, **B:** Animals, **C:** Children, **D:** People with Disabilities

Answer: D [21]

These and other questions (which appeared on screens that closely mimicked the design format of *Who Wants to Be a Millionaire?)* all produce a jarring, discordant effect, albeit for different reasons. If, for example, the question pertaining to thrush produces a sense of discomfort for some contestants/audience members, then it is because thrush and other issues pertaining to women's health do not—with the exception of commercials for so-called 'sanitary' products—feature in the public sphere generated by the media. What is, however, disturbing (on both thematic and formal levels) about the questions pertaining to concentration camps and the legal consequences of the rape of disabled people, is the degree to which they short-circuit the experience of pleasure associated with the contestant/audience's capacity to answer the question. If, for example, in response to the first question about the geographical location of former concentration camps, the contestant/audience member is able to answer the question correctly, the sense of discomfort produced by the memory of the camps and the atrocities that occurred there both outweighs the pleasure gained from providing the host with the correct answer, and makes it very difficult for the contestant/audience member to proceed in an enthusiastic manner to the next question.

Figure 2: Schlingensief poses a question to one of the *Quiz 3000* contestants. © Thomas Aurin

The integral relationship between Schlingensief's critical re-enactment of popular, mass-produced, television formats and the self-described 'atonal' character of his work is rendered further apparent in an interview with Alexander Kluge in which Schlingensief reflects on his 'compulsion' to replay certain scenarios, characters and events.[22] As he makes clear, however, this process of re-enactment is not driven by a desire to produce an exact copy of that which is being reproduced. 'If', he states, 'I say, out of a desire for perfection, I can re-enact it exactly, that's not it'.[23] Rather, in a similar vein to Adorno's analysis of the sense of discord produced by atonal music, what fascinates Schlingensief about this mode of re-enactment is the 'inconsistency' that emerges as a result.

In the opening scenes of *Freakstars 3000*, this sense of 'inconsistency' is immediately felt. The reproduction, however, is not a parody of the original because *Freakstars* sticks too closely to the conventions of the format, which are reinforced and undermined simultaneously. This dual process comes into play in the opening moments of the film via the male voiceover that introduces us—in a very familiar, generic tone—to what is to come: 'Watch cool, young people, fulfil their dreams of a career in music, with talent and 100 per cent dedication! Hear German originals use song to highlight the problems of the non-handicapped!'[24] This opening sequence is followed soon after by a Monty Pythonesque opening credit sequence that features, among other images, animated diagrams of a cross-section of a human brain, and an anatomical measuring device that appears throughout the audition process. This montage sequence is followed by an image of one of the contestants, Horst Gelonnek, who stands at the front of the star-spangled stage and enthusiastically welcomes the audience to the show.

In the following scenes, which are located in the Thiele Winkler Home, Schlingensief stands before the contestants and explains how the audition process will proceed, while the voiceover states, in a very cheesy tone: 'From Germany, Austria, and Switzerland, they've come from all over to fulfil their dream of becoming a real Freakstar 3000!' Before the audition process begins, however, we are presented with a montage of clips which feature reproductions of a diverse range of television formats including, among others: *The Hit Parade*; a home shopping show; a weather program hosted by Schlingensief regular Mario Garzaner; and political talk shows entitled *Freakmann* (*Freak Man*) and *Presse Club* (*Press Club*) in which the politics of Jörg Haider, Hitler and the NPD (National Democratic Party) are discussed alongside other topics such as the status of the German press, and love and sex in contemporary Germany. Clips from each of these 'programs' appear throughout the course of the film, prompting viewers to consider the various ways in which other television formats could be re-enacted and transformed as a result.

Schlingensief's main focus, however, is the casting show format and, as the auditions begin, the gap between *Freakstars 3000* and its reality template immediately generates a sense of discord that produces a very interesting, destabilizing effect. As Adorno and Eisler write in *Composing for the Films* (1947) of the discord generated by an experimental film scoring practice:

The aim of [...] an antithetic utilization of music will not be to introduce the largest possible number of dissonant sounds and novel colours into the machinery, which only spits them out again in a digested, blunted, and conventionalized form, but to break the mechanism of neutralization itself.[25]

In *Freakstars 3000*, the 'dissolution of tonality'[26] produced by the 'lack of fit' between the *Freakstars* contestants and the so-called 'ideal' types who ordinarily feature on such programs immediately 'breaks the mechanism of neutralization' bestowed on such formats by a culture industry that thrives on the promotion of stereotypes and the reproduction of the status quo. Instead of a crowd full of Justin Timberlake or Beyoncé wannabes, we are presented with contestants of diverse ages and backgrounds who perform (some confidently, others tentatively) an eclectic collection of numbers, including: German folk tunes; an anti-war song by Udo Lindenberg; a selection of poems; and a song by Karel Gott, who was Austria's representative in the 1968 *Eurovision Song Contest*. In contrast to the judgemental atmosphere that pervades the casting show format, the mood generated by the audition process is predominantly light-hearted and positive, and Schlingensief is very supportive in encouraging those participants who are nervous and/or lacking in confidence. When Werner Brecht, for example, nervously declares that he only received a C minus in music, Schlingensief states that he himself received an F, and Brecht's audition proceeds with the support of another contestant.

This 'lack of fit' between the original and the reproduction also generates much humour not because, as some critics have suggested, Schlingensief is 'making fun' of the disabled contestants, but because the program is very effective in rendering viewers conscious of the stereotypes, norms, and clichés according to which such programs operate. In this regard, *Freakstars 3000* is highly successful in undermining the neutral, automated mode of engagement that Adorno associates with the standardized products of the culture industry, because it encourages the audience to question how—and with what effects—such products actively shape our perception of what it means to be 'normal' or 'disabled'. Indeed, as the cheesy voiceover informs us in the opening minutes of the film, song is employed in *Freakstars 3000* 'to highlight the problems of the non-handicapped', and it is clearly the perceived prejudices and shortcomings of the audience—rather than any 'shortcomings' of the contestants themselves—at which Schlingensief's criticism is levelled.

In Schlingensief's productions, however, criticism is never straightforward. As attested by the open, ambiguous, unresolved form characteristic of his work, he is not driven by a desire to pedagogically instruct the audience on the 'best way' to approach the issues and ideas raised by his work.[27] Rather, in keeping with his delineation of a non-alienated form of pleasure, he is much more interested in encouraging viewers to reflect on their own prejudices, and to think critically and creatively about the material at hand.

Schlingensief himself describes this active, critical mode of engagement as a form of 'self-provocation', because he argues that it is the responsibility of the viewer to work through the feelings, issues, and prejudices aroused in them by the material in question.[28] In a similar vein to Adorno's delineation of the active, creative mode of engagement fostered by Schönberg's atonal compositions, Schlingensief's atonal re-enactment of the casting show format challenges the audience to become active co-producers in the meaning-making process.

Tell me what to think

As revealed by the large number of viewer comments entered on the *Freakstars 3000* online guestbook[29], not all members of the audience are comfortable with Schlingensief's provocative, non-pedagogical approach. Indeed, in keeping with Adorno's analysis of the passive, non-participatory mode of reception fostered by the culture industry, a number of viewers noted that they felt uncomfortable while watching the film because they were unsure how they were *supposed* to respond. 'I want to know', one viewer noted,

> whether I can die laughing without thinking about my morals or whether what has been concocted there is serious? [...] I find it simply so priceless. [...] Am, however, really SERIOUSLY confused. Have unfortunately absolutely NO idea what it is.[30]

'The three of us', another viewer wrote,

> are watching the film and we don't know what is meant by it. Should we be reflective, amused, or disgusted? [...] We have come to the conclusion that the whole production is a send-up of disabled people and that such a thing should not, under any circumstances, be broadcast on television.[31]

The comments of another viewer expressed a similar sentiment:

> Am I just humourless, full of prejudice, not prepared to see sick and disabled people on television? No idea. [...] In any case, I was thinking about how remarkably far our (German?) society has developed since the Third Reich and Hitler: then, all 'freaks' were locked away or 'euthanized', we have now come so far that we amuse ourselves at their cost, and thoroughly take the Mickey out of them, in order to then celebrate what liberal and unprejudiced people we are![32]

The view expressed both here and in the previous quote, that Schlingensief is simply making fun of the disabled contestants, is one that was well represented in both the media and in guestbook comments that appeared at the time of the film's release. However, in their ambivalence about the appropriateness of featuring disabled people on such a program, such comments would seem to support, rather than undermine, one of the key points that Schlingensief is seeking to make: That 'the freak is the situation itself, which forces us to make a distinction between what is and isn't normal'.[33]

Indeed, as Schlingensief makes clear, the discomfort experienced by some viewers while watching the film/program could be seen as a hangover from the Third Reich and from Nazi policies according to which the contestants would, indeed, be viewed as 'freaks'. These policies, which were put in place in the 1930s, dictated—among other things—that the 'hereditarily defective' be sterilized and/or 'euthanized' in order to 'cleanse' the German *Volk*.[34] Schlingensief is very upfront in seeking to make this connection explicit. By introducing anatomical measuring devices at the start of the program, and by superimposing images of those devices on footage of contestants as they participate in the audition process, Schlingensief confronts viewers to question the degree to which certain National Socialist ideals of what constitutes a 'normal' and/or 'desirable' citizen retain a certain currency in the contemporary media and popular culture spheres.

As is the case with much of Schlingensief's work, this questioning is prompted by a process of re-enactment: in this case via the playing out—and evocation of—names and policies that are clearly derogatory and that, during the Third Reich, resulted in mass murder. In this context, the title *Freakstars 3000* serves as a provocation to—rather than an expression of solidarity with—those audience members who view the public representation of disabled people as somehow 'inappropriate', 'distasteful', or 'uncomfortable'. Through the presentation of interviews in which the contestants discuss their lives, loves and interests, and by providing a very diverse group of people with a space in which they can express their enthusiasm for music and performance, Schlingensief challenges the audience to question why—and with what effects—disabled people are largely excluded from the public sphere generated by the media.

In stark contrast to Adorno's delineation of standardized television formats that 'channelize audience reaction' and promote an 'identification with the status quo'[35], the significance of *Freakstars 3000* lies in the degree to which it encourages viewers—in a playful, humorous, but nonetheless serious way—to think critically and creatively for themselves. Moreover, by reproducing the form and effects of an experimental, atonal music practice within the structure of a popular and widely accessible television format, Schlingensief has gone some way to bridging the gap between art and popular culture: those 'torn halves of an integral freedom' that, for Adorno, '[did] not add up'.[36]

Endnotes

1. Kluge, A. (2001), 'Das Halten von Totenschädeln liegt mir nicht!/Christoph Schlingensief inszeniert Hamlet', *News & Stories*, SAT 1, December 16. This discussion has been reproduced in Heineke, T. and Umathum, S. (eds.) (2002), *Christoph Schlingensiefs Nazis Rein*, Frankfurt am Main: Suhrkamp, p.122.

2. Schlingensief, C. (1998), 'Wir sind zwar nicht gut, aber wir sind da', in J. Lochte and W. Schulz (eds.), *Schlingensief! Notruf für Deutschland. Über die Mission, das Theater und die Welt des Christoph Schlingensief*, Hamburg: Rotbuch Verlag, p.19. *RTL Samstag Nacht* was a comedy sketch show that screened on RTL in Germany in the 1990s. Unless otherwise noted, all translations from German language sources are my own.

3. Horkheimer, M. and Adorno, T.W. (2002), *Dialectic of Enlightenment: Philosophical Fragments* (trans. Edmund Jephcott), Stanford: Stanford University Press, p. 109.

4. Adorno, T.W. (2002), 'On Popular Music', in R. Leppert (ed.), *Essays on Music* (trans. Susan H. Gillespie), Berkeley and Los Angeles: University of California Press, p. 458.

5. Ibid.

6. Ibid., p. 459.

7. Adorno, T.W. (1989), *Introduction to the Sociology of Music* (trans. E. B. Ashton), New York: Continuum, p. 30.

8. Adorno, T.W. (1990), 'Arnold Schoenberg 1874—1951', in *Prisms* (trans. Samuel and Shierry Weber), Cambridge, Massachusetts: The MIT Press, p. 149.

9. Adorno, T.W. (2002), 'The Dialectical Composer', p. 203.

10. Adorno, T.W. (1990), p. 150.

11. Adorno, T. and Eisler, H. (1994), *Composing for the Films*, London and Atlantic Highlands: The Athlone Press, p. 9.

12. Ibid., p. 26.

13. Ibid., p. 41.

14. See, for example, Schlingensief's comments in this regard in Kluge, A. (2001: 128).

15. Schlingensief, C. (2005), 'My work always has something to do with a change of perspective' (interviewed by Hans Ulrich Obrist), in A. Koegel and K. König (eds.), *AC: Christoph Schlingensief—Church of Fear*, Köln: Museum Ludwig and Verlag der Buchhandlung Walther König, p.19.

16. Schlingensief, C. (2004), 'Kunst und Gemüse: Eine Erklärung', in C. Hegemann (ed.), *Theater ALS Krankheit*, Berlin: Alexander Verlag, p. 2.

17. These include *Talk 2000* (1997), *U 3000* (2000), and *Die Piloten/The Pilots* (2007). Although the latter series has not been broadcast on television, Cordula Kablitz-Post has produced a film that documents the production of the 'pilot' episodes. The documentary, which is also entitled *Die Piloten*, is available on DVD via Avanti Media, which has also released a DVD compilation of the *Talk 2000* episodes.

18. See www.freakstars3000.de/. Accessed 8 June 2009.

19. For an analysis of the various strategies of re-enactment employed by Schlingensief in this production, see Forrest, T. (2008), 'Mobilising the Public Sphere: Schlingensief's Reality Theatre', *Contemporary Theatre Review*, 18:1, pp. 90–98. See also Solveig Gade's analysis of the strategy of 'perfomative recitation' employed by Schlingensief in the context of his 1998/1999 *Wahlkampfzircus—Chance 2000*/Election Circus—Chance 2000, in Gade, S. (2005), 'Playing the Media Keyboard: The Political Potential of Performativity in Christoph Schlingensief's Electioneering Circus', in R. Gade and A. Jerslev (eds.), *Performative Realism: Interdisciplinary Studies in Art and Media*, Copenhagen: Museum Tusculanum Press, pp. 19–49.

20. For an overview of the performance, see Kümmel, P. (2002), 'Der Mann mit der Moralkelle. "Ordnen Sie folgende KZ von Nord nach Süd": Christoph Schlingensief parodiert Günther Jauchs Rateshow', *Die Zeit*, No. 13, 21 March, http://www.zeit.de/2002/13/200213_quiz3000_xml. Accessed 8 June 2009.

21. These and other questions that were posed on the 'pilot' version of the 'program' staged at the Volksbühne can be accessed on the official *Quiz 3000* website: www.quiz3000.de/fragen16.3.pdf Accessed 8 June 2009.

22. Schlingensief C., in Kluge. A. (2001: 114).

23.   Schlingensief, C., in Kluge, A. (2001), p. 128.

24   All quotes from the film are taken from the English language subtitles that appear on the *Freakstars 3000* (2003) DVD released by Filmgalerie 451.

25.   Adorno, T. and Eisler, H. (1994), p. 87.

26.   Footnote 2, Ibid., p. 41.

27.   See, for example, Schlingensief's comments in this regard in relation to a discussion about *Bitte Liebt Österreich*, in Kluge, A. (2000), 'Theater der Handgreiflichkeit/ Christoph Schlingensief's Wiener Container', *News & Stories*, SAT 1, 22 October.

28.   Schlingensief quoted in Anonymous (2007), 'Keine Wiener-"Konzentrationswoche"', *Die Presse*, June 7.

29.   The guestbook can be found at: http://www.freakstars3000.de/. Accessed 15 April 2009.

30.   *Freakstars 3000 Gästebuch*, entry 27 (10 August 2004). Accessed 15 April 2009.

31.   Ibid., entry 20 (10 August 2004). Accessed 15 April 2009.

32.   Ibid., entry 51 (10 August 2004). Accessed 15 April 2009.

33.   Schlingensief, quoted in Straub, J. (2003), 'Wir sind alle krank', *Spiegel Online*, 19 November, http://www.spiegel.de/kultur/kino/0,1518,274587,00.html. Accessed 25 April 2009.

34.   Poore, C. (2007), *Disability in Twentieth Century German Culture*, Ann Arbor: University of Michigan Press, pp. 75–78. This book provides a comprehensive analysis of the representation of disability in German culture spanning the Weimar period up until the early years of the twenty-first century.

35.   Adorno, T.W. (2001), 'How to Look at Television', in J.M. Bernstein (ed.), *The Culture Industry: Selected Essays on Mass Culture*, London and New York: Routledge, pp. 165; 164.

36.   See Adorno's letter to Walter Benjamin (dated 18 March 1936) in Adorno, T. et al. (1990), *Aesthetics and Politics*, London and New York: Verso, p. 123.

THE FUSION AND CONFUSION OF ART AND TERROR(ISM): *ATTA ATTA*

Brechtje Beuker

In the aftermath of the terrorist attacks of September 11, German composer Karlheinz Stockhausen shocked the public by referring to the attacks as the greatest work of art of all time. Many took his remark to refer to the fact that the terrorists had calculated on the live broadcasting of the second airplane's crash into the Twin Tower, thus creating a media event of an unprecedented scale. Because the images of the collapsing tower were created and distributed in 'real time', they produced a sense of threat (to the) here and now, making it possible to think of the attacks as having a certain performative quality. Not only were they 'staged' in front of an audience, but this public staging was also a prerequisite for the attacks to generate meaning. After all, what distinguishes terrorism from many other forms of violence is that it operates primarily on a symbolic level, where it aims for the highest degree of psychological, not material damage. Thus, rather than representing acts of violence whose meaning precedes their mediation, the media images of 9/11 were very much part of the destructive acts themselves.

While the terrorists' instrumentalization of modern technologies and the performative mode of the attacks were widely acknowledged, Stockhausen was criticized for his use of the term 'artwork' and, moreover, his apparent appreciation of the attacks themselves. Within days, the composer made an exculpatory statement in which he accused the press of quoting him out of context and misinterpreting his words.[1] But as is so often the case with media scandals, the damage was done and Stockhausen's clarification failed to have its intended effect. Instead, his (misinterpreted) comparison became a contributing factor to post-9/11 debates that evolved around the relationship between violence and the media, terror(ism) and art, fiction and reality.

That Stockhausen's controversial remark was given serious consideration became strikingly clear when Berlin's Volksbühne am Rosa-Luxemburg-Platz organized a round table entitled 'Attaismus-Seminar'—the second project in a series of events focusing on the intertwinement of politics and crime. From 2–20 December 2002, the theatre made its rehearsal space available to a group of artists and cultural critics so that they could engage in lectures, discussions and artistic interventions dealing with the connections between terror(ism) and art. Among the participants were the philosopher Peter Sloterdijk, the artists and scholars Bazon Brock and Peter Weibel, the Hungarian author Péter Nádas, the chief dramaturge of the Volksbühne Carl Hegemann as well as Christoph Schlingensief. Taking the ideas discussed during the seminar as a starting point, Schlingensief collaborated with Volksbühne actors and members of his professional 'family' to create the theatrical production *ATTA ATTA—Art Has Broken Out!*, which premiered on 23 January 2003 and which was performed approximately once a month for a period of more than a year. *ATTA ATTA* marked the beginning of a larger endeavour, often referred to as the 'attaistic project', which further includes Schlingensief's production of Elfriede Jelinek's *Bambiland* at Vienna's Burgtheater (2003), his piece *Atta Bambi Pornoland* for the Schauspielhaus Zürich (2004), as well as the movies shown as a part of these productions.

Figure 1: Schlingensief and Peter Sloterdijk at the Attaismus-Seminar. Photo: David Baltzer.

The overall goal of the Attaismus-seminar was to establish an alternative discourse to the explanatory and unifying narrative framework that the US government and the majority of the American media constructed after 9/11 in an attempt to contain the excessive and disruptive nature of the attacks and to justify a politics of retaliation. As Judith Butler has argued, the rhetoric of firm action, patriotism and heroism that emerged almost immediately was not only symptomatic of the widespread denial of a newly experienced vulnerability, but also of the unwillingness to acknowledge the involvement of the western world in the political and economic conditions that provided the breeding ground for the terrorist attacks.[2] In this respect, Butler's ideas are in line with those of other influential critics such as Slavoj Žižek and Jean Baudrillard. In their essay collections *Welcome to the Desert of the Real!* (2002) and *The Spirit of Terrorism* (2003) respectively, they asserted early on that Islamic terrorism and, in particular, the practice of suicide bombing can be understood as a means via which the underprivileged can effectively resist the hegemony of global capitalism.[3] Viewed from this perspective, the terrorists' message of death is, paradoxically, also a message of life, i.e., a way to insist on their otherwise marginalized existence. When, in a world dictated by exchange value, those with limited access to financial and political power choose death and self-sacrifice as their currency, they force the hegemonic system into a kind of double bind: the system *either* has to pay back with death and destruction (thereby ridiculing its superior claims at fighting efficient and 'clean' wars) *or* renounce the currency of death and acknowledge the existence of an external set of values (thereby revealing the contradictions within global capitalism).

This viewpoint, however, was largely overlooked by the western public that clearly recognized the symbolic meaning of 9/11, but interpreted it according to convenient black and white schemata. In the United States and Europe alike, the perception of an Islamic threat to western civilization led to a revival of old dichotomies; opposing Christian and Muslim worlds, liberal democracy and religious fundamentalism, modern Enlightenment and pre-modern darkness. At the same time, expressions of anti-Islamic sentiment revealed the tensions lingering in Europe's multicultural societies, where the failure to integrate those who had migrated to western Europe since the 1950s was seen by many as a key cultural and political problem. In Germany—a country with a Muslim population of a little over three million—the struggle to accept cultural diversity as a social reality and, consequently, to rethink what constitutes German national identity has split public opinion. Whereas conservative politicians have repeatedly proclaimed that all citizens should subscribe to the basic values of the western 'core culture' (*Leitkultur*), their critics have rejected the coercive nature, or even the very idea of such a concept in favour of a more pluralist notion of collective identity. This divergence could be seen quite clearly in 2003, when a heated public debate evolved around the Federal Constitutional Court's decision to overturn a ruling that prohibited Muslim teachers from wearing a headscarf when employed at a public school.[4]

Despite shared anxieties over Islamic fundamentalism, German-American relations took a turn for the worse when, less than two years after 9/11, Washington announced that it condoned pre-emptive military action against Iraq as a necessary means to win the 'war on terror'. After an initial phase of solidarity with the largest NATO-ally, German citizens and politicians openly criticized the United States' unilateral politics, viewed by many as a manifestation of imperialism. The opposition was, however, not entirely lacking in bias. For German chancellor Gerhard Schröder, distancing his social-democratic party (SPD) from George W. Bush's foreign policies became a crucial strategy in his campaign for re-election in the fall of 2002.

Revisiting the violent legacy of the avant-garde

Not surprisingly, the left-leaning Volksbühne picked up on the climate of declining support for the United States' response to international terrorism when it planned its 'Attaismus-Seminar'. Weary of the kind of 'shock management', as Sloterdijk called it,[5] that employed collective mourning and fear of the Muslim Other for geopolitical purposes, the seminar participants were more interested in approaching the issue of terrorism through a process of self-questioning. By focusing on what Žižek refers to as western society's 'passion for the Real'[6]—i.e., a longing for an authentic experience of violence and excess typical of the twentieth and twenty-first centuries—they broke decidedly with the popular practice of portraying the traumatized West in the role of victim while demonizing the terrorists. Through the exposure of the attacks' distinctly modern features, as well as their underlying ambiguities, the speakers at the seminar hoped to deconstruct the one-sided media coverage and shed light on the issue of terrorism without buying into the culture of fear that was being orchestrated and instrumentalized by government officials. In particular, they focused on an ambivalence that had revealed itself in Stockhausen's reference to the greatest work of art, namely the intrinsic double nature of violence. As the interdisciplinary scholarship on violence known in Germany as '*Gewaltforschung*' has emphasized, what makes violence so complex is, in part, its capacity to simultaneously disable and enable, destroy and produce, horrify and fascinate.[7] In the eyes of Sloterdijk, Stockhausen's remark demonstrated this fascination with violence's productive force and had to be understood as the 'legitimate reaction' of an artist envying the criminal his successful, most radical fulfilment of the 'driving dynamics of the art perpetrator' (*Antriebsdynamik des Kunsttäters*).[8]

Assuming that the artist and the terrorist share not only the need for a public platform but also a strong belief in the value of transgressive action, the question of what distinguishes one from the other is less trivial than it may seem at first. In fact, the Stockhausen-controversy opened up a variety of related questions, many of which have a long tradition in modernist art: Can art enter the realm of reality? Does art have fixed borders that prohibit labelling violent events as works of art? Is art autonomous and subjected to its own laws, thus surpassing common moral and legal structures? Can art serve as a weapon in pursuit of political goals?

Formulating answers to these questions has been a fundamental endeavour of various avant-garde movements, whose representatives experimented with aggressive and boundary breaking art forms in order to undermine the (aesthetic) establishment presumed responsible for political or social stagnation. For the historical avant-garde, Hanno Ehrlicher notes:

> Violence becomes part of a radical cultural critique that aims to overcome modernity by actionist means. In the self-perception of numerous artists between the turn of the century and the First World War, the contradictions and antagonisms of the bourgeois cultural order had aggravated into a crisis that could no longer be solved by means of rational strategies, but only overcome in a heroic exertion.[9]

From early thinkers such as Antonin Artaud and the Dadaists to the Vienna Actionists and Elfriede Jelinek in the post-war period, artists have questioned the notion of a repressive rationality and insisted on the need for an aesthetic of shock, radical rhetoric, and violent imagery. In doing so, they deliberately played with their own image as 'intellectual' or 'aesthetic terrorist'. However, over the years this trope had to be re-evaluated because the experiences generated by the First and Second World Wars, as well as Germany's encounter with left-wing terrorism in the 1970s, rendered the avant-garde project problematic. In Austria, for example, the initial belief in the progression of society through the destruction of cultural symbols gave way to the idea that an aesthetic of transgression could serve a culture of remembrance. What motivates Jelinek and the Vienna Actionists to employ provocative methods is the wish to expose the country's failure to confront its Nazi past.

Although, according to some, the avant-garde became obsolete a long time ago and should be declared dead, the recent terrorist spectacles pose a challenge to those who both want to hold on to its legacy and consider its future in a postmodern society.[10] For how should one envision the validity of the avant-garde agenda if the fusion of art and life that it aimed to achieve has reached its ultimate form in the violent theatrical performances witnessed by millions? Furthermore, in view of contemporary society's saturation with images of real and virtual destruction, an aesthetic concept that builds on ruptures, terror, and transgression unequivocally runs the risk of replicating, rather than disrupting or transforming, existing cultural norms. Precisely this dilemma became a key issue in the Attaismus-debates, in part because several of the participants were closely involved with the avant-garde art scene—Brock and Weibel took part in Happenings in the 1960s while Schlingensief has been celebrated as 'the avant-garde artist of our times'.[11] For Weibel and Brock, revisiting the crisis of the avant-garde was a necessary step in critically assessing the cultural implications of twenty-first century terrorism.

The theatrical terror of *ATTA ATTA*

The title of the theatre production *ATTA ATTA—Art Has Broken Out!*, and the neologism 'Attaismus' chosen by Schlingensief to describe the extended project, refers— on the one hand—to Mohammed Atta, the suicide pilot of the attacks of 9/11. On the other hand, the sound and repetitive use of its short syllables remind us of Dada, the anti-bourgeois movement whose origin coincided with the beginning of World War I. Thus, the title immediately reveals the avant-garde tradition in which Schlingensief's work can be understood. Peter Weibel defines 'Attaismus' as 'the sum of all possibilities left open by previous avant-garde movements'.[12] For Schlingensief, however, the comparison with the avant-garde or Dadaism is insufficient:

> Attaism is Dadaism or something like that, that's not enough in my opinion. But it's about some kind of movement contained within it. The point is to commit an act of betrayal against oneself or to find a discourse exposing one's own vulnerability. Not as a showcase [*Schauelement*], however, but as a description of one's personal pleasure in this very moment.[13]

The term 'Attaismus' clearly plays with the linguistically correct term 'atavism', which designates the return to a previous (or even primitive) phase in human development. In this sense, the double 'atta' phonetically resembles baby language, while it semantically signals Mohammed Atta's as well as modern art's relapse into a state of being or form of behaviour that can be associated with the bliss of innocence as well as with barbarism. Analogous to Derrida's famous 'differance', the 'v' that is simultaneously absent and present (as a trace) in 'Attaismus' draws us into the game of signifiers and confronts us with the impossibility of fixed meanings. The line dividing lust from barbarism, pleasure from fear, and good from bad appears to be as fragile as the two slashes shaping the letter. The ambivalence of the title *ATTA ATTA* and the term 'Attaismus' is a first indication of a deconstructionist procedure that is characteristic of the entire production. Although it takes place in a conventional theatre, it breaks with the unambiguous framework of the classical drama with its narrative plot and psychologically differentiated figures. The *mise-en-scène* is not designed to create the illusion of a fictional world, but rather to emphasize the creative process that is the foundation of every theatrical performance. With its disjointed scene changes and its concurrent use of video clips and scenic action, *ATTA ATTA* supports an aesthetic of presence and corporeality that undermines the logical strategies we employ to conceptualize violence and neutralize its horror.

Because the conceptualization and narration of violence in a linear, rational fashion according to conventional cause-and-effect-relationships is a preferred method for those seeking to assert their political and ideological dominance, Schlingensief deliberately calls the traditional narrative model into question. Instead of offering an easily consumable or even recognizable statement on terror(ism), he invites the audience to join him in his search for the meaning of violence, a search for which he does not guarantee an end. The play of signifiers that unfolds between the various segments of the performance is nearly endless. Without a clear and coherent narrative, viewers are free to make their own connections between the thematic fields of the performance. Verbal and scenic references to Schlingensief's work as a film-maker, to his debut as an opera director, and to his parents' dislike for their son's work identify art as one of those fields, while also linking the artist's struggle to escape bourgeois domesticity with the desire to become a terrorist. The set design—which combines a German living room with a camping ground that could function equally well as an Al-Qaeda training camp—further underscores the connection between a western lifestyle and Muslim fundamentalism. In addition, Schlingensief blurs the boundaries between East and West through his use of music and costumes, including a chasuble and a Middle Eastern thawb to symbolize both the Christian and Islamic religions. But for all these familiar symbols, the lack of common schemes of cause and effect makes it impossible to recognize either an explanation for, or a condemnation of terrorism. Rather, the performance foregrounds just how futile any effort to make sense of an inherently senseless phenomenon is. This is not to say that the spectator cannot gain an understanding of terrorism, but this understanding is as intuitive and subjective as the one around which Schlingensief builds his production.

In a TV interview, Schlingensief has explained the importance of this subjective approach to the representation of violence as follows:

> The desire for violence that I know derives from my own petty bourgeois background and from my personal fear, a fear that instills in me the need to find an image for this very fear. That means that I want to experience myself, I want to get the sense that I'm alive again, and since I cannot do that in a way that would make ten other people unhappy, I can express it in a form of violence against myself. I would suspect that, in many cases, what comes into play when people resort to violence is the fact that they do it to co-punish themselves or to get a sense they're alive.[14]

Consequently, Schlingensief does not strive in *ATTA ATTA* to comment on the events of 9/11 from a safe, critical distance (claiming a moral high ground he does not believe exists) but seeks, rather, a proximity to the terrorists by re-enacting the events and by releasing his own aggressive drives. As is the case with most of his work, in *ATTA ATTA*, he plays the leading part, appearing as 'dramatic' figure Christoph Schlingensief; entertainer, moderator, and commentator all in one. A detail worth mentioning here is the wig Schlingensief wears throughout the performance, which closely resembles his own hair. It is a typical example of what Jörg van der Horst describes as Schlingensief's

Figure 2: Schlingensief and Irm Hermann in *ATTA ATTA*. Photo: David Baltzer.

preferred use of 'metacommentary', a method that calls regular distinctions between reality and fiction into question.[15] While Schlingensief's reference to himself—by means of the wig—offers the promise of his authentic presence, it simultaneously exposes the claim to authenticity as mere simulation as he is clearly performing himself. When Schlingensief liberates the terrorist in himself and revisits the violent fantasies of the avant-garde, he does so within this context of ironic, ostentatious self-portrayal.

Although Schlingensief emphasizes that 'Attaismus' is not adequately described as Dadaism, the references in *ATTA ATTA* to the avant-garde and, in particular, to actions or happenings of the 1960s and 1970s run like a thread through the production, and they concern both the form and the content of the performance. While following a basic script, each performance is characterized by considerable variations and improvisations, giving

ATTA ATTA the 'here-and-now' quality of an action. This is due in part to the mentally disabled performers, some of whom play their part as rehearsed, while others seem to forget the script and take matters into their own hands. With regard to the scenic content, *ATTA ATTA* copies avant-garde actions with canonic status. In imitation of the Vienna Actionists—a group of artists who attempted to overcome the traditional canvas by painting on objects and bodies, and who later abandoned the idea of painting altogether, moving on to even less conventional events which included public defecation and masturbation—Schlingensief creates paintings with his buttocks, smears paint on a naked woman, and turns the stage into a mess with butter, flour and water. One of the performers portrays Hermann Nitsch, a prominent representative of the Vienna Actionists, whose orgiastic adaptations of medieval mystery plays are referenced. Schlingensief appears with a fake hare and dressed in a felt blanket, thereby conjuring up the image of Joseph Beuys from his action pieces *How to Explain Pictures to a Dead Hare* (1965) and *Coyote: I Like America and America Likes Me* (1974). What makes the Beuys-connotation relevant here is not so much the fact that the latter action took place in a gallery located in the shadows of the Twin Towers. More importantly, the images symbolize the programmatic connection between Schlingensief's theatre and the work of Beuys, whose vision of a fusion of art and socio-politics led to his famous statement that 'every human being is an artist'.[16] In *ATTA ATTA*, Schlingensief examines the ramifications of this statement which, in previous years, had inspired him to work with homeless people, neo-Nazis, and other social outcasts, and which now seems to confirm the validity of Stockhausen's assertion that the terrorists of 9/11 were artists. After all, if every human being is an artist, and a terrorist is a human being, then a terrorist is an artist, someone who cannot be denied his/her capacity (or even right) to creatively construct social reality, but who can be criticized for the way in which he/she chose to express this creative potential.

The cross-fertilization of Beuys' and Stockhausen's ideas leads to another, flawed syllogism: if a terrorist is an artist, and every human being is an artist, then every human being is a terrorist. In Schlingensief's theatre of free associations, precisely this non-logical 'truth' emerges. It is the kind of truth that is often repressed and that needs to reveal itself through embodiment, not through speech. When Schlingensief lets loose, taps into his own aggressive energies and runs amok, he offers the audience a glimpse of the destructive forces that lurk in every human being.

In this regard, *ATTA ATTA* brings to mind Artaud's comparison of theatre with the plague, a disease that kills without leaving visible traces of material destruction. Artaud makes this comparison 'because like the plague [theatre] is a revelation, urging forward the exteriorisation of a latent undercurrent of cruelty through which all the perversity of which the mind is capable, whether in a person or a nation, becomes localised'.[17] It is important to note that the theatrical model envisioned by Artaud veers away from mimetic representation, and that the term cruelty should, therefore, not be taken too literally. Rather, within this schema, it should be viewed as a metaphor for those relentless, dark, and chaotic forces of life that, if unleashed in reality, would pose a threat to the individual or society as a whole. Through an unsettling use of symbols, gestures, light and sound, Artaud wants to liberate these powers in the theatre, thus reminding his audience of their hidden existence. Like Artaud's 'Theatre of Cruelty', Schlingensief's 'Theatre of Fisticuffs'—to borrow Alexander Kluge's term—is a theatre of exposure and revelation and it operates on a sensual and spatial level more than on a discursive one.[18] But unlike Artaud, Schlingensief is interested in using some forms of physical aggression in order to deprive his viewers of their sense of security and complacency and to let them experience a sense of terror.

The actors in *ATTA ATTA* attempt to achieve this goal by breaking down the 'fourth wall'. Using part of the auditorium as a performance space, they literally produce 'in-yer-face theatre'.[19] When Schlingensief displays aggression towards the other performers or threatens to kill a chicken, viewers have to ask which ethical rules apply in the theatre or, more precisely, which rules they are willing to accept. When he destroys a part of the set, there is a fear that the aggression will leap over to the spectators' seats, as does indeed happen occasionally. Apart from deafening sounds and an overkill of images, *ATTA ATTA* contains several moments in which (part of) the audience experiences a more direct physical threat. At one point, an actor repeatedly and with force shoots a soccer ball into the auditorium, seemingly unconcerned if it hits a spectator (which it sometimes did). While making a mess with paint, butter and water, Schlingensief more than once targets both fellow performers and audience members. Although this causes great merriment for some, others leave in anger after being soiled or embraced by a wet and dirty Schlingensief. Aggressive verbal reactions from audience members are not uncommon, and I once observed a woman who felt she had to keep Schlingensief at a distance by kicking him. Apparently, even part of the bourgeois and bohemian audience of the Volksbühne—generally familiar with the kind of productions one may expect from Schlingensief—is not insensitive to his self-ironic provocations.

A movie shown on two large screens during the greater part of the performance further contributes to the production's terrorizing tactics. In the movie (that seems to be filmed in a rather amateurish manner) the camera follows the famous German actress Hannelore Elsner and her companions as they meet in a restaurant and walk through Berlin. Viewers attending *ATTA ATTA* for the first time wonder whether they are watching a live recording (they are not). This question becomes more urgent near the end of the performance, when we see the group around Elsner enter the Volksbühne and change into Ku Klux Klan outfits, seemingly ready to storm the auditorium. One of the actors from the movie does indeed come in and makes his way to the stage, followed by a camerawoman who films his actions. The camera's gaze is immediately projected onto the screens. Thus, the movie not only produces a sense of suspense by means of the content of the video clip but, moreover, heightens the anticipation of terror as a result of its confusing and disorienting juxtaposition with live action. For the audience, the smooth transition between pre-recorded footage and live-recording and the simultaneous observation of immediate and mediated acts challenge the differences—both on a conceptual and empirical level—between here and elsewhere, presence and absence. While it may seem at first that *ATTA ATTA*'s excessive use of filmic material diminishes the affective and experiential potential of the performance, the opposite is true. The confusion and insecurity caused by the interaction of different media strengthens rather than reduces the power of theatricality, which is the power to initiate an at times enjoyable, at times disquieting process of transformation.

Symptomatic of the theatrical is that it comes into being and passes away at the same time, making it difficult to locate and situate. In Samuel Weber's definition, theatricality is 'a problematic process of placing, framing, situating', and it emerges 'where space and place can no longer be taken for granted or regarded as self-contained'.[20] For this reason, he argues, it is possible to think of terrorism as possessing a theatrical quality.[21] In today's globalized world, terrorism defies conventional spatial constructions because there is no clear opponent in the form of a nation state or an 'axis of evil', no recognizable face, and no guarantee that violence originates from some other social and geographical environment than one's own. *ATTA ATTA* exposes precisely this connection between terrorism and theatricality. When Schlingensief and his co-actors constantly slip in and out of different roles, while also changing the audience's role from spectator to participant and from voyeur to aggressor, they undermine processes of personification and identification—and thereby stabilization. And when the performance space itself becomes difficult to locate and situate, theatre refuses the function of a place where terrorism's spectacle can be confined. Thus, the performative violence of *ATTA ATTA* does not only constitute itself through physical aggression and the overstraining of the senses, but also through the oscillation of spatial boundaries and the loss of orientation that is produced as a result.

What makes Schlingensief's contribution to the debate about terrorism, art, and media unique is that he does more than recycle and remix the violent images with which we are so familiar, either from apocalyptic Hollywood movies, the ongoing stream of news reports, or modern art. By pursuing the avant-garde goal of bridging the gap between art and life, and by bringing the reality of terror to the auditorium, he thematizes Žižek's notion of a postmodern 'passion for the Real' in an exaggerated gesture of self-conscious theatricality. It is precisely through the exposure of the theatrical in the real that *ATTA ATTA* manages to confront the contradictory nature that lies at the heart of our fascination with images of violence and destruction. Psychologically, this fascination can be explained by the individual's need to construct him/herself as a stable subject. In order to accomplish this sense of psychic stability, it is necessary to identify with a safe and stable location. Projecting violence onto an image that represents an Elsewhere fulfils the desire to imagine oneself at this place of (mental) stability and wholeness. However, this position of unity is, of course, an illusion to begin with because it requires the spectator to occupy two imaginary places simultaneously. The realm of safety cannot exist without its exact opposite: that of feared destruction. Schlingensief's boundary breaking spectacle opens up the abyss of this double occupancy. It forces audience members to observe their own gaze, contemplate their role as spectator, and question their libidinous motivation for attending a performance on the topic of terrorism. The fact that the audience's response to Schlingensief's transgressions oscillates throughout the performance between delight and abhorrence allows for moments of critical reflection on the emotional investment in fictions of violence. It is, however, the kind of critical reflection that lacks any promise of exoneration. Those who had hoped that *ATTA ATTA* would offer a satisfying explanation for, and moral distance from, the attacks of 9/11 leave the theatre empty-handed. Schlingensief does not help close the wound inflicted by the attacks. On the contrary, he rubs salt into the wound as he teaches his audience a highly discomforting lesson about the human desire for violent fantasies.

The tapestry of new and recycled images, sound fragments, and self-reflexive comments on the connections between violence and art that Schlingensief creates in *ATTA ATTA* demonstrates that neither the violence of 9/11—nor his own theatrical terror—should be understood as the irruption of authenticity in a world of simulation. Rather, *ATTA ATTA* portrays the terrorist attacks as moments in which familiar fictions of violence entered and shaped reality. And yet, in spite of this awareness of the conflation of fictional and actual destruction, the production does not abandon the hope that art's relation to death can be of a different nature. In the final scene, Schlingensief compares the role of the artist with Scheherazade, whose continuous storytelling saved her from execution. In this tradition, he suggests, art should continue to explore its potential as an alternative to the discourse of death. Its message may be disturbing, but as long as the performer prolongs his tale of fear and aggression, the transformation of aesthetic terrorist into suicide bomber remains forever unfinished.

Endnotes

1. On his website, Stockhausen explains the situation as follows: 'At the press conference in Hamburg, I was asked if MICHAEL, EVE and LUCIFER were historical figures of the past and I answered that they exist now, for example Lucifer in New York. In my work, I have defined Lucifer as the cosmic spirit of rebellion, of anarchy. He uses his high degree of intelligence to destroy creation. He does not know love. After further questions about the events in America, I said that such a plan appeared to be Lucifer's greatest work of art. Of course I used the designation "work of art" to mean the work of destruction personified in Lucifer. In the context of my other comments this was unequivocal.' 19 September 2001. Homepage Karlheinz Stockhausen: http://www.stockhausen.org/message_from_karlheinz.html. Accessed 6 September 2007.

2. In her essay collection *Precarious Life: The Powers of Mourning and Violence*, Butler calls for critical reflection on the social and discursive practices of mourning that followed the events of 9/11, arguing that these practices serve the political line of US-unilateralism while failing to contribute to the process of gaining profound insights in the circumstances leading to the attacks. See Butler, J. (2004), *Precarious Life: The Powers of Mourning and Violence*, London and New York: Verso.

3. See Žižek, S. (2002), *Welcome to the Desert of the Real! Five Essays on September 11 and Related Dates*, London and New York: Verso, pp. 33–57, and Baudrillard, J. (2003), *The Spirit of Terrorism* (trans. Chris Turner), revised ed., London and New York: Verso, pp. 11–35 and 50–64.

4. For an overview of the central issues of the headscarf debate, see the website of Germany's Federal Institute for Political Education: http://www.bpb.de/themen/ NNAABC,0,0,Konfliktstoff_Kopftuch.html. Accessed 15 July 2009.

5. Sloterdijk, P. (2003), 'Erschütterung des Erschütterungs-Managements', in C. Hegemann (ed.), *Ausbruch der Kunst*, Berlin: Alexander Verlag, pp. 56–86, here p. 60.

6. Žižek, S. (2002), p. 5. Žižek borrows the term from the French philosopher Alain Badiou, who uses it in his—at that time still forthcoming—*Le siècle* (Paris: Éditions du Seuil, 2005).

7. For a discussion of the ambivalent nature of violence see, for example, Heitmeyer, W. and Soeffner, H. (eds.) (2004), *Gewalt. Entwicklungen, Strukturen, Analyseprobleme*, Frankfurt am Main: Suhrkamp.

8. Sloterdijk, P. (2003), p. 58. All translations of German texts cited in this chapter are my own.

9. Ehrlicher, H. (2001), *Die Kunst der Zerstörung: Gewaltphantasien und Manifestationspraktiken europäischer Avantgarden*, Berlin: Akademie Verlag, p. 35.

10. For a discussion of arguments made by proponents and opponents of the alleged death of the avant-garde, see Langston, R. (2008), *Visions of Violence: German Avant-Gardes after Fascism*, Evanston, Illinois: Northwestern University Press, pp. 3–22.

11. Theatre critic Robin Detje uses these words in a review of *Bambiland* that appeared in the influential magazine *Theater heute*. He furthermore argues that the notion of the 'death of the avant-garde' becomes questionable in the light of Schlingensief's successful revival of this movement. Detje, R. (2004), 'Wie er tut, was wir nicht lassen können', *Theater heute*, February, pp. 12–14, here p. 13.

12. Hegemann, C. (ed.) (2003), *Ausbruch der Kunst*, Berlin: Alexander Verlag, p.120.

13. Ibid., p. 83.

14. The interview is part of a documentary by Rainer Ostendorf entitled *Lust auf Gewalt*. In this documentary, which was broadcast by WDR in 1997, Ostendorf investigates the remarkable interest in excessive theatrical violence in the 1990s.

15. Van der Horst, J. (2002), 'Theater als Baustelle. Schlingensiefs Theater im Antitheorietest'. Homepage Christoph Schlingensief: http://www.schlingensief. com. Accessed 8 March 2005, no pagination.

16. Beuys has repeatedly explained this thesis, which is central to his expanded notion of art (*erweiterter Kunstbegriff*). 'Artist' here does not refer to a painter or sculptor, but to the individual's innate creativity that allows him/her to shape and change society. Adriani, G., Konnertz, W., and Thomas, K. (eds.) (1994), *Joseph Beuys*, revised ed., Köln: Dumont, p. 178.

17. Artaud, A. (1993), *The Theatre and Its Double* (trans. Victor Corti), Monteuil, London and New York: Calder, p. 21.

18. The German term used by Kluge is '*Theater der Handgreiflichkeit*', which is also the title of a television interview he conducted with Schlingensief: Kluge, A. (2000), 'Theater der Handgreiflichkeit/Christoph Schlingensiefs Wiener Container', *News & Stories*, Sat 1. As revealed in Kluge's foreword to this book, the term can be translated as 'theatre of fisticuffs' or 'visceral theatre'. It thus captures both the violent quality and the physical, energetic and non-intellectual nature of Schlingensief's theatre.

19. The term 'in-yer-face-theatre' gained popularity in the United Kingdom in the 1990s, where it was used to describe a dramatic genre that demonstrates an exceptional preoccupation with sex, violence, and drugs and that often employs shocking tactics. Well-known representatives are Sarah Kane, Patrick Marber and Mark Ravenhill.

20. Weber, S. (2004), *Theatricality as Medium*, New York: Fordham University Press, p. 315 and 300.

21. Weber discusses the connection between terrorism and theatricality in Chapter 14 of *Theatricality as Medium* (2004), in which he elaborates on society's desire to perceive terrorism as a spectacle, i.e., something that is localizable. The spectacle seems to promise the separation of the here (auditorium or living room) from the elsewhere (stage, screen), although in reality it always occurs in relation to the place of the spectator.

MEDIA PLAY: INTERMEDIAL SATIRE AND PARODIC EXPLORATION IN ELFRIEDE JELINEK AND CHRISTOPH SCHLINGENSIEF'S *BAMBILAND*

Morgan Koerner

Burgtheater, Vienna, 18 March 2004, 7:30pm: The audience has just taken their seats for Christoph Schlingensief's production of Elfriede Jelinek's theatre text *Bambiland* (2003). Although scheduled to begin at 8pm, Schlingensief and a handful of his troupe are already on stage. Schlingensief sets up props and paints while Horst Gellonek rants to the audience, sings nonsensical songs, and bangs on the stage with a hammer. This opening pre-performance largely recycles the opening minutes of Schlingensief's previous production *ATTA ATTA—Art Has Broken Out* (2003). But one prominent addition is present: from a loudspeaker at the side of the stage, a computerized voice recites the beginning of Jelinek's theatre text *Bambiland* in a continuous loop. As I thumb through Jelinek's text in the program in an attempt to follow the computer, I suddenly notice a conspicuous audience member enter one of the box seats on the ground floor: Elfriede Jelinek. Schlingensief spots her as well from his position on the stage, waves at her, smiles, and returns to the prelude to his chaotic, excessive and multimedial reaction to her theatre text.

The scene I witnessed at the Burgtheater illustrates the unique position of *Bambiland* within Schlingensief's oeuvre as a theatre director and performance artist: never before had Schlingensief staged a theatre text by another author. The theatre critic Peter Kümmel responded to the world premiere by claiming that it was not a true premiere at all, that it had more to do with Schlingensief's own aesthetics than Jelinek's text, which only appeared in small doses throughout the performance and was often drowned out by other voices.[1] But in a statement to the press, Jelinek herself claimed that Schlingensief had understood her text well:

I am thrilled. It was one of the most overwhelming reactions that my texts have ever received. Even though not much of the text appears [in the performance], it corresponds to my method of writing. This text is an amalgam of media reports about Iraq, and Schlingensief amalgamised it once more with this overwhelming visual level.[2]

Schlingensief responded to Jelinek's collage of media citations with an excessive multimedia patchwork of his own that combined multiple video projections with citations from neo-avant-garde performance traditions. He thereby translated Jelinek's intermedial writing strategies to the stage. Whereas Jelinek can only simulate the semiotic systems of television in her writing, Schlingensief has the very 'stage of intermediality' at his disposal: the theatre.[3] As Frieda Chapple and Chiel Kattenbelt argue, the theatre functions as a 'hypermedium' that can serve as a space 'in-between' different media.[4] Within its own boundaries, the theatre can thus effectively 'stage' and reflect upon other media.[5] In line with this strategy, Schlingensief's *Bambiland* displays overwhelming televisual and filmic images but juxtaposes them with live performance art. He thereby combines an investigation of 'infotainment' and televisual representation with an exploration of the modalities of live, avant-garde performance. On a textual level, Jelinek's *Bambiland* presents a dilemma about the role of authorship in the age of media saturation: how can a writer respond to a real, horrific event that has always already been mediated by television infotainment? In effect, Schlingensief's staging shifts Jelinek's predicament from the realm of writing to that of live performance: what can a theatre ensemble do in response to both the cultural dominance of televisual media as well the presence of real suffering and violence in the world?

The above question is not unique to *Bambiland*, but rather pervades Schlingensief's performance work. One of his more theoretical answers to the question came during his performance piece and pseudo-political campaign *Chance 2000* (1998), when he referred to both political rhetoric and humanist notions of 'dialogue' as belonging to what he termed 'System 1': a language of consensus that negates individual difference and excludes the abnormal.[6] Schlingensief's goal in *Chance 2000* and elsewhere has been to subvert dominant language systems by refusing to play by their rules.[7] In order to avoid the clarity and consensus of 'System 1', Schlingensief emphasizes confusion over clarity and nonsense over sense, creates a cacophony of voices and images, incessantly subverts and undermines his own position, and emphasizes open-ended play in his performances. It is thus notable that Schlingensief agreed to 'premiere' a satirical text about the 2003 invasion of Iraq. Journalists and scholars alike tend to agree on a satirical impetus in Jelinek's writing,[8] one that would seem to go counter to Schlingensief's refusal of categorization and clarity. Between the hot topic of US-Imperialism, the long-standing tradition of the anti-war play, and the alleged critical position of Jelinek, the text *Bambiland* provided a minefield of temptations to make a clear statement and thereby fall into the confines of 'System 1', that is to say, into a binary system of opposition and critique.

The following chapter explores how Schlingensief navigates these pitfalls and responds aesthetically to the loaded question of media representation in *Bambiland*. The first two sections investigate the confluences between Jelinek and Schlingensief's methods. Schlingensief, I argue, emphasizes Jelinek's more playful and open-ended strategies and thereby interprets her aesthetic differently than the usual pigeonholes of satire and ideology critique. In the final section, I examine Schlingensief's own strategy of parodic exploration vis-à-vis both media and performance art traditions.

Elfriede Jelinek's *Bambiland*: Intermedial satire and ludic excess

The 2004 Nobel laureate Elfriede Jelinek's literary oeuvre is best known for its incisive critique of gender relations, consumer culture, xenophobia, and the legacy of fascism in her home country of Austria. Since she emerged as a writer in the 1970s, Jelinek has gained the reputation of a fierce moral critic. Aided by her own comments in interviews, journalists usually mention Jelinek's feminist and Marxist affiliations and highlight her moral outrage and cultural pessimism. Literary scholars more interested in her texts than her biography come to similar conclusions. Marlies Janz, in her seminal monograph on Jelinek's writings up to the mid-1990s, argues that her aesthetic of linguistic collage and citation serves the larger goal of ideology critique and the deconstruction of societal myths.[9] Yet ironically, the notion of Jelinek as the 'Cassandra of German language literature and theatre'[10] has itself become a myth that obscures other prominent aspects of her writing: her playful, associative style, humour, and self-reflexive irony. Jelinek's texts abound with parodic citation, excessive wordplay, comic and grotesque gags, jokes ranging from the absurd to the insipid, and ironic self-subversion of the authorial voice. While some of these comic strategies indeed serve a satirical impetus, their excessive presence in her oeuvre underscore an ambiguous open-endedness that often goes neglected in interpretations of her work.

Since the 1990s, Jelinek herself has emphasized the open-ended nature of the writing in her theatre texts. Beginning with *Wolken Heim/Cloud-Cuckoo Land* (1990), she has increasingly written post-dramatic theatre texts, namely theatre pieces that depart from traditional notions of character, dialogue and plot.[11] These lengthy language collages demand directorial intervention: her directors must not only cut large portions of the text, but also negotiate how to stage what are often prose pieces without clear stage directions. Yet surprisingly, many critics and scholars continue to discuss whether Jelinek's directors remain faithful to the original texts: did the director retain Jelinek's critical impetus in the production and thus translate Jelinek's critique to the stage?[12] This question is problematic insofar as it neglects Jelinek's associative aesthetic and her own willingness to collaborate with the stars of director's theatre since the mid-1990s.[13]

A turning point in theatre productions of Jelinek's texts came in 1994, when Frank Castorf staged her play *Raststätte oder Sie machens alle/Services or They all do it*[14] in Hamburg. One of the last Jelinek plays to have discernible characters and a plot, *Services* had already premiered at the Burgtheater under Claus Peymann, a director best known for his reverent stagings of Thomas Bernhard plays. While Peymann more or less stuck to Jelinek's text, Castorf put it through the grinder of radical director's theatre, adding his own associations and comic disruptions, doubling characters, and changing large segments of the play. After the success of Castorf's production, Jelinek increasingly submitted her theatre texts to the elite of German directors' theatre and eliminated stage directions and authorial advice, as she notoriously noted at the beginning of her 180 page *Ein Sportstück/A Sport Play* (1998): 'The author doesn't give many directions, she has learned this in the meantime. Do what you want'.[15] In the 1990s, it seems, Jelinek discovered a process of creative collaboration with directors in which she encourages (if not forces) them to respond to her associative texts with further associations. This strategy challenges the notion of Jelinek as 'a writer who wishes to leave little doubt as to the political dimension of what she has to say'.[16]

Jelinek's theatre text *Bambiland* exemplifies the tension between satirical impetus and playful excess that underlies her oeuvre. Aesthetically, *Bambiland* offers a ludic citational collage: in fifty pages of prose without characters and a clear speaking voice, Jelinek mixes and changes citations from Aeschylus' *The Persians*, Nietzsche, and, most prominently, voices from 24 hour news coverage of the 2003 invasion of Iraq. In terms of content, it is difficult not to read *Bambiland* as a biting satire of news reporting about the Iraq war: the text presents this flow of television information and images from the war as a distraction from critical thought. At points throughout the text, the critical voice of a television viewer emerges amongst the media citations and expresses the desire for a non-sensational, non-ethnocentric portrayal of events.[17] Every time this voice questions the media portrayal, however, it is immediately distracted by descriptions of war technology or light-hearted entertainment stories such as the coverage of dolphins searching for mines in the gulf.[18] Throughout *Bambiland*, the text repeatedly returns to long descriptions of tomahawk missiles and other technology, which the speaker anthropomorphizes and treats as more important than the human protagonists. The ironic undertone of these exaggerated passages renders Jelinek's critique of so-called infotainment obvious. Television coverage creates a spectacle of technology and hides the violence, horror, and true motivations of the war. The text's final image, which describes the detonation of a tomahawk missile as an ejaculation,[19] underscores the critique present throughout *Bambiland*, namely that television news presents a voyeuristic fetishization of war. But *Bambiland's* satirical edge is not only directed at the media, but also at the television viewer, who is portrayed as passive and unable to obtain any critical distance from the televisual spectacle.[20] Yet despite the obvious critique of television news coverage, the text does not offer a stable outside position from which to judge events.[21] The voices in *Bambiland*, including the authorial voice, occur within an inescapable system of media language and images.

However, while the text does not offer a position outside of media simulacra, it does give an example of how to respond from within the system. The text models how one can appropriate and undermine the language and images of media infotainment. *Bambiland* simulates and simultaneously displaces media language in a playful and comic fashion. The following passage mimics the commentary and questions of reporters and news pundits, but through comic repetition and associative jumps, spins the commentary in absurd directions:

> How is our little Lord Bush doing? Fine, thank you. You can't be serious about what I'm finding here, it's got to be anything but. Serious. Seriously, somehow I always seem to find the seriousness lacking here. Where has it gone? You burdensome, burdensome burden of grief, have you made off with the seriousness? Aren't you the one who brought it on in the first place? Come out with it already, who and where is complaint's client? Who are the clients of corporate complaint? Sure, it's all pretty much done for out there, well, ok, not quite, not yet, but soon. And we've all become clients. Consumers. Customer Kings. Well, now that we're the consumers, it's about time we get around to complaining![22]

Obviously, this passage aligns with the aforementioned critique of war infotainment, which belittles the seriousness of real suffering and turns the viewer into a passive consumer. But the excessive and repetitive wordplay in the original German text also indicates a ludic writing stance that pursues linguistic associations. In the original German, the text jumps alliteratively and associatively from *des Kummers Kunden* (complaint's client) to *des Konzerns Kunden* (clients/customers of corporations) and the statement *Was müssen wir doch künden, da wir doch Kunden sind?* (what do we have to announce/cancel, now that we're customers?). And even as the text points to the gravity of the war, the language takes on a comical tone. For example: Jelinek mixes the gravitas of Aeschylus's inverted genitives (*des Kummers Kunde* [complaint's client]) with colloquial language and comic repetition. Moreover, the language parodies the short sound bites and repetitions of news reporting in a way that implies an active consumer stance, one which parodies media language in order to pursue other associations. In her initial 'stage directions' for *Bambiland*, Jelinek encourages her directors to react to her own text in a similar manner:

> I don't know I don't know. Just stick a knit stocking cap on it, the kind with a tassel on top like my dad used to wear with his old overalls while building our little single-family home [...]. That's all folks.[23]

Instead of any serious directions on how to stage the text, Jelinek offers what seems to be a private association, one that models how readers and directors might add their own personal connotations to the text. Jelinek thereby emphasizes the primacy of the theatrical realizations of her directors and aligns her theatre pieces more with open-ended postmodern play than with the insistence on a single meaning associated with ideology critique. Given this predilection, it begins to make sense why she chose Christoph Schlingensief to stage *Bambiland*.

Intermedial polyphony: Schlingensief's performative transformation of *Bambiland*

Schlingensief's world premiere of *Bambiland* reduces Jelinek's text but translates many of its themes and strategies to the stage.[24] Whereas Jelinek's *Bambiland* only evokes television through language, Schlingensief's production offers an array of intermedial strategies that thematize—and bring to mind—television viewing. The stage itself contains multiple video screens, two of which flank the proscenium of the Burgtheater while yet another stands on the revolving set at the back of the stage. Throughout the production, the screens show video segments that range from night bombings of Baghdad to a US documentary film of surgery undertaken during the Vietnam War. The most imposing visual imagery, however, appears on a fourth, larger screen: the set's thin curtain, where a black-and-white film by Schlingensief entitled *Atta in Bambiland* is projected for three quarters of the play. At points throughout the production, the curtain rises but *Atta in Bambiland* continues, superimposed across the actors on stage. The set itself thematizes television: a living room with a television stands stage left, where an actor playing Schlingensief's mother sits facing the television and the audience. The right front of the stage serves as a set for a televised political party meeting/press conference while on the larger rotating stage behind the curtain, an omnipresent film crew follows the actors. Furthermore, the performance opens with a long address by Schlingensief to a video camera, and throughout the production many of the actors position themselves towards the on-stage film crew and not towards the audience. The stage for the production presents two films: the recorded film *Atta in Bambiland* and the film that the ensemble creates live on stage. The production thereby visualizes the inescapable omnipresence of media images in Jelinek's text *Bambiland*.

The film *Atta in Bambiland*, which provides the most imposing images in the performance, dovetails at several points with Jelinek's satire of television news reporting and its effect on viewers. Filmed at night in Vienna, the black-and-white film follows at least three distinguishable groups: Schlingensief's disabled troupe members Horst Gelonnek and Mario Garzaner, who pose as embedded war reporters; a group of protestors who stage a march; and a bourgeois group who, dressed in formal evening wear, walk through the streets of Vienna, ride in a horse-drawn carriage, and visit a restaurant. While these images are loosely associated with themes in Jelinek's text,[25] the most striking alignment with *Bambiland* occurs when the actions of a couple and their friends take a voyeuristic and pornographic turn. Thirty minutes into the film, the group enters a space that resembles a movie theatre and gazes in pleasure at the camera. As this scene is projected on the curtain, images of night bombings over Baghdad appear on the other video screens to the side of and behind the curtain. This juxtaposition associates voyeuristic pleasure with media coverage of the war; the trance-like state of the actors indicates the passive and uncritical viewing stance satirized in Jelinek's text. The film's pornographic finale, which concludes circa ten minutes before the end of the performance, continues this critique but directly addresses the audience at the Burgtheater. In this final sequence, two women masturbate a young man with an American flag while the bourgeois couple watches from behind. All of the actors in this scene look towards the camera and thus outwards towards the audience; meanwhile, an actor on stage who has recited lines from Jelinek's text throughout the production approaches the screen with her back to the audience and raises her hands towards the erect penis in the centre of the shot. As the scene reaches its climax, everyone in the shot continues to look towards the camera and yell, in English, 'look at this picture, look at this picture!'[26] The finale creates a visual equivalent to the ejaculating missile with which Jelinek concludes *Bambiland*. It equates sensationalist news coverage with pornography and fetishized patriarchal power and can thus be understood to critique the monolithic, one-sided perspective of infotainment.

While the film translates some of the more obviously critical elements from Jelinek's text, the production as a whole proliferates the chorus of competing voices already present in *Bambiland*. The film *Atta in Bambiland* and the other projections do not appear in isolation. Schlingensief and his troupe perform alongside and in front of the film and the other projections, and the actors also interrupt and compete with each other while on stage. The performance's opening segment already contains opposing voices: in the initial minutes, the actors perform concurrent with a computerized recitation of Jelinek's *Bambiland*. The performance thus begins with competing voices and images: Horst Gellonek's rantings and Schlingensief's stage preparations contrast with the 'official' text of the play. In Schlingensief's opening monologue, he speaks in tandem with Gelonnek, who sits at his side and repeats everything he says, and Brigitte Kausch who, across the stage on her couch in the role of Schlingensief's mother, berates him, throws organic carrots at him, or harangues the audience. Later, the voices multiply even further as more actors appear at different points on the stage. At one point towards the end of the performance, at least six different actors recite lines and act out or improvise scenarios at the same time, which results in complete cacophony.

Unlike Jelinek's text, in which the different voices occur in the linear progression of syntax, the voices in Schlingensief's performance occur concurrently and thereby overwhelm, disorient, and confuse the viewer in search of meaning. The opposition

Figure 1: Polyphony turns into cacophony: Several groups of actors recite lines from Jelinek's text and improvise scenes simultaneously. Photo: Georg Soulek.

between the video screens and the simultaneous voices in the live performance underscores an issue at the heart of Schlingensief's production. On the one hand, the production attempts to avoid the over-simplified narratives of news reporting, as satirized in the film's pornographic finale. In other words, the overwhelmingly clear pornographic images contrast with the incoherence of the onstage performances. On the other hand, the film screens invoke not only the media, but also the tradition of political theatre. The film screens in *Bambiland* allude to Erwin Piscator's multimedial epic theatre of the 1920s and 30s, which featured projections and documentary footage.[27] But whereas Piscator's theatre aimed to educate his audiences and activate their critical thinking, Schlingensief and his troupe attempt to avoid the trappings of clear critique. The imposing finale, in the form of *Atta in Bambiland,* can therefore also be associated with the kind of political theatre that Schlingensief's live performance seeks to avoid. Put differently, both media infotainment and political theatre cast a shadow over Schlingensief's performance and serve as representations of a reality that his production attempts to avoid in its search for other modes of perception and thought.

Enter mediality! Schlingensief's method of parodic exploration

Schlingensief's *Bambiland* attempts to respond to media coverage of the War in Iraq without falling into the predictable grooves of media satire or anti-war theatre. His aesthetic solution to this predicament is one that permeates his stage and television performances: parody. In her seminal work on parody in twentieth century art forms, Linda Hutcheon makes the much-cited assertion that parody is a form of 'imitation characterised by ironic inversion' or 'repetition with critical distance'.[28] Hutcheon's definition moves away from the traditional definition of parody as ridiculing or mocking imitation and argues that parody's imitative strategies need 'not always [be] at the expense of the parodied text'.[29] While the word 'para' can mean 'against', it can also mean 'besides' or 'next to'.[30] This double meaning characterizes the inherent ambiguity of parody: the comic imitation of another text or style can indicate both distance from and homage to the original. And while comic effect is an indispensable component of parody, the laughter elicited need not be critical.[31] Instead, parody can also result in the pleasure of recognition and, as Simon Dentith reminds us, it 'can be irreverent, inconsequential, and even silly'.[32] This definition of parody explains why Schlingensief uses it as a primary aesthetic strategy: it provides a means to explore and displace both media aesthetics and theatre history without committing to a specific message. In other words, parody serves as an aesthetic strategy of playful exploration.

Schlingensief's *Bambiland* includes his signature parodies of the talk show and political rally formats. Schlingensief begins the performance with a talk show parody: on a couch, he offers an opening monologue and then interviews fellow actors for the video camera, but as previously noted, the scene devolves into multivocal chaos. The talk show parody provides a format in which Schlingensief and his ensemble improvise and explore associations. The 'political rallies' that take place during the performance offer a similar framework. At four separate points, Schlingensief and the ensemble gather together at a podium on stage right. Above the podium hangs a flag that combines a swastika and a deer, a reference to the play's title *Bambiland*, which associates Austrian culture (the novel *Bambi*) and global entertainment (Disney) with fascist tendencies. Yet what happens below the flag is hardly as clear. In each meeting, different speakers offer statements that range from Jelinek citations to random improvisations to banal interludes, such as when an actor in a *Hanswurst* (Viennese version of the harlequin) costume sings a silly song. The actors enact a political press conference but offer diverse and random statements that lack both the order of a real press conference and the moral clarity of satire. Literally under the banner of Jelinek's media critique, the actors improvise nonsensical interludes that elude the teleological thrust of satire. The motto of the press conference seems to be 'anything goes'—the group are allowed to try out whatever ideas or associations they choose and the statements differ in each performance.

More prominent than the media parody in *Bambiland* are Schlingensief's parodic re-enactments of performance art. In the opening 'talk show' sequence, Schlingensief presents himself and his cast as a group of artists who are producing a video application for the Oberhausen short film festival. In this sequence Schlingensief aligns himself and his fellow actors with the goals of performance art but constantly ironises his statements, such as when he notes that his ensemble works in the tradition of 'Günther Brus, Hermann Nitsch and Klaus Bachler'. Brus and Nitsch were co-founders of the neo-avant-garde group the Viennese Actionists, whereas Bachler was the manager of the Burgtheater Vienna at the time. Here Schlingensief implies that neo-avant-garde strategies have already become institutionalized and lost their revolutionary potential. But despite this open recognition, Schlingensief *enacts* action and body art on the stage throughout the performance. At times, these (re)enactments have a comic effect: when, in the initial sequence, Schlingensief charges a canvas with a paint brush, stabs it, and declaims, 'Ha! You didn't anticipate that, you asshole', he appears to mock the obsession with innovation and unpredictability in avant-garde performance traditions. Other examples, however, lack the humorous distance of the opening segments. Like the Viennese Actionists, Schlingensief attempts to exchange aesthetic distance for an immediate experience of the artwork. Schlingensief not only places himself in the middle of his own production, but throughout it, he incessantly immerses his own body in different artistic media (paint, feathers, flour, butter). In the performance that took place on 11 May 2004, his excessive exploration of body art led to apparent physical exhaustion and nausea. While he parodies performance and body art, Schlingensief is forced to relinquish all distance and explore the different strategies with his body on stage. His approach thus exemplifies the ambiguous position of parody: he ironises neo-avant-gardes but at the same time pays homage to their experimental attempts to find other means of expression and experience.

When considering the significance of Schlingensief's exploration of performance art, it is important to remember that it appears within a multimedial maze of semiotic excess. The experimentation with body art and citations from the Viennese Actionists occur next to multiple video projections, recitations from Jelinek's *Bambiland*, and interventions by other actors. A segment towards the end of the performance exemplifies this semiotic excess. While the film *Atta in Bambiland* continues on the main curtain, a documentary film that shows operations in Vietnam appears on the other three screens. Schlingensief emerges in front of the curtain with a deer-sized 'Bambi' doll, a physical reminder of Jelinek's text, and begins to recount the infamous Joseph Beuys action *Iphigenia/ Titus Andronicus* (1969).[33] An actor behind the transparent curtain then interrupts Schlingensief with lines in the first person plural from Jelinek's *Bambiland* that justify why 'we' shot a bus full of seven Iraqis because they did not stop in time at a road block. Thereafter, Schlingensief continues to recount the Beuys action but simultaneously creates his own action art: he places two nudes in a tableau, throws paint on them, and then pours so much paint on his head that he is forced to vomit.

Figure 2: Enter mediality: Schlingensief, stage centre, has doused himself with paint, and continues to recount the Joseph Beuys performance *Iphigenia/Titus Andronicus* while performing a tableaux with two nudes and a deer-sized Bambi doll. Meanwhile, clips from operations on American soldiers during Vietnam run on the three screens, and the black-and-white film *Atta in Bambiland* is projected onto the stage's thin curtain. Photo: Patrick Hilss.

This sequence creates a connection between Schlingensief's performance, the Iraq war, and the neo-avant-gardes of the 1960s. The scientific videos of operations thematize the media's claim to objective portrayals that we also hear from the speaking 'we' in Jelinek's *Bambiland* that is recited from behind the screen. Schlingensief's allusion to Beuys provides a counter-example to the media images. Beuys' actions, many of which were performed during the Vietnam War, emphasized a subjective, ephemeral social experience. Schlingensief follows his allusion to Beuys with action art of his own that results in his own real experience of nausea and exhaustion. In contrast to the media voices from Jelinek and the scientific mediation of the documentary film, Schlingensief's physically challenging performance models an active subject who immerses himself in and experiments with the medium instead of passively viewing from the sidelines.

Conclusion

It now becomes clear why Jelinek expressly chose Schlingensief to premiere her theatre text. Both Jelinek the writer and Schlingensief the director/performance artist engage in similar strategies. Jelinek immerses her authorial voice within media citations and refuses to indicate a space 'outside' the matrix of media representation; yet her citational collage satirizes media reporting on the Iraq War. While the media may be omnipresent for Jelinek, the text models an active viewer who attempts to turn media representation on its head and explore other possibilities for signification. In Schlingensief, Jelinek chose a director who personally places himself at the centre of chaotic, multimedia productions and thereby mimics the way in which the authorial voice in Jelinek's text explores media citations by immersing them within media language. After the announcement of Jelinek's Nobel Prize for literature, Schlingensief made the following statement to the press:

> Instead of maintaining distance, Elfriede Jelinek engages with the world, almost compulsively exposes herself to the world, sees and finds elements and creates something new from them—and she challenges others to appropriate the world. In our collaboration she has challenged me not to revere her texts but to use them to form my own systems.[34]

Schlingensief's description of Jelinek reveals a good deal about his own approach. Instead of a distanced analysis or critique of war reporting or, for that matter, the effectiveness of neo-avant-garde performance, Schlingensief opts to enter the media in question, to immerse himself within both televisual images and, quite literally, performance art. Both the distance and the clarity of a critical or analytical standpoint are out of place in Schlingensief's *Bambiland*, which obsessively explores and appropriates citations from Jelinek, media aesthetics, and avant-garde performance in the attempt to open up, not to close down or fixate, new systems of signification. In applying his strategy of parodic exploration and appropriation to *Bambiland*, Schlingensief has also provided a new perspective of Jelinek's own writing and indicated that Jelinek's texts are more open-ended than feuilleton writers and literary scholars would have us believe.

Endnotes

1. Kümmel, P. (2009), 'Nicht schuldig! Christoph Schlingensief überrollt Elfriede Jelineks "Bambiland" an der Wiener Burg', *Zeit Online*, 17 December, http://www.zeit.de/2003/52/Bambi-Land. Accessed 5 May 2009.

2. *NEWS.AT*, 'Bambiland: Jelinek begeistert von Schlingensief', 17 December, http://www.usq.edu.au/library/help/referencing/harvard.htm#Web_documents_and_sites. Accessed 5 May 2009. My translation.

3. Kattenbelt, C. (2006), 'Theatre as the art of the performer and the stage of intermediality', in F. Chapple and C. Kattenbelt (eds.), *Intermediality in Theatre and Performance*, Amsterdam: Rodopi, pp. 29–39.

4. Ibid., p. 20 and 24.

5. Ibid., p. 37.

6. Hegemann, C. and Schlingensief, C. (1998), *Chance 2000. Wähle dich selbst*, Köln: Kiepenheuer & Witsch, p. 17.

7. Gade, S. (2005), 'Playing the media keyboard. The political potential of performativity in Christoph Schlingensief's electioneering circus', in R. Gade and A. Jerslev (eds.), *Performative Realism*, Copenhagen: Museum Tusculanum Press, pp. 39–40.

8. When she was awarded the 2004 Nobel Prize in Literature, journalists inevitably highlighted the societal critique that permeates Jelinek's oeuvre (see, for example, *FAZ.NET* (2004), 'Nobelpreisträgrin Jelinek. Beschimpft und Gefeiert', 8 October, http://www.faz.net/s/Rub1DA1FB848C1E44858CB87A0FE6AD1B68/Doc~EA48 818C90D34C3F950FC3809FCF20F3~ATpl~Ecommon~Sspezial.html. Accessed 3 June 2009. Jelinek supports this understanding of her work in countless interviews, where she repeatedly mentions her stance as a Marxist and Feminist, states that her writing is inspired by moral indignation, and insists that her texts are politically

engaged. See Roeder, A. (1989), *Autorinnen: Herausforderungen an das Theater*, Frankfurt am Main: Suhrkamp, p. 141. Literary scholars generally interpret Jelinek's oeuvre along similar lines, for example, as ideology critique (Janz, M. (1995), *Elfriede Jelinek*, Stuttgart: Metzler), as a continuation of the moral impetus of the Enlightenment (Kurzenberger, H (2000), 'Die heutige Schaubühne als moralische Anstalt betrachtet. Über das Erbe der Aufklärung im postdramatischen Theater der Elfriede Jelinek', *Forum Modernes Theater*, 15:1, pp. 21–30), and as satirical literature fueled by 'outrage and fury against the injustices of the world and its multiple manifestations in language' (Lamb- Faffelberger, M. (2007), 'The Audacious Art of Elfriede Jelinek: *Tour de Force* and Irritation', in M. Konzett and M. Lamb-Faffelberger (eds.), *Elfriede Jelinek. Writing Woman, Nation, and Identity. A Critical Anthology*, Madison: Farleigh Dickinson University Press, pp. 48–49).

9. Janz, M.

10. The director Claus Peymann (2004) used this epithet to describe Jelinek when she won the Nobel Prize in Literature. 'Elfriede Jelinek. Literaturpreis für Skandalautorin', *Stern.de*, 7 October, http://www.stern.de/unterhaltung/buecher/: Elfriede-Jelinek-Literaturnobelpreis-Skandal-Autorin/530838.html. Accessed 10 May 2009.

11. For more on postdramatic theatre, see Lehmann, H.-T. (1997), *Postdramatic Theatre* (trans. K. Jürs-Munby), London: Routledge; Poschmann, G. (1997), *Der nicht mehr dramatische Theatertext. Aktuelle Bühnenstücke und ihre dramaturgische Analyse*, Tübingen: Niemeyer.

12. Kümmel's question about whether *Bambiland* had truly been premiered provides a paradigmatic example of journalistic assumptions about 'translating' Jelinek to the stage. In her discussion of Einar Schleef's production of *A Sports Play* (1998), Linda DeMeritt phrases a question that underlies scholarly discussions of Jelinek plays on the stage: 'The issue is whether the staging, like the text, is able to ground its superficiality within the seriousness of societal critique'. DeMeritt, L.C. (2002), 'Staging Superficiality: Elfriede Jelinek's *Ein Sportstück*', in L. C. DeMeritt and M. Lamb-Faffelberger, *Postwar Austrian Theater. Text and Performance*, Riverside: Ariadne, p. 258.

13. *Regietheater* or 'director's theatre' indicates a directorial approach in which the handprint and interpretation of the director becomes more important than acquiescence to the playwright's voice or intentions. The most prominent German proponent of director's theatre in the 1990s was the Volksbühne Berlin's manager Frank Castorf, who was

notorious for radically changing canonical plays on stage. For a discussion of Jelinek's collaborations with the stars of director's theatre, see: Honegger, G. (2007), 'Bodies that Matter', *Hunter Online Theater Review*, March, http://www.hotreview.org/articles/bodiesthatmatter.htm. Accessed 24 May 2007.

14. Jelinek, E. (1998), *Services or They all do it. A Comedy*, in *Cat and Mouse (Sheep)*, *Gregory Motton. Services, Elfriede Jelinek* (trans. Nickl Grindell), London: Methuen Drama, pp. 65–132.

15. Jelinek, E. (1998), *Ein Sportstück*, Hamburg: Rowohlt, p. 7.

16. Fiddler, A. (1994), 'There Goes That Word Again, or Elfriede Jelinek and Postmodernism', in J. B. Johns and K. Arens (eds.), *Elfriede Jelinek: Framed by Language*, Riverside: Ariadne, p.141.

17. Bärbel Lücke describes this voice as the 'non-dispossessed tone of an artist-author voice' that transcends the other citational voices in the text (my translation). Lücke, B. (2004), 'Zu *Bambiland* und *Babel*. Essay', in *Bambiland. Babel. Zwei Theatertexte*, Hamburg: Rowohlt, pp. 229–271.

18. As the authorial voice in the text indicates; 'Now, just when I get to the part I consider worthy of discussion, along comes that dolphin again to distract me, as animals always manage to do for me, even when I'm on the verge of breaking the bonds of love and morals in one fell swoop.' Jelinek, E. (2007), *Bambiland* (trans. L. Friedberg), http://ourworld.compuserve.com/homepages/elfriede/. Accessed 17 May 2009.

19. 'Finally, he shoots his wad. I thought he was never going to come. So. Now that's the end of that, too' (Jelinek, E. [2007]).

20. Lücke, B. (2004), p. 44–45.

21. Cf. Beuker, B. (2006), 'Theaterschlachten: Jelineks dramaturgisches Konzept und die Thematik der Gewalt am Beispiel von *Bambiland*', *Modern Austrian Literature*, 39:3, p. 63; Blödorn, A. (2006), 'Medialisierung des Krieges; Mit Susan Sontag in Elfreide Jelineks *Bambiland*', *Gegenwartsliteratur: ein germanistisches Jahrbuch* 5, p. 157.

22. Trans. L. Friedberg.

23. Ibid.

24. The following discussion of Schlingensief's production is based on my experience as an audience member on 18 March and 11 May 2004, as well as repeated viewings of a recording of the performance from 11 May. I am grateful to Meika Dresenkamp for making the live recording available to me.

25. Both embedded reporting and peace protests figure at different points in the text *Bambiland*.

26. This quotation appears in Jelinek's *Bambiland* and is taken from a US-American father whose son died in the war; he appeared before a news camera team and addressed President Bush, saying, 'He was my only son. Look at his picture, Mr. President!' *Bambiland. Uraufführung*, Theatre Programme, Burgtheater, 2003/4 Season, p. 68.

27. See Fiebach, J. (2004), 'Piscator, Brecht, und Medialisierung', in M. Schwaiger (ed.), *Bertolt Brecht und Erwin Piscator, Experimentelles Theater im Berlin der Zwanzigerjahre*, Vienna: Verlag Christian Brandstätter, pp. 113–14.

28. Hutcheon, L. (1985), *A Theory of Parody. The Teachings of Twentieth-Century Art Forms*, New York: Methuen, p. 6.

29. Ibid.

30. Harries, S. (2000), *Film Parody*, London: BFI, p. 5.

31. Roßbach, N. (2006), *Theater über Theater. Parodie und Moderne 1870-1914*, Bielefeld: Aisthesis, p. 36.

32. Dentith, S. (2000), *Parody*, London: Routledge, p. 37.

33. This performance took place at the 'Experimenta 3' theatre festival in Frankfurt. Beuys appeared alone on stage with a white horse while recorded voices recited lines from Goethe's *Iphigenia* and Shakespeare's *Titus Andronicus*. Birringer, J. (1991), *Theatre, Theory, Postmodernism*, Bloomington: Indiana University Press, p. 13.

34. *suedeutsche.de* (2004), 'Eine Realistin, es ist schwer, ihr standzuhalten', 7 October, http://www.sueddeutsche.de/kultur/13/407788/text/19/. Accessed 31 May 2009.

SCHLINGENSIEF'S ANIMATOGRAPH: TIME HERE BECOMES SPACE

Roman Berka

I am on the way to becoming a butterfly or I am on the way to a crucifixion.
On the way to Golgotha I'd still like to experience something![1]
(Christoph Schlingensief)

The borders between individual projects, as well as the various artistic fields in which Christoph Schlingensief moves, are always in flux in terms of time, content, form and genre. Within the flow of Schlingensief's work, *The Animatograph* is a particularly multilayered, long-term project, which he developed between 2004 and 2007. The various stations of the animatograph are interwoven with each other on a conceptual level. At the same time, however, each station works as a self-contained project that takes on a different form depending on the context in which it is located, be it in a public space, an opera house, a theatre or a museum. In this chapter, I will sketch the various phases of *The Animatograph* project in order to describe the gradual development of this unique form of artistic expression, which goes hand-in-hand with the creation of an independent system of meaning. In doing so, I will argue that *The Animatograph* marks the decisive point in Schlingensief's oeuvre when the film-maker, TV host, action artist, and theatre and opera director enters the realm of fine art and opens up the space of the museum for his work.

'Ur-Animatograph Parsifal'

The Animatograph developed out of Schlingensief's Bayreuth production of Richard Wagner's opera *Parsifal* (2004–07), which he later described as the 'Ur-Animatograph'.[2] He did not stage *Parsifal* as a moving drama of redemption with a happy ending, but as a commemoration of death. At the centre of the production stood the:

Evolution of Parsifal from a naïve, proud go-getter to a guilt-ridden man, conscious of death and aware of his own mortality, who leads his life out of compassion for others and who, although king by the end, will, like all others, only find redemption through death.[3]

The drama, inscribed in a mystical cycle of birth, death and rebirth, turns into a kind of passion play. At the moment of his death, all of the images of Parsifal's life pass over him once again. In realizing the story scenically as an endlessly extended near-death experience, Schlingensief took Wagner's stage directions and Gurnemanz's paternal words to Parsifal literally; he had a revolving stage contructed for the Bayreuth production that could spatialize time:

> Parsifal: I scarcely tread, yet seem already to have come far.
> Gurnemanz: You see, my son, time here becomes space.

> (Gradually, while Gurnemanz and Parsifal appear to walk, the scene has changed perceptibly: the woods have disappeared, and in the rock faces a gateway has opened, which closes behind them.)[4]

By constructing a revolving stage, Schlingensief dissolved the static nature of the traditional Bayreuth stage. In doing so, he created the possibility of a theatre setting in permanent motion, with new scenes continually passing by. Most notably, however, Schlingensief employed film as a primary dramaturgical element for the first time in Bayreuth. Film fragments were projected from several projectors onto ever-shifting scenery and curtains over a revolving stage dimly washed with light. The result was a permanently mutating artistic stage organism on which a never-ending flow of images was superimposed.

Wagner's music was an important component of Schlingensief's artwork, but only one part among many in the conglomeration of the whole. It had, as the philosopher Boris Groys remarked, the function of a ready-made, which was paradigmatically indicated by a picture of Marcel Duchamp's *Fountain* (1917) as a prop.[5] The transfer of prefabricated objects into an artistic context, where they become charged with new meaning and proclaimed as works of art in their own right, has become standard practice since Duchamp. The technique of the ready-made also belongs to Schlingensief's modus operandi. As will be discussed later on, he unabashedly uses material and images produced by other artists like Joseph Beuys or Dieter Roth, and integrates them into his own work. This artistic technique, which he employed in *Parsifal*, and exponentialized upon in his animatographic project, found its apogee in *Mea Culpa: A ReadyMadeOpera* (2009), which premiered in Vienna's Burgtheater in March 2009.

Life machine and soul illustrator

The central phrase from Schlingensief's *Parsifal* production—'Time here becomes space'—becomes the constitutive idea of his animatograph projects, for which the Wagner opera served as a predecessor. Their basic element is a revolving stage installation, equipped with building elements, props and screens: a performance surface for action as well as a projection surface for filmic works. The animatograph thus offers the viewer both a frontal view and a literal entry point into the installation. From different locations around the room, films are projected onto the mobile stage.[6] If the viewer enters the revolving stage, he himself becomes an integral part of the animatograph—a projection surface and actor whose entrance brings it to life. As Schlingensief's dramaturge Jörg van der Horst explains: 'The person is the organ which activates the spatial structure, the "life machine". His eye is the camera which records the world.'[7] Expanding on this point, Schlingensief states: 'The Animatograph is not an artificial eye, not a camera but a human visual organ. It is the viewer seeing himself and, in doing so, leaving traces, the way images leave traces on the retina.'[8]

The term 'Animatograph' itself stems from Robert William Paul (1869–1943), one of the most important English film pioneers. In 1896, Paul introduced his first film projector—the Theatrograph—to the public, a device that he later dubbed the Animatograph.[9] Schlingensief borrows this term, elaborating on it in the process: 'Anima is the soul. Animatograph is the name of one of the first image-projecting apparatuses. The animatograph illustrates what happens in the soul, it is a soul illustrator.'[10]

Dark phase and actionistic photo plate

Schlingensief experienced his artistic 'socialization' as an assistant to the German experimental film-maker Werner Nekes. It was already his dream in the 1980s 'to combine all the media in which I have worked until now with the viewer to create a total organism (*Gesamtorganismus*)'.[11] Nekes explained to Schlingensief that it is only the inertia of our nerves that makes watching films possible[12]: eighteen or more images per second are required for the movement of film to be perceived as flowing. The temporal gap between two individual images is called the 'dark phase'. The individual pictures are perceived as continuous movement through the stroboscopic effect of the sequence of frames and the after-image which leaves light on the retina. Schlingensief expands on the 'dark phase' as follows:

> The dark phase is a pupation phase. After the dark phase comes new life. But the dark phase is equally alive, because the dark phase first makes the creation of life possible [...] I also relate the dark phase to society. For me

this dark phase concerns those who stand in darkness. This is the actual power. Not the flash, I'm the flash, I flash a lot. [...] For me it is a matter of things that are briefly illuminated.[13]

Metaphorically speaking, the animatograph functions as an 'actionistic photo plate'.[14] An essential cornerstone of the animatograph concept is the idea that it travels, stopping in various places around the world, including those outside specifically artistic domains. For example, in certain locations in Iceland and Africa, the animatograph was purposefully made accessible to people who normally do not have anything to do with art. The intention is for viewers to use the installation, activate it and apply it to their daily lives and culture, thus recharging the animatograph through daily interactions, religious rites, artistic acts and relics. The actions are documented on film and in photographs and flow back into the installation at subsequent stops by means of projections, photos and sound documents. The 'actionistic photo plate' illuminates the locations of its travels and superimposes the images on each other, thus gradually generating a hyperprojection—a picture of a universal culture. The charged animatographs can then, in turn, be reincorporated into the art contexts of the opera house, theatre, museum, or gallery, to be exhibited and recharged again.[15]

Illuminated obsessions: *Iceland Edition*

The first animatograph, *Iceland Edition—House of Obsession* (2005) revolved in the basement of the Klink & Bank Art and Culture Centre in Reykjavik from May to June 2005 as part of the Reykjavik Arts Festival. Schlingensief had travelled with his team around the island beforehand and organized actions to take place at various locations in preparation for the actual presentation of the animatograph. After navigating the stairs down to the basement, visitors could wander through a labyrinthine structure and, via gaps in the partitions, were directed through rooms full of action photos, working materials, and architectural models of historic Icelandic sites, before arriving in the room with the actual animatograph. Films that had been created during the preparatory actions were projected onto a revolving stage with a diameter of 8 metres.

Filming for this animatograph took place in Thingvellir, among other locations. Thingvellir lies in a seismically sensitive zone, where Eurasian and American continental plates break through the earth's core and drift apart eight millimetres per year, which is reflected in an impressive, volcanic landscape. Today, Thingvellir is a national memorial and ceremonial site where the Althing—a prototype parliament with a legislative assembly—met annually from 930 AD. In a parliamentary decree, the Althing of the year 999 or 1000 decided that, in Iceland, paganism would be replaced by Christianity.[16]

For this project, Schlingensief immersed himself in the natural and cultural history of Iceland and, in particular, its mythology. The oral poetry, sagas, and songs about the gods and heroes of Old Norse mythology are summarized in the *Edda*, which is the most important source of Nordic-Germanic mythology. It provides a cosmological, eschatological elucidation of the world from the creation of the earth to its demise (*Ragnarök* = final fate of the gods) and resurgence. Although the *Edda* poems are pagan myths, they were first transcribed after Iceland's Christianization and therefore also reflect Christian ideas. In drawing upon the *Edda* as a model for his actions, Schlingensief thus taps into an endless cosmos of images for the animatograph.[17]

In the actions and films, Schlingensief overlays pagan with Christian images; the *Edda* with the Bible, the *Nibelungenlied* with Grail legends, and the pagan father of the gods Odin with Jesus. Superimposed on these images are quotes from Joseph Beuys, Jonathan Meese, and the Vienna Actionists, among others. In the richly painted animatograph installation—which is inscribed with lines from the *Edda* and animated with projections— the mythical-mystical layering of image, sound, and text is raised to a higher power. Schlingensief does not recount linear histories, but produces rhizomatic visual worlds: the various set pieces are all interwoven, with images systematically juxtaposed and superimposed in an attempt to avoid prescribed meanings. For Schlingensief, it is the images that are of prime importance: 'Images must be created. That has always been the idea behind my entire work.'[18] The production of images is Schlingensief's great obsession, and the animatograph became an obsessive machine for producing them.

From the Beuys-Roth Academy to Wagner's *Gesamtkunstwerk*

For the opening of the Iceland animatograph, an event performed by Schlingensief and others took place in a small room entitled the 'Beuys-Roth Academy'. The performance served as an affectionate and satirical homage to Joseph Beuys and Dieter Roth. References to Beuys, who is obsessively quoted in the animatograph, regularly feature in Schlingensief's work. New, however, is his intensive preoccupation with Dieter Roth. Throughout his career, Beuys had developed theories with a social-utopian thrust. His 'plastic theory' became the theoretical basis for his practical attempts to expand our concept of art—a process that led to the development of what he described as 'social sculpture'. The question of how humans can become sculptors of the 'social organism' is central to his oeuvre, and he coined the famous statement: 'Every human is an artist.'[19]

While Beuys developed concrete ideas for a future social model, Dieter Roth (who lived primarily in Iceland from 1957) did not follow similar intentions. In fact, he decidedly repudiated such models. Beginning in 1964, Roth assembled objects from organic materials, which he later termed 'decomposition objects and images'.[20] A gradual decomposition of these objects—often made from foodstuffs—was an intentional part of their conception. Roth, however, was not interested in the extinction resulting from decomposition, but rather in making the process of decomposition visible. Beginning in the 1980s, Roth captured all aspects of his studio in detailed material images. He integrated things that had surrounded him during the process of creation (such as paint, tools, packaging materials, etc.). Some of these assemblages were specially lit, so that viewers had the impression that the studio itself was being declared a work of art.[21] While Beuys' works were materialized vehicles for transporting certain ideas, Roth's works clearly pointed to their own materiality and processual nature.

In the Iceland animatograph, Schlingensief alluded to Beuys not least by means of a drawing of a right angle in a corner of the 'Beuys-Roth Academy', which was a short-hand expression for a Beuysian 'Fat Corner' (*Fettecke*) which, for Beuys, was a materialization of his 'plastic theory' and a symbol of rational, rather than intuitive, thinking. In addition, a blackboard with allusions to the *Edda* and other animatographic set pieces functioned as a performative homage to Beuys and his ideas. Dieter Roth was quoted through the use of edible materials (which Schlingensief combined with wild actionism) and through the arrangement of the animatographic installation as a kind of studio setting. Through his appropriation and citation of the work of both artists, Schlingensief thus positioned himself in a field of tension composed of these diametrically opposed artistic concepts.

Richard Wagner was indirectly also cited in the installation. Against the background of the historic Icelandic parliamentary site in Thingvellir and his own fundamentally democratic attitude, Schlingensief alludes to Wagner's tract *Die Revolution* (1849).[22] He proclaims in an affirmative inversion: 'Destroy Thingvellir!', 'Destroy Parliament!' because he conceives of democracy—in its current form—as a 'pack of lies'.[23] Affirmation is thus another artistic strategy: he exaggerates the picture of societal conditions to unmask them. Where, for Wagner, the destruction of the status quo is only the precondition for creating a social *Gesamtkunstwerk* (total work of art), for Schlingensief, only the call for destruction remains ('Destroy Parliament!'). No Schlingensiefian *Gesamtkunstwerk* comes about in the Wagnerian sense of the term: there can be no question of a self-contained, total interpretation of the world, for this path implies a notion of totalitarianism,[24] which Schlingensief strongly opposes. The concept of such a totalizing artwork fundamentally contradicts his artistic intentions. As he states: 'The great *Gesamtkunstwerk* does not exist for me, in my eyes it is no longer even possible. I need the unfinished.'[25]

Schlingensief himself has always guarded against attempts to label his work as art that attempts to change the individual or the world. On the other hand, he describes himself as a 'moralist' and he seeks, via his work, to poke a finger into societal wounds.[26] Many of his projects, especially those produced between 1997 and 2003, sought to produce a concrete socio-political, social-sculptural impact beyond the realm of art discourse. Nevertheless, in contrast to Beuys and Wagner, Schlingensief has not sought to develop a social utopian world model or a *Gesamtkunstwerk*. Following his public social-sculptural interventions—such as the founding of the party *Chance 2000* in 1998, and the publicly staged, fictional deportation of migrants in the Big-Brother-spoof *Please Love Austria* (2000)—and his earlier excursions into the institutional field of fine art (such as at the Biennale in Venice in 2003), with the animatograph Schlingensief finally entered the protected realm of art. For him, the museum became an experimental laboratory in a Rothian sense: a space within which he has moved away from direct social and political intervention. In an inversion of the Beuysian statement 'I hereby resign from art' (which is the title of a graphic work from 1985), I would argue that the animatograph project marks Schlingensief's 'entry into art'.

German edition: *Odin's Parsipark*

After the animatograph had recorded the site from which parliamentarianism originated in Iceland, it travelled to an historic site of dictatorship and barbarism. Its second stop, in August 2005, was in Neuhardenberg near Berlin, where the Nazis had built a secret military airfield in 1934. One of the last battles of the Second World War raged in the area around Neuhardenberg in April 1945 and, during the GDR period, the National People's Army used the airfield. It was against this historical background that Schlingensief put his 'actionistic photo plate' into action.

In the woods beside the airfield, where derelict military barracks remain, Schlingensief built *Odin's Parsipark*. The centrepiece of this huge trail of installations—where there were four revolving stages—was the new, large animatograph titled *Ragnarök/Götterdämmerung* (Twilight of the Gods). Visitors could navigate their own route through the performative course, walking through stuffy, dilapidated barracks arranged with monitors, video beamers, objects and thematic installations. Dim living room lamps lit the way through the dark Neuhardenberg forest. In *Odin's Parsipark*, the animatographic principle of rhizomatic image, and meaning-superimpositions were carried on obsessively. The *Edda*'s world of the gods was combined with images from the Second World War (including images of Hitler and Stalin), while further images from *Parsifal*, Hitchcock's films, the Viennese Actionists, Beuys and Roth featured in the mix. In the accompanying brochure, Schlingensief reflected on his plans for the animatograph:

> My dream of the path of this organism would be to build [...], at some point, in three or five years, a sixteen meter large Animatograph, surrounded only by a screen, on which all existing films overlap one another permanently and in this manner become their own story; a story that I myself can no longer correct. It is written by an Animatograph.[27]

The Neuhardenberg project took one step further in the direction outlined by Schlingensief above. The image machine had—as an 'organism'—taken on a life of its own.

Africa Edition: *The African Twintowers*

On its third station, the animatograph also followed the trail of the destruction of democracy. Although the project failed in light of Schlingensief's original plan, it turned out to be a productive source for the further development of his concepts. In October 2005, he travelled with his team to Lüderitz in Namibia, which is located in the former German colony of Southwest Africa. The *Edda* world of images continued in Africa and was mixed with images of colonialism. The journey was, for Schlingensief, an exploration of the German colonial period, especially the bloody suppression of the Herero Revolt by German troops in 1904. The African animatograph was set up in the middle of the Lüderitz Township 'Area 7': a newly constructed settlement for the poor made up of uniform corrugated iron huts. A wooden ship entitled the 'Arch', which had been painted with animals by the children of the township, was resplendent on the stage. The ship had previously been laboriously pulled—*Fitzcarraldo* like—through the desert for several kilometres to the revolving stage. Unlike Schlingensief's other animatographs, the African animatograph was really taken over by the inhabitants of 'Area 7' and utilized as a stage, both during the days-long construction process and during the performance that took place on the final evening, when Schlingensief's team and the inhabitants of 'Area 7' came together for a big party.

In addition to setting up the animatograph, Schlingensief's plan was to shoot his first feature film since 1997: *The African Twintowers*. As indicated by the title, Schlingensief planned to stage the catastrophe of September 11 in an African slum as a statement against globalization and the decadence of the so-called First World. In a problematic manner, the dead in New York were juxtaposed with the horrendous number of people who die in Africa each day, but who—unlike the victims of 9/11—do not draw the media's attention. The animatograph was to be the film set for this undertaking. Another 'storyline' concerned the construction of an opera house in an African slum and, in an allusion to the Wagner festival in Bayreuth, a Bach festival was to be held in a township. [28] In his typically affirmative manner, Schlingensief criticized the (neo-) colonial importation of western culture to the Third World. But this artistic strategy of affirmation (which is frequently employed in his work) did not really work outside the western context. As Schlingensief was well aware, in Africa it did, instead, appear a bit cynical.[29] Lüderitz, however, became the site of an artistic crisis: Schlingensief threw away the screenplay and staged a confrontation with the medium of film itself. After three weeks of shooting without a script, 180 hours of footage remained, and the project was deemed unworkable by several editors.

Figure 1: *The Animatograph—Africa Edition: The African Twintowers*, Township 'Area 7', Lüderitz, Namibia, October 2005. Photo: Aino Laberenz.

The failure of the film in Africa was a symptom of the fact that Schlingensief had lost interest in the film or, more to the point, lost interest in producing a film in a conventional manner. While he had never been interested in linear narrative structures, he was now no longer interested in making a film with a beginning, an end, opening titles and credits. As he explained: 'Whether in the theatre or in the cinema: it starts on the left, finishes on the right; there is the beginning, there is the end. A fundamental mistake.'[30] It is clear that, in Namibia, Schlingensief was searching for a new form of artistic expression that was no longer compatible with the way in which he had previously produced films: 'I don't,' he states, 'need this two-dimensionality anymore [...].'[31] What he wanted was a new three-dimensionality.

With the animatograph as a surface for projection and a platform for action, Schlingensief had found a vehicle to realize his ideas of a spatio-temporal extension of film: 'Time here becomes space.' By projecting endless loops of independent film sequences onto screens on the revolving stage, sequences are created which overlay one another and which together produce a film with neither a beginning nor an end. For the viewers who move on and through the animatograph, a film that edits itself is born through the overlapping images produced in the doubled movement of stage and viewer and in the multiple projection sources. With the animatograph, Schlingensief not only broke open the frontal screen set-up of the cinema, he also did away with linear narrative. As Schlingensief puts it: 'Actionist films were made of scenes which take place to music or come about completely on their own. The results can no longer be controlled. The camera is merely the attempt to maintain distance.'[32] For Schlingensief, the animatograph was thus the culmination of—and the solution to—an artistic crisis. [33]

Area 7—St. Matthew's Expedition

The fourth station of the animatograph can be viewed as the climax of this long-term project: *Area 7– St. Matthew's Expedition* (2006) which took place on several evenings in January, March and May 2006 at the prestigious Burgtheater in Vienna. Austrian author and Nobel Laureate Elfriede Jelinek wrote a theatre text especially for the production. In a similar vein to the film shoot in Africa, which did not result in the production of a feature film, *Area 7* did not result in the production of a conventional theatre play. The actors again did not know what they were required to do. Instead of traditional rehearsals, material actions were carried out in the style of the Vienna Actionists. These were filmed, and the result was the production of an installation that was accompanied by a series of performances. The installation extended throughout the auditorium (the rows of seats were mostly removed) as well as over the main stage of the theatre. A small animatograph rotated in the auditorium, and the revolving main stage became a large animatograph in itself. The African animatograph, with the boat that had been especially transported from Lüderitz, served as the centrepiece of the installation on the main stage.

In the auditorium, visitors could wander through the installation and on the main stage they were guided in groups by actors (or Schlingensief himself) as if through a museum exhibition. The professional and non-professional actors largely represented famous artists: Andy Warhol, Joseph Beuys, Yoko Ono, the Vienna Actionist Hermann Nitsch, the German artist Jonathan Meese and Michael Jackson. Throughout the evening, there were performances, actions and concerts featuring these fake artists. Only rock poet Patti Smith (who had previously accompanied Schlingensief to Africa) was 'real'.

Figure 2: *Area 7—St. Matthew's Expedition*, Burgtheater Vienna, January 2006. Photo: Georg Soulek.

In *Area 7*, Schlingensief expanded and exponentialized upon the principles of the animatograph that I have described above. The use of available props, the intentional production of fakes, and various strategies of appropriation are authorial acts in the sense of the ready-made. This time, however, he reflected on the conditions of art production and the art market in particular, as well as on his own 'entry' *into*—and particular way of dealing *with*—art. Set pieces and props from *Area 7* were acquired by collectors and thereby immediately absorbed into the art market. At the same time, his witty homages to other artists, and his satirical reflections on the art production process, ensured that he retained an ambivalent distance from the art scene. With the culmination of the animatographic project, Schlingensief had thus finally made his way into the art system, after having generated a system of his own.

The differentiation of the Schlingensief system

The world of images that constitute the animatograph—or, as I would put it, the 'Schlingensief system'—achieved its highest degree of differentiation in Vienna. Building upon previous incarnations of the animatograph (with its mythological, religious and political themes) Schlingensief also incorporated images of science and, more than ever, art into the structure. He appropriated images and signs from all societal fields, rearranged them in a syncretic act in the huge *Area 7* installation, and thus created his own projection of society and its social systems. *Area 7* had, as Schlingensief himself has stated, a 'model character'.[34] But he did not create a model of the world that conveys a particular world view. Instead, he took known models and turned them on their head: scientific formulas were re-written, history and works of art were re-interpreted, myths and ideologies were toppled. Schlingensief destroyed known conceptual frameworks and thereby relativized reality. However, the themes and images of the animatograph nonetheless formed a system of meaning that was coherent *in itself*. Schlingensief had—in the terms of system theory—paradigmatically shown how an autopoietic social system comes into existence.[35] The differentiation of the 'Schlingensief system', to paraphrase Niklas Luhmann,[36] did not just begin with the animatograph, but reaches its apogee in the animatograph itself, through which the viewer gets physical access to the system.

In Schlingensief's 'parallel universe', however, relativity does not mean complete arbitrariness, but suggests instead that there are no clear solutions to social problems, be they scientific, political, ideological or religious. With this relativization of given situations and the creation of subjective realities, Schlingensief is in accord with the findings of system theory and constructivism.[37] In his animatographic installations, he takes the step taken by science in regard to the realization of the relative nature of reality, and thereby opens an endless field of possibilities for art production. As a result, the central interpretation of the animatograph has to be: there is *no* one possible interpretation. The animatograph eludes unambiguous interpretations on account of its conceptual composition. This is the reason why the 'Schlingensief system' can never be a concrete world model in the sense of a Beuysian social design or a Wagnerian *Gesamtkunstwerk*.

Kaprow City

The last large project that operated under the name of an animatograph was *Kaprow City* (2006–07) at the Volksbühne in Berlin (September 2006 to March 2007). By this time, however, the concept had already moved far beyond its actual starting point in Iceland. The mythological imagery disappeared, and Schlingensief tried 'to take the Animatograph away from the myth machine of the *Edda* to become an Animatograph of the 21st century'.[38]

In *Kaprow City* (which was simultaneously an art installation, a play, a happening and a live film) a giant installation was built on the Volksbühne's revolving stage. The viewers were guided through eighteen small rooms that actively played with the idea of a fourth wall. The original event that moulded the concept of the happening as an art form, *18 Happenings in 6 Parts* (Allan Kaprow, 1959), served Schlingensief as a model for *Kaprow City*, as did Kaprow's earlier 'environments'.[39] As in *18 Happenings in 6 Parts*, actors performed simple actions in Schlingensief's installation, such as squeezing oranges, and the rooms were exuberantly decorated. To the beat of a gong, viewers were asked to change rooms rhythmically. Thus they themselves became actors in the happenings. In accordance with Schlingensief's preference for producing 'viscous' films (in which eighteen rather than 24 frames per second are projected so that the 'dark phase' between the images comes into being), *18 Happenings in 6 Parts* in *Kaprow City* mutated, in Schlingensief's words, into '18 happenings in one second. [...] That's what it's about. These eighteen happenings are arranged in a circle. That's the film spool.'[40]

The installation, however, also functioned as a film set with cameras, and a film was simultaneously shot live, edited, and projected onto a screen in the auditorium. Schlingensief chose a theme for the live film via which he could once more question mediated and staged reality: in this case, Princess Diana's fatal accident in 1997. With this film, he recreated the final, unpublished pictures of the accident and, in doing so, reconstructed the last hour of Diana's life, which was caught by media cameras down to the smallest detail. The theatricality and mediated nature of reality were thus unmasked, and images of Nordic mythology were followed by those of a 'modern myth'. In more general terms, it is clear that the animatograph concept was transformed in *Kaprow City*, which marks the beginning of the end of the animatograph as a long-term project.

Expansion of the dark phase

The works that followed *Kaprow City*—some still planned as part of *The Animatograph*— were finally realized without the application of the 'Animatograph' label, although some of its actionistic, filmic and theatrical principles continued to be applied. During this period, Schlingensief turned again to film, experimenting with what he has described as an 'expansion of the dark phase'.[41] The black and white short films and film sequences that he produced for his new projects became increasingly 'viscous', with dark intervals of up to a few seconds between shots. This work went hand-in-hand with his first large solo exhibitions in museum spaces: *18 Images per Second* (2007) at the Haus der Kunst in Munich and *Cross Mutilation* (2007–08) at the Migros Museum für Gegenwartskunst in Zurich. As Schlingensief himself has noted: 'The museum work is an important step. I make use of the museum as a sheltered, cloistered space. For thinking, for experimentation, this space is great.'[42] The museum, he continues, is a 'zone of fear', because he has to encounter himself there, which, for him, is a process of 'productive self-torture' and 'self-provocation'. As Schlingensief stated in a panel discussion, it is this zone—where the images 'originate and are negotiated'—that constitutes the 'dark phase'.[43]

After his first solo museum exhibitions, Schlingensief reanimated and further transformed the animatograph concept.[44] This innovative form of artistic expression constitutes the spatialization of the flow of time in his projects: it enables him to integrate earlier and current projects, as well as all of the artistic fields (including film, theatre, opera, performance and fine art) in which he moves, into an overall work. In terms of form, this means an expansion beyond traditional modes of expression: looped film projections onto the fluid curtains of accessible, revolving stage installations vs. films with a beginning and end on the taut, orthogonal silver screen in the black box of the cinema; open productions with untrained performers, professionals and audience participation vs. conventional theatre or musical theatre in the temples of high culture maintaining the performer-audience dichotomy; changeable environments in an extra-institutional context vs. hermetic art exhibitions in the White Cube. With his animatographic installations, Schlingensief has thus not only found his way into the art market and traditional museum spaces, he has also developed a truly independent art form that enables him to open up new experimental fields that transgress traditional domains of art.

Endnotes

1. My special thanks for advising, translating and editing go to Fatima Naqvi. Schlingensief in *Area 7—Matthäusexpedition von Christoph Schlingensief* (2006), Programme Book of *AREA 7*, Issue 130, Season 2005/2006, Burgtheater Wien, p. 48.

2. See Ahrens, G. (2005), 'Das Universum hat keinen Schatten', (Christoph Schlingensief in conversation with Gerhard Ahrens) in *Der Animatograph—Odins Parsipark*, brochure accompanying *Odins Parsipark*, Stiftung Schloss Neuhardenberg, pp. 6–8, esp. p. 6.

3. Hegemann, C. (2005), 'Alles schreit. Notizen zu Christoph Schlingensiefs Parsifal', in Hegemann, C., *Plädoyer für die unglückliche Liebe. Texte über Paradoxien des Theaters 1980–2005*, S. Umathum (ed.), Berlin: Theater der Zeit, Recherchen 28, p. 241.

4. See Wagner, R. (1948), *Parsifal. Ein Bühnenweihfestspiel*, Vienna: Globus Verlag, pp. 27–28. On this crucial sentence in *Parsifal* see also Brock, B. (1983), 'Der Hang zum Gesamtkunstwerk', in H. Szeemann (ed.), *Der Hang zum Gesamtkunstwerk. Europäische Utopien seit 1800*, 2nd ed., Aarau and Frankfurt am Main: Verlag Sauerländer, pp. 22–39, esp. p. 27.

5. See Groys, B. and Hegemann, C. (2004), 'Wir sind die Welt. Wir sind die Kinder', in Hegemann, C. (ed.), *Theater ALS Krankheit* (booklet for *Kunst und Gemüse, A. Hipler*, a production by Christoph Schlingensief at the Volksbühne Berlin), Berlin: Alexander Verlag, pp. 6–16.

6. See van der Horst, J., 'Der Animatograph—Eine "Lebensmaschine" von Christoph Schlingensief', http://www.schlingensief.com/projekt. php?id=t052&article=theorie. Accessed 29 April 2009.

7. Ibid.

8. Schlingensief in Ibid.

9. See Low, R. (1997), *The History of the British Film 1896–1906*, London: Routledge, pp. 23–24 and p. 113.

10. Schlingensief in 'Schlingensiefs Animatograph—Einleitung', http://www. schlingensief.com/projekt.php?id=t052&article=einleitung. Accessed 27 April 2009.

11. Schlingensief in van der Horst, J., 'Der Animatograph', l.c.

12. See Obrist, H. U. (2005), 'Meine Arbeit hat immer mit dem Blickwechsel zu tun' (Christoph Schlingensief in conversation with Hans Ulrich Obrist), in Koegel, A. and König, K. (eds.), *AC: Christoph Schlingensief: Church of Fear*, Köln: Verlag der Buchhandlung Walther König, pp. 9–15, esp. p. 10.

13. Schlingensief in Dander, P. and Frensch, V., 'Schlingensief-ABC' in Haus der Kunst (ed.) *18 Bilder pro Sekunde*, brochure accompanying Schlingensief's exhibition *18 Bilder pro Sekunde* (*18 Images a Second*) at the Haus der Kunst in Munich, 25 May – 16 September 2007 (Munich, 2007), pp. 9–14, esp. p. 11.

14. van der Horst, J., 'Der Animatograph', l.c.

15. Ibid.

16. See Genzmer, F. (2000), *Die Edda. Götterdichtung, Spruchweisheit und Heldengesänge der Germanen*, 5th ed., Kreuzlingen/Munich: Diederichs, pp. 9–24.

17. See van der Horst, J., 'Der Emmaus-Effekt oder das Wunder von Pingvellir' in Koegel, König (eds.), *AC: Christoph Schlingensief: Church of Fear*, l.c., no pagination.

18. Schlingensief, C. (2006), 'Ich bin für die Vielfalt zuständig', in C. Reder (ed.), *Lesebuch Projekte. Vorgriffe, Ausbrüche in die Ferne*, Vienna: Edition Transfer, Springer, pp. 125–140, esp. p. 139.

19. For an introduction to the Beuysian concepts of 'plastic theory', 'social sculpture' etc., see Harlan, V., Rappmann, R. and Schata, P. (eds.) (1984), *Soziale Plastik. Materialen zu Joseph Beuys*, 3rd edition, Achberg: Achberger Verlag, esp. pp. 56–61 and pp. 102–103.

20. See Vischer, T. and Walter, B. (eds.) (2003), *Roth-Zeit. Eine Dieter Roth Retrospektive*, catalogue, Baden: Müller, esp. pp. 77–78 and pp. 95–97.

21. Ibid., p. 195–197.

22. After the tractate *Die Revolution* (1849), in the same year Richard Wagner wrote his constitutive works *Die Kunst und die Revolution* and *Das Kunstwerk der Zukunft*, in which he formulated his conception of the *Gesamtkunstwerk*.

23. Schlingensief in Buhre, J. (2005), 'Die Demokratie ist ein Wäschetrockner', in *Planet Interview*, 8 April, http://planet-interview.de/christoph-schlingensief-04082005.html. Accessed 29 April 2009.

24. See Brock, B. (1983), 'Der Hang zum Gesamtkunstwerk', l.c., p. 28.

25. Schlingensief, C. (1998), 'Wir sind zwar nicht gut, aber wir sind da', in Lochte, J. and Schulz, W. (eds.), *Schlingensief! Notruf für Deutschland*, Hamburg: Rotbuch Verlag, pp. 12–39, esp. p. 27.

26. Schlingensief, C. (1998), p. 34.

27. Schlingensief in Ahrens, G. (2005), 'Das Universum hat keinen Schatten', l.c., p.7.

28. See *The Animatograph* (2006), PDF-booklet ed. by Thyssen-Bornemisza Art Contemporary—T-B A21, Vienna, pp. 24–27; and: http://www.schlingensief.com/downloads/the_animatograph.pdf. Accessed 26 October 2007.

29. See the discussion between Schlingensief and the Namibian farmer Friedhelm von Seydlitz, 'Laßt uns machen!', http://www.schlingensief.com/weblog/?p=55. Accessed 22 August 2009.

30. Schlingensief, C. (2006), 'Ich bin für die Vielfalt zuständig', l.c., p. 132.

31. Schlingensief in Philipp, C. (2005), 'Is there anybody out there? Erster Teil des Schlingensief Drehtagebuchs (19.10.2005)', http://www.schlingensief.com/weblog/?p=42. Accessed 27 April 2009.

32. Schlingensief (2006), 'Ich bin für die Vielfalt zuständig', l.c., p. 131.

33. The 'failed' film *The African Twintowers* was finally presented as a museum installation consisting of eighteen monitors, on which the same number of uncut film sequences of various lengths were shown simultaneously. In 2009, *The African Twintowers* appeared as a documentary film about the 'impossibility of making a linear film'. See: http://www.filmgalerie451.de/film/the-african-twintowers/. Accessed 7 May 2009.

34. Schlingensief in Kluge, A. (2006), 'Der Animatograph—Christoph Schlingensiefs Erste-Hilfe-Koffer gegen Tiefsinn', *News & Stories*, SAT 1, 8 January 8. See also Brock, B., 'Eine großartige Tat!', http://www.schlingensief.com/weblog/?p=98, 18.11.2007. Accessed 27 April 2009.

35. See Luhmann, N. (1998), *Die Kunst der Gesellschaft*, 2nd ed., Frankfurt am Main: Suhrkamp, p. 499.

36. Luhmann, N. (1994), *Die Ausdifferenzierung des Kunstsystems*, Bern: Benteli Verlag AG.

37. Simon, F. B. (2006), *Einführung in Systemtheorie und Konstruktivismus*, Heidelberg: Carl Auer Verlag, pp. 40–55.

38. Schlingensief in Laudenbach, P. (2006), 'Jetzt sage ich die Wahrheit', interview with Christoph Schlingensief in *tip*, Issue 19, p. 63.

39. See Ursprung, P. (2003), *Grenzen der Kunst. Allan Kaprow und das Happening - Robert Smithson und die Land Art*, München: Verlag Silke Schreiber, p. 50 and pp. 76–87.

40. See Schlingensief, C. (2006), '18 Happenings in einer Sekunde', lecture before the opening of *Kaprow City* for staff and students, published in the programme accompanying *Kaprow City*, Volksbühne Berlin, no pagination.

41. As paradigmatically inserted in his black and white silent film *Fremdverstümmelung* (2007).

42. Schlingensief in Stähli, S. (2007), 'Ich muss nicht mehr den wilden Mann spielen', interview with Christoph Schlingensief in *Zürcher Tagesanzeiger*, 6 November 6, p. 24.

43. Schlingensief in a public discussion on 22 July 2007 with the curator Stephanie Rosenthal and film theorist Georg Seeßlen on the occasion of his exhibition *18 Bilder pro Sekunde* at the Haus der Kunst in Munich.

44. See Hart, K., 'Geister in São Paolo. TREM FANTASMA—Erster Prototyp einer Operngeisterbahn', 18.11.2007. http://www.schlingensief.com/projekt. php?id=a002. Accessed 25 June 2009.

CITIZEN OF THE OTHER PLACE: A TRILOGY OF FEAR AND HOPE

Florian Malzacher

> Illness is the night-side of life, a more onerous citizenship. Everyone who is born holds dual citizenship, in the kingdom of the well and in the kingdom of the sick. Although we all prefer to use only the good passport, sooner or later each of us is obliged, at least for a spell, to identify ourselves as citizens of the other place.
>
> (Susan Sontag[1])

Perhaps the most alarming thing is this: that there is a narrative plausibility even to Christoph Schlingensief's cancer—as if plausibility had anything to do with life and death. We narrate our lives backwards; in retrospect, decisions seem inevitable, coincidence feasible, and the hand of fate consequential. Just as the Romantics believed that illness and early death were the result of a poetic sensibility. Just as we see an inner logic, a dramaturgy in the lives of famous people and are disinclined to read them as mere products of circumstance.

The neo-romantic Schlingensief has, in his work and interviews, always narrated his life in this way: as an ultimately coherent—albeit circuitous—development. He has expanded upon this narrative onstage and enlarged it via his incursions into public spaces, which in turn were taken up by the media so that they, too, have chronicled his life as it were a novel. And because Schlingensief and the world around him tend to notch things up more than just a little, he has considerably overextended the arc between life and art, as was demonstrated (if not before) in his 2004 production of *Parsifal* in Bayreuth. If an artist and his interpreters equate the two ends of this arc so strongly, couldn't it be that the work actually writes the life? That life adheres to a desirable (because plausible, because aesthetically beautiful) logic? And, at some point, it seemed as if this life were no longer being narrated backwards, but forwards. Like a serialised novel or a film or, to cite Schlingensief's 2008 production *A Church of Fear for the Stranger in Me*:

Are we perhaps a lie? Are we a film, a film lasting barely a moment? Are we the thoughts of a madman? Are we a printing error? Are we a premonition? The picture that forms in one's imagination much earlier than the events via which we participate in life occur? [...] Are we a future fact that has not yet come about?[2]

Parsifal is Wagner's final opera, an artistic and ideological legacy replete with religious motifs—from the revelation of the monstrance to the Eucharist. Following Schlingensief's surprising appointment as the director of a new production of this opera, time and again comparisons were made between him and its title figure[3]: Parsifal the 'pure fool' who, as a Germanised figure of salvation, redeems the world through compassion, and Schlingensief—for whom compassion and redemption, albeit often misunderstood as irony, were always central motifs in his work—who tilts in apparent naivety at windmills. Or at Klingsor.

The wider resonance of the Parsifal story was also soon to be extended by the concrete situation of the artist himself. Even with someone like Schlingensief, who has effected so many surprising yet convincing artistic turnarounds, it was difficult to imagine what might follow the supposed highpoint of a production at the Bayreuth Festspielhaus. The *enfant terrible*, trash filmmaker, scandalous performer, and TV provocateur had entered the heart of bourgeois culture. It would be difficult for an artistic career to reach a more established or esteemed position than this. The life story appeared complete—catharsis had to follow. Schlingensief, too, did not resist the temptation of ennobling his life and art with the possibility of its early end. In fact he repeatedly mentioned that death could, indeed, follow his production of *Parsifal*.[4]

Theatre as illness, illness as theatre

Schlingensief's fascination with illness and death did, however, not begin with *Parsifal*. Rather, it is a fascination that is also apparent in his early films. Blood is vomited in *Mother's Mask* (1988) and *Menu Total* (1986) contains the eerie white-coats-and-doctors scene that would later be incorporated into the video segment of *Mea Culpa: A ReadyMade Opera* (2009). For Schlingensief, the motif of illness has various functions and meanings. It becomes a symptom of what society has suppressed, of something (the National Socialist past, incest, rape) that breaks out because it can no longer be restrained. But, in contrast to Antonin Artaud (who likened the theatre to the plague with its grotesquely transformative power), the outbreak of illness in these cases does not mark a turning point, a new social beginning, or a resurrection from the smoking ruins. It does not have a cathartic effect; it merely brings the truth to light, without leading to insight. The truth serum of illness does not heal—even though redemption is another central motif in Schlingensief's work - perhaps for the very reason that it cannot be attained.

The fact that Schlingensief likes to bring up the subject of societal illness has less to do with the desire to provoke than with compassion, indeed with a vicarious suffering that sometimes lends him a touch of the messianic. The supposition of irony or even cynicism is usually incorrect here—techniques of the inauthentic or of distancing are largely foreign to Schlingensief. Rather, it is primarily the techniques of non-integration and non-resolution that are essential to his work.

Above all, it is death—which cannot be integrated into life or art—that marks the limits of what can be spoken about and portrayed. Although more or less always a taboo, death has a central place in theatre, which—sometimes more of a psychoanalytical therapy meeting, and sometimes closer to an archaic ritual—attempts to say, or at least allay, the unsayable. Illness and death also epitomise the uncontrollable. When Schlingensief includes disabled and amateur performers together with other means of producing coincidence or chaos in his shows, he creates an incursion of reality that brings us back to theatre's most basic principle: being in a space together with other—real—people, with the possibility of mistakes, failure, malfunction and, as Heiner Müller emphasised, even the possible death of an actor or fellow viewer[5]. Theatre has always flirted with its ephemerality and transience, claiming an element of evanescence and non-reproducibility as its essential quality. Yet, for centuries, great value has been placed on its supposed capacity for precise reproduction. Schlingensief's theatre, however—and this was particularly the case during the 1990s and early 2000s—is usually impossible to reproduce identically night after night.[6]

'Is this part of the piece?' asks the genuinely confused amateur performer Peter Müller, alias Johannes Heesters, the one-hundred-year-old entertainer and operetta singer in *Art and Vegetables, A. Hipler* (2004). It is exactly the contravention of classical ideas of good dramaturgy that creates space for reflection and demands that we take a position when timing goes askew, or when the overview is lost, when nothing happens, or too much. Schlingensief, who likes to maintain complete control over his work, goes to a great deal of trouble to evade this control himself. His work with disabled performers, for example, has precisely this aim: these performers push the limits of theatre because they are unable or unwilling to remain within them. They break through the illusion, representing both the other and the real. They constitute reality, insofar as reality is possible in the theatre.

Illness and death are thus metaphors for the greatest possible loss of control, for the ultimate failure of the system. Yet Schlingensief had never—prior to his own illness—put the threat of death on stage with such concreteness as in *Art and Vegetables*.[7] Angela Jansen, an ALS patient who was forty-nine years old at the time, had to be brought to the theatre every evening by ambulance. ALS—amyotropic lateral sclerosis—is a usually fatal disease of the motor neurons. The body is afflicted with a gradual paralysis that can lead to total immobility, including that of the vocal and breathing apparatus. Angela Jansen has been on artificial respiration for years. On stage she speaks with the aid of a machine that can recognise the movements of her pupils and form the letters on which her eyes focus into words and sentences—a little like writing an SMS. Although *Art and Vegetables* deals with the art world, Bayreuth, Schönberg's opera *From Today to Tomorrow*, Johannes Heesters and much more, at its centre is the provocative, moving and barely visible presence of Angela Jansen and her illness. 'Theatre ALS [*as*] illness,' says Jörg Immendorf[8] on tape at the opening of *Art and Vegetables*. 'Towards the garden, that is, vegetables—they are killing us. Towards art. Towards the selves. They are ... still ... moving. Theatre as illness. Everyone declares war on decay. Towards the garden, that is, vegetables [...].'

Cancer is one of the diseases that Susan Sontag has identified as being 'spectacularly [...] encumbered by the trappings of metaphor.'[9] It lends itself so well to projection because it is seen as 'intractable and capricious,' as incurable and impossible to overcome: 'A disease not understood—in an era in which medicine's central premise is that all diseases can be cured. Such a disease is, by definition, mysterious.'[10]

Schlingensief too has repeatedly used illnesses metaphorically in his work, but in *Art and Vegetables* he was primarily concerned with awakening sympathy for the concrete situation of Angela Jansen, and with raising awareness about her disease. With the onset of his own illness, the artistic preoccupation with sickness and death became central to his work in a largely un-metaphorical sense. In mid January 2008, Schlingensief was diagnosed with lung cancer. In late January he underwent an operation to remove an entire lung. During the chemotherapy that followed, he suffered an embolism but appeared, nonetheless, to have coped tolerably well with the severe medical interventions. Although greatly weakened, he directed an opera from his hospital bed.[11] Shortly afterwards, he began rehearsing an evening for his friends and acquaintances that was performed on the studio stage of Berlin's Maxim Gorki Theatre in July 2008. In November, it was revived in a revised version entitled *The Current State of Things*.[12]

The Current State, like his later pieces (*A Church of Fear for the Stranger in Me* and *Mea Culpa*) is essentially based on tape recordings that Schlingensief started to make shortly after his diagnosis in January 2008 and that continued (with a few additions) until mid April. These tapes—often immediate, direct and intimate—are a strikingly honest and ruthlessly emotional record of events that fluctuates between abysmal, hopeless despair and an almost manic optimism. On the small studio stage of the Gorki Theatre, these texts—either played on tape or spoken by actors—come across as disturbingly private, partly because Schlingensief has always needed very large spaces in which to stage his work. In *The Current State*, a screen stands just in front of the first row and everything is close-up and intimate. Hospital scenes in light-comedy style overlap with Schönberg's *Erwartung* (Expectation) op. 17, Schlingensief's ensemble of disabled actors sing a song, the performance almost dissolves, often behind gauze as if we were viewing a dream, or a nightmare.

The tendency to keep one's own illness secret, as if it were something scandalous, remains quite common—particularly in relation to cancer—although less so than at the time of Susan Sontag's assessment of the disease. Schlingensief, who has always treated the private realm as an object of artistic inquiry, again chose to go public:

I can of course remain silent about my illness, my fear of death, but I don't want to. I want to talk about sickness, dying and death. To talk against this culture of ostracism that bans the ill from speaking. I am moulding a social sculpture from my illness. And I am working on an extended concept of illness. It isn't about being a delegate for the suffering; it is simply about [generating] visibility.[13]

Schlingensief has discussed his ordeal in three theatre pieces, the book version of his dictaphone diary entries, and in numerous interviews (some on lightweight television talk shows), and, in doing so, he has successfully retained a sense of control over its reception (after initially forbidding his lawyers to report in any way on his illness). If, at first, the tape recordings had a primarily therapeutic function, the theatre performances and the diary that appeared in early 2009[14] are not simply gushing confessions, but clearly formed works that are an attempt to stay above water in the face of an illness that Schlingensief—along with so many others[15]—experienced as a fundamental affront: 'I'm so insulted, *so* insulted and hurt by this thing. At forty-seven. It really is an unbelievable insult!'[16]

A monstrous church of fear

A Church of Fear for the Stranger in Me (which premiered on September 21, 2008) begins and ends on a sombre note. Even on entering the former factory in Duisburg, where the production took place, it is obvious that it is going to be about life's 'big' questions. The audience forms a congregation, separated by a wide central aisle as in the nave of a church. The seats are hard and, at the front, there is a monstrance bearing one of Schlingensief's x-rays. A film triptych flickers in the grainy black and white of early cinema where the apse is still hidden by a half-curtain. A magnified cancer cell, ghostly in front of a black background: a moon, a new moon, framed by a shimmering ray of light like an eclipsed sun.[17] Some lettering flashes up: EXIT—as if there were an exit from this evening that leads deep into Schlingensief's illness. The way he lies there, recorded on video, fatally ill a few months before, crying, in despair: 'Please don't touch me. Please don't touch me now. I don't want anyone to touch me anymore.' The plaintive voice and the ailing man are uncanny, unpleasant, distant and intrusive at the same time—in short, obscene. 'For those who live neither with religious consolations about death nor with a sense of death (or of anything else) as natural, death is', according to Sontag, 'the obscene mystery, the ultimate affront, the thing that cannot be controlled'.[18] Do we want to see this? Do we want to get so close to him? Is it honest sharing, exhibitionism, or emotional blackmail?[19]

A Church of Fear takes up many scenes and motifs from *The Current State of Things,* but detaches them from the oppressively immediate, unbroken privacy of the former piece, generalising them, but without affording us the opportunity to gain the necessary reflective distance from their monstrosity.[20] Too close, too much, too honest, too vulnerable. In his need to confide, Schlingensief infringes the rules of propriety. He imposes himself, talks uninterruptedly about himself, his life, and his experiences. Despite musical interludes by Bach, Wagner and others (mostly interpreted by the black-garbed, twin-like singers Friederike Harmsen and Ulrike Eidinger) and quotations from Joseph Beuys, Heiner Müller or Friedrich Hölderlin, *A Church of Fear* is, above all, a long monologue: a monologue of despair, a megalomaniac attempt to grasp the ungraspable, to enable the ultimate insult of mortality to be talked about. Not to deny it, but to lay it bare.

Schlingensief speaks via a polyphony of voices. Sometimes via Margit Cartensen, whose unmistakable cadences seem to merge with the breathless, often faltering tone of the dictaphone recordings. Sometimes unctuously derisive (Stefan Kolosko), sometimes childishly naive (Mira Partecke), sometimes with smiling friendliness (Angela Winkler), the disharmonious cacophony of earlier works is bundled into an inner monologue. As in *The Current State of Things*, Super-8 films taken by his father of Christoph as a child on the Baltic Sea—with mother, waves, sand and wind—are contrasted with Schlingensief's dictated report on his medical results:

> Have this death cut out of you [...] as soon as possible [...] And what comes then [...] is a new life. This means that from Saturday you will live a new life. It'll be quite different from your previous one, with no big plans for the next year or so [...] The prognosis for this kind of thing is not good [...] Only a few people make it [...].

While Schlingensief as a young boy plays on screen with a toy gun, dances and runs about, his forty-year-older self concludes that the life he has known is now over: 'But you have to know,' he quotes his doctor in a shaky voice, 'that you're living every day as if it were also your last...' The voice fails. 'That's what he said.'

In moments like these, the theatre and its actors retreat almost entirely, as if Schlingensief can no longer bear the continual presence of other people and needs a few minutes of quiet. The piece becomes a video installation in which old family films are interspersed with early Fluxus and actionist recordings (for example by Nam June Paik and VALIE EXPORT), the rotting hare from *Parsifal*—a Beuys citation—and the re-enactment of Fluxus material. But this does not last for long: Schlingensief needs at least a touch of unpredictability—even if it is more of a quotation of former chaos than real chaos itself. From out of the gloom, Achim von Paczensky and Kerstin Grassmann emerge. They are old friends from Schlingensief's ensemble of disabled performers, and together they recite a Dadaist chorus (which rhymes in German): 'The Oberhausen Short Film Festival is the best short-film festival! Avant-garde! Marmelade! Avant-garde! Marmelade !' No comic relief, since even this usually nonchalant couple is too inhibited

Figure 1: A tableau from *A Church of Fear for the Stranger in Me* with the three projection screens visible. Photo: David Baltzer.

by the situation. But at least a brief moment of respite is offered through which we get an inkling of why the performance is subtitled *A Fluxus Oratorio*. Life goes on.

The chamber play finally overbalances towards the middle of the performance when the screen-curtain lowers, vastly opening up the space and revealing a huge church apse, high windows, and an altar. The ministrants (a role that Schlingensief performed as a boy) file in with a full gospel chorus and a children's choir.[21] A large deployment—and suddenly the loneliness is interrupted as if an entire family had arrived at the patient's sickbed. Sixty or seventy people stand in rows around the altar in a group portrait with a female pope.[22] In this performance, Schlingensief does not shy away from either adversaries or pathos. Beuys' famous phrase—'He who shows his wound will be healed.

He who conceals his wound will not be healed'—is the biblical reference for this sermon. What better summary of Schlingensief's highly psychoanalytical credo? Despite it also being perverted or perfected on afternoon chat shows, Schlingensief takes the claim to the extreme by literally putting everything on stage: deep self-doubt ('I can't love myself like this'), thoughts of suicide, and again and again, of course—as in many previous works—his contradictory, traumatic relationship to his parents, here in the form of ritual accusations against his mother, who didn't visit him because she was too afraid. At the same time, Schlingensief elevates this theatre of avowal and confession into the realm of the allusive and celebrates a symbolically overloaded funeral rite for someone who has—for now—survived.

In reverse gear—quoting the rewinding of a film—the choirs are drawn back down the nave through the middle aisle until only the core ensemble remain, and Schlingensief finally appears himself. Not as a live director, a frenzied challenger of his own production, but as the leading character who—despite having been present throughout the performance—finally appears onstage. With eyes wide open, he once again radically raises the stakes: he embodies Jesus, celebrates the mass, and quotes from the Bible: 'This is my body, which is broken for you [...]'—only to rebel furiously against the passivity of the victim that has set the tone of the preceding hour:

> Subject oneself to voluntary suffering? Oh yeah? Doesn't that mean the desire to reach an end on the timeline? Is Jesus deceiving himself here? Because subjecting yourself voluntarily means, "Right, shoot me now!" We know it from kitsch films, but it doesn't help us at all in reality, because the human spirit is too small to cultivate the generosity of saying, "You finish me off!" [...] Lord, forgive me my delusion, for the organism consists of the brainstem, but the brainstem persists even once the shot has been fired. Hallelujah!?

The saviour turns away from pure doctrine and towards the artistic avant-garde: 'Do this in remembrance of me: Fluxus!' The sacramental host is thrown to the crowd and the mass becomes a happening.

At the end of the evening, long after Schlingensief has left the stage and silence and darkness have returned, the circle closes. Once again, the oppressive video recording of the frightened, whimpering patient flickers across the screen. 'Touch me not'. *Noli me tangere*' says Jesus in the New Testament, telling Maria Magdalene not to detain him: do not touch me for I am going elsewhere. The eternal virgin has grown up. Going elsewhere. 'You will live a new life.' But Schlingensief has reinvented himself before and, as much as he has changed, he has also remained himself.

Mea Culpa: A double healing in Africa

In November 2008, a routine examination surprisingly revealed more than ten new pea-sized metastases in Schlingensief's remaining lung.[23] The additional dictaphone recordings and the revival of *The Current State of Things* give a sense of his despondency about everything beginning yet again, and the prognosis is worse than ever. Schlingensief undergoes many different therapies, one of which includes taking a new type of pill that promises relief and, for whatever reason, a few weeks later the metastases have disappeared. It seems to be a good omen for the forthcoming rehearsals of Schlingensief's third production about illness.

Mea Culpa: A ReadyMade Opera (which premiered on March 20, 2009 at the Burgtheater in Vienna) is, by Schlingensief's standards, a relatively quiet and ordered piece, cheerfully serene and, all in all, clearly oriented towards the future. It is, as Schlingensief has pointed out, 'the part where one had got rid of the metastases, but was still perplexed because of almost having accepted dying very soon. One had sensed death, was already elsewhere. Nothing remains as it was.'[24] However much Schlingensief holds Wagner and Bayreuth responsible for his cancer,[25] he is—nonetheless—unable to let them go. Since his production of *Parsifal*, motifs, quotations or whole passages from the opera have repeatedly made their way into his work. Through Schlingensief's own illness, the wound of Amfortas, his suffering, and the futile efforts of Kundry to heal him have entered the spotlight. Like Amfortas, who may only be healed by the touch of the weapon that inflicted the wound, Schlingensief seeks the touch of the music he partially blames for his illness.

Mea Culpa also begins with the first act of *Parsifal*. It is initially reminiscent of *A Church of Fear* where distance from the subject matter had proven impossible for both the director and the audience. The powerfully suggestive music, the solemn singing, and the flickering gloom of the video projection create an emotional space in which stage and auditorium merge. But it soon becomes clear that, this time, Schlingensief wishes—via an explicit and uncharacteristic use of irony—to generate a sense of distance. Four black nurses appear, as if in a prelude to some soft-porn fantasy, and Amfortas seeks his recovery in sexual convergence with Kundry and appears to have some success: 'I am healed! I am healed!'

Shortly afterwards we find ourselves in an Ayurvedic clinic, very much like the one in Bad Schandau where Schlingensief took a cure. Margit Carstensen plays its director, Irm Hermann functions as a kind of house poet, and the space is populated with gurus and patients. Schlingensief is also among them, but is played by Achim Meyerhof who—with his thick glasses and green velvet suit—bears little resemblance to the original. He does, however, have Schlingensief's manner of speaking down to a T. Throughout the production, Fritzi Haberlandt variously appears as Schlingensief's partner Aino Labarenz, or as Oda Jaune, the widow of Jörg Immendorf.

While *A Church of Fear* is largely static—aligned along an apse—*Mea Culpa* turns on its own axis in a very lively fashion. The rotating stage is employed by the designer Janina Audick to evoke an array of very different, overlapping zones, some of them more associative spaces, others naturalistic (including sanatorium rooms reminiscent of those described in Thomas Mann's novel *The Magic Mountain*, a chapel, a boarded tomb, an opera house in Africa) over which a multitude of video material is laid (some of it found, some newly shot, some from old films and productions). The principle of sampling, quoting, and stealing seems to be carried to an extreme here. Aside from Schlingensief's dictaphone notes, the texts are taken from Goethe, Nietzsche, Beuys, Žižek, Jelinek, and Nancy, among others. The filmic music was written by Arno Waschk in the style of Wagner, Bach, and Mahler, etc. to produce a *ReadyMade Opera*. That is to say, Schlingensief draws on what is at hand and places it—à la Duchamp—in a different context. His context.

Figure 2: One part of the revolving set of *Mea Culpa: a ReadyMade Opera* revealing the clinic. Photo: Georg Soulek.

The evening is very clearly structured. It largely adheres to the dramaturgy of 'the story so far' and more or less narrates exactly that until, towards the end, it turns to the future and beyond. The production's three parts are equated with three different concepts of healing: wellness and Ayurveda characterise the first; the second alternates between Dionysian orgy, shamanism, and Catholicism. The third act is occupied with an attempt to seek recovery in Africa, an idea that Schlingensief by no means intends only metaphorically: his long-cherished plan to set up an opera house there has become very concrete in the meantime.[26] For Schlingensief, the 'Dark Continent' is to induce a double cure: on the one hand his own (he has repeatedly and explicitly connected the construction of this building with the recovery of his own health);[27] on the other, this anti-Bayreuthian opera house is intended to heal a cultural wound, as Meyerhoff/Schlingensief announces at the opening of the building staged in the third act of *Mea Culpa*:

> It really is about infecting oneself. We can no longer go on sending a few Goethe Institute types over to Africa to show people how to do culture. Here it's about bringing ourselves into an exchange of experience, and not from the top down or from the bottom up always giving culture, etc. as if it were some kind of gift [...] It's about taking away as much as we are given [...].

The third act—or Africa—also brings this world and the next together. The opening crowd is still gathered for a Miss Africa contest when the ghosts from Schlingensief's own life appear: Andreas Ahrens, an old school friend who killed himself at the age of nineteen when he was unhappily in love with Schlingensief; Schlingensief's father, who wants to persuade his son to join him in the hereafter. The series of deathly temptations ends with the movingly fragile interpretation of Isolde's *Liebestod* by the aged opera singer Elfriede Rezabek. But, despite these temptations, Meyerhof/Schlingensief closes the curtain: 'That was really lovely, I thank you all so much, but I don't want to yet, no, I simply don't want to yet.'

Schlingensief, who distributes the Eucharist as the Messiah in *A Church of Fear*, is a strange saviour. He has the world revolve around him because it is *his* world. It comes about with him, and it expires with him as well. Church nave, operatics and loaded symbolism claim nothing more than: this is my world, in which I have to put together my own beliefs, my own standards, and my own will to survive.

'Vote for yourself' was the slogan Schlingensief gave his party *Chance 2000*. What sounds egotistical or egocentric is, for him, the only way to generate equality and genuine collectivity. 'Believe in yourself.' A church nave filled with individual churches. Schlingensief is not only a romantic, he is also an existentialist: the birds in the forest don't sing when he isn't there.

– Translated by Michael Turnbull

Endnotes

1. Sontag, S. (1978), *Illness as Metaphor*, New York: Farrar, Straus and Giroux, p. 3.

2. In *A Church of Fear*, Mira Partecke quotes Salvador Elizondo in an abridged and revised form.

3. E.g. Peter Michalzik in the *Frankfurter Rundschau* (17 July 2004): 'When I first heard that Schlingensief, the pure fool, was doing *Parsifal*, I thought: that's perfect'.

4. See, for example, Schlingensief's remarks in *Der Tagesspiegel* (26 July 2004): 'I am convinced I'll get cancer after *Parsifal*, like Heiner Müller.' Or in the *Frankfurter Rundschau* (17 July 2004): 'I'm very moved when I hear that *Parsifal* was Wagner's departure from the world. Deep inside I have imagined that it's my departing piece [...] I have the feeling as if everything has boiled down to *Parsifal*. I've often thought I'll probably get cancer after *Parsifal*, or a stroke, or that a car accident will happen.'

5. 'The specific thing about theatre is not the presence of the living audience, but the presence of someone who may actually die.' In Kluge, A. and Müller, H. (1996), *Ich bin ein Landvermesser. Gespräche mit Heiner Müller, neue Folge*, Hamburg: Rotbuch Verlag, p. 95. In *A Church of Fear*, Schlingensief varies this sentence to have Angela Winkler say: 'The special thing is not the presence of the living priest or the living congregation, but the presence of someone who may actually die.'

6. This element has been somewhat suspended in operas like *Parsifal*, but also in *A Church of Fear* and *Mea Culpa*, in which Schlingensief appears very little on stage, or not at all, and does not influence the performance from outside while it is taking place.

7. Premiere at the Berlin Volksbühne on 17 November 2004.

8. Jörg Immendorf, one of the most successful post-war painters, himself suffered from ALS and died in 2007.

9. Sontag, S. (1978), p. 5.

10. Ibid.

11. Carl Hegemann, Anna-Maria Mahler and Sören Schuhmacher realized *Joan of Arc—Scenes from the life of St. Joan* by Walter Braunfels (premiere 27 April 2008 at the Deutsche Oper Berlin) from Schlingensief's notes and instructions.

12. Premiere 13 November 2008 on the studio stage of the Maxim-Gorki-Theater in Berlin.

13. Schlingensief, C. (2009), *So schön wie hier kanns im Himmel gar nicht sein!*, Köln: Kiepenheuer & Witsch, p. 243.

14. Ibid.

15. "'Why me?" (meaning "It's not fair") is the question of many who learn they have cancer'. Sontag, S. (1978), p. 38.

16. Schlingensief, C. (2009), p. 72, and Margit Carstensen in *A Church of Fear*.

17. The idea of the 'Stranger in Me', which Schlingensief alludes to in the title, takes up the widespread analogy of cancer as a kind of 'demonic pregnancy' (Sontag, S. (1978), p. 14), and is familiar from countless science-fiction films, the most well-known of which is probably Ridley Scott's *Alien* (1979). 'Cancer is the disease of the Other. Cancer proceeds by a science fiction scenario: an invasion of "alien" or "mutant" cells, stronger than normal cells. [...] Cancer could be described as a triumphant mutation, and mutation is now mainly an image for cancer'. Sontag, S. (1978), p. 68.

18. Sontag, S. (1978), p. 55.

19. The feelings that Schlingensief provokes are, in this way, in line with society's attitude to illness in general: cancer 'is felt to be obscene—in the original meaning of the word: ill-omened, abominable, repugnant to the senses' (Sontag, S. (1978), p. 9).

20. The piece is, in fact, difficult to discuss within the categories of theatre criticism. It is noticeable that most critics expressed their remarks favourably but cautiously. Only the *Frankfurter Allgemeine Zeitung* declared that 'the evening [was] all that— on the one hand this, on the other hand that, and both of them at once. But it cannot be criticized. All that remains is the wish for a swift recovery'. *Frankfurter Allgemeine Zeitung* (23 September 2008).

21. The gospel chorus 'Angels' Voices' and the children's choir of the Aalto-Theater.

22. Played by the growth-restricted Karin Witt, also an old friend from Schlingensief's previous work.

23. Schlingensief, C. (2009), p. 235.

24. Christoph Schlingensief in the programme of *Mea Culpa* (2009), p. 8.

25. 'I have come to the strong conviction that during the Bayreuth time I crossed a boundary in my life. In my imagination I have always played a little with the death wish. [...] But with *Parsifal* it was no longer a game. [...] I wanted to do the production so well that I let the music send me on the very trip Wagner intended. [...] I now believe that it really is the music of death, dangerous music that doesn't celebrate life, but death. Wagner was squirting poison'. Schlingensief, C. (2009), p. 171.

26. Schlingensief is indeed fervently pushing ahead with the setting up of such an opera house—probably in Burkina Faso. Despite his illness, he has frequently travelled to Africa and has meanwhile received promises of financial support from official sources such as the German Foreign Ministry.

27. See Schlingensief, C. (2009), p. 46, et al. and 'Of course I'd be happy if this Africa project were to turn out to be the road that leads to victory over the disease' (p. 65).

BLURRING BOUNDARIES/CHANGING PERSPECTIVES: AN INTERVIEW WITH CHRISTOPH SCHLINGENSIEF

Florian Malzacher

Your work always builds on itself and develops further certain themes, motifs, and also aesthetic approaches. Mea Culpa *has now become the third part of a trilogy about your illness with cancer.*

I have certainly produced work that was deliberately and purposefully developed to attract attention and nothing more. But sometimes that was a mistake because doing that turned out to be completely uninteresting. The best things were those that developed unintentionally, where the work, for example, came into being as a result of an invitation out of the blue. That is even more clearly the case with the three pieces about cancer. They came out of nowhere – out of the shock that came with this illness. And, of course, it turned everything upside down. Suddenly all of my 350 kilometre-per-hour plans— my life at the time was super fast—were brought to a halt. But at the same time I didn't see any reason to brake because cancer has to do with death and with the limitations of time that one has, but that wasn't really clear to me at the time. It was actually a massive disruption. Like something that wants to prevent you from doing the work that is pulling at you. When I looked at the X-ray, I suddenly became very hot, as if I had made a huge mistake. The first thing I felt was a certain sense of guilt. In that moment, I probably already sensed: This is really such an insane rupture it is almost impossible to imagine. And then a flood of questions followed: What happens now? Operation? Radiotherapy? Chemotherapy? Will I still exist after the operation? And will I still have a voice afterwards? Because the doctor thought that he might have to remove my vocal nerves. And then you wake up and you can speak—that was really such a relief. Then my appetite returned and I came to terms with the whole situation, so I was optimistic. That is something that has remained with me. That is to say: I always have moments when I think: This is great, things go on. And then I fall to pieces again, you know: A complete nervous wreck, with absolutely no idea about how to cope with it, and I just think: It's all over. And there is no way of driving a wedge between myself and it, or of flinging open a window.

It was thus pure expediency to say: good, if you have fear, then talk about fear. So the old automatism returned: If you have a problem, don't think it away, deal with it. Then use it, grab it, and channel your sorrow into a comrade-in-arms. So I had to give form to it, create images, in order to cope with it and at first I thought: We will make a film as soon as I get out of hospital. A comedy about someone who has cancer and who only meets crazy people. Then I thought: That would just be the old sales and suppression strategy, i.e. how do I give form to it in a way that people notice that I'm in control—and of course I'm not in control of it at all! It's the complete opposite. It is probably the hardest experience of my life. In this case, I can stand neither above nor below it. This time I have definitely landed somewhere else. I am in it.

You made notes with the help of a dictaphone...

Yes, even in the first weeks, I recorded nearly every day what I experienced there and what happened when the doctor or the palliative nurse came etc. And in the evenings, I didn't listen to it again. I did, however, cry and talk into the device, when nobody was there. It wasn't a speech, or material, at that stage, for a book. It was simply a collection of everything that was racing through my head at the time. And then I had the idea of making a piece out of it—which I began to rehearse in the flat... from an automated bed with a remote control from the hospital. That was immediately a flop because, as a result of the Chemo, I wasn't able to continue. Aino, my girlfriend at the time and now my wife[1], tried to reconstruct the material that I had worked on laboriously in the flat, on the rehearsal stage of the Maxim Gorki Theater. That resulted in the first performance of *Zwischenstand der Dinge* (*The Current State of Things*) which took place in a very intimate atmosphere with no press allowed. I made it while still in shock. Guests were invited solely via a text message—no other announcement was made. We had sixty or seventy seats for people including neighbours and friends, but also Bob Wilson and Volker Spengler, Werner Schroeter, who has cancer himself, Martin Wuttke... And because it was an evening without pressure and without a discussion afterwards, it was an incredible source of power for me: We pulled it off. Somehow it worked.

At that point I thought: Stick with this theme. And *Zwischenstand* was further developed into *Kirche der Angst* (*A Church of Fear for the Stranger in Me*) for the Ruhr-Triennale, as a sort of requiem or 'cancer mass'. It was a huge success yet a different kind of success than previously. Something really happened between the audience and us – it was sincere and, to a certain extent, tragic. I also appeared in a short scene at the end of the performance that utilized the liturgy of a Catholic mass. But on the fifth or sixth evening, I thought: That's enough. I don't want to make touring theatre, or something, for people with cancer. That can't be the case and it has no future. And then came the third part in the Burgtheater Vienna and, with it, the risk that people would perhaps think: Yeah, yeah, here he goes again about his illness… But then the situation changed again. The metastasen suddenly disappeared as a result of a tablet, something which, according to the doctors, wasn't really possible in that period of time. After four or five weeks, I had a CT scan in which none could be found! How does that come about? The third part of the trilogy is concerned with life going on. What do you do, when you step back into reality, but you can't perceive it as real because you previously thought you were already dead?

Figure 1: *A Church of Fear for the Stranger in Me*, 2008. Photo: David Baltzer

When someone dies, it is the loneliest path there is. It is not about hand-holding or whatever: My father smiled at the end. That was, however, a smile that I couldn't understand. Was it, perhaps, the smile of someone face to face with a secret society that had taken him in? To see that was a heavy burden for me because he also told us that, in two weeks, he would be dead. And in two weeks he was dead. They are exceptional circumstances and we lack the criteria for working through them.

Can one actually grasp something like that in a production?

It can only function via music, and perhaps also via beliefs, i.e. individual beliefs. One couldn't go further with some sort of objective realism. Only through that which is ritualistic, almost sacred can one produce something that is befitting and moving. And the third part *Mea Culpa* was perhaps the most difficult: an uncertain resurrection, a celebration of life in the face of the inevitability of death.

In the middle of the stage, almost invisibly, I presided over the church, that is, the *Kirche der Angst*. Within it the ritual continues and someone there celebrates a requiem while outside are the treatment rooms and life follows its normal course... It is once again an argument [*Auseinandersetzung*] with the realization that redemption is actually a concept that is completely misunderstood, and which one connects with something great and sublime. But redemption is the most individualistic, small, and awful step that there is. Because he who is done for, who seeks only to be redeemed gives himself over to total loneliness and surrenders everything that makes him who he is. That he is then told that everything will be fine and that he can cope—this is not really what is on his mind...If one has been through such a situation and come through it, one has more interest in people than before. One sees them differently. I look at them as if I were already standing a step outside of them. One looks at them perhaps not more exactly, not analytically, but longer. Humans and human life gain a different value. Everything is no longer taken for granted.

Sometimes of course, I slip into old mechanisms in my work, but they don't really come through. It doesn't become a show, because I don't want that anymore. The distance is greater.

Previously you were always on stage and committed to being involved. It was precisely this lack of distance that defined your work. From the earliest theatre productions on, you had to be able to join in, because otherwise you couldn't respond to the reactions of the public and the actors' routines. And now suddenly this composure?

Yes. I already had that with *Kirche der Angst*, when I simply pull back and my team reconstructs the work. And then I say, let's put that in for now, and I lean back and look at it. Previously I didn't permit such a situation. I didn't want to see it. I didn't want anything finished which is why I hesitated until the premiere. I was downright afraid that it would be finished. Now I mould the 'sculpture' more in my mind, and no longer believe that I have to work on it with an axe, hammer and a chisel. Now I can turn off more quickly. I am more interested in the total composition, which means that I need to be able to observe everything. And I also don't fiddle around with the actors' bodies as I used to and flip out in front of their faces, so that they no longer know how they should act. In the past, I always had muscular pain in the evening, because I actually wanted to play all of the roles. And now I just write the texts and concentrate more on looking. That is my job.

Figure 2: *Mea Culpa: A ReadyMade Opera,* Burgtheater, Vienna, 2009. Photo: Georg Soulek.

Your previous work was, in part, shaped by a notable paradox: you are, on the one hand, a complete control freak—you can't leave the actors alone on the stage—and, on the other hand, you produce permanent chaos in order to limit or thwart your own control. Has control become less important for you?

It could well be. It pleases me when things evolve more from themselves. I have less strength, but I think more. The whole time, I occupy myself with the texts, images and particularly the music. And at night I search for pieces of music, which is something I didn't previously do. I try to respond when someone doesn't understand something, whereas in the past, my immediate reaction was: Out! These days, someone will leave rather than me having to say he should no longer be there. But the control is greater, because I see it as an image, as a composition. I have to feel it first. Previously I almost had to catapult myself into a trance at each rehearsal.

The musicality that I have with opera is now more and more important. With theatre, one thinks a lot, und that is something that one can make great use of, but the structure is easily lost. The opera has more stability and provides a framework which is organic and not compulsive. A singer has to accept that he sings, he can't just jump around. And for that reason, we don't do a lot of theatrics with them, they should simply sing. I don't believe them anyway when they start to introduce their pretence of naturalism.

So more the image of the whole—there is still control, but less getting tangled up in the details, in order to see the larger arc...

...and to also accept that this is simply how it is now. And not, as in the past, change something in the last few weeks and cut the text, so that the whole production dies in the process. I don't do that anymore, because I really fight hard for the subject matter. And even if the text is, at first, a jumble of words, the music clarifies what is happening. I now think in a very musical way. When you are lying in bed, there are not a lot of alternatives... I thought a lot while I was in bed, spoke a lot, read a lot but also listened to a lot of music. In terms of your question about rhythm, it is also interesting when you are simply lying there with an embolism. You simply do not have any chance of producing rhythm.

Is the work then more disembodied? Less physical?

Yes, I believe so... In the past we pulled viewers onto the stage, bound them, and then smeared them with Nivea cream; a latent form of rape or something. It was, in any case, so corporeal that people went out and cried, because they couldn't handle the violence that had befallen them during their visit to the theatre. We found that pretty great and exciting.

Although at times we also had a bad conscience. That I hurt people because I pulled them onto the stage was, perhaps, justifiable at the time, but at the moment, I have no connection to it, even a certain sense of disgust. Because that type of act makes the arrogant claim that: We are the ones who see through everything and will show you that we are breaking the rules and acknowledge no taboos. This attitude has become rather alien to me now. One can also employ theatre as a place where one can think. Back then, however, I couldn't do that, because I felt virtually compelled to get into fights on the stage. We only enjoyed it when there was a ruckus. I don't want to say that that was completely wrong—there were indeed great nights. Often, there were metaphysical moments as well. But people change.

The explicitly and concretely political work that emerged in this period—Kühnen 94, the party Chance 2000, the Vienna Container-Project Please Love Austria, the Hamlet production with the Neo-Nazis in Zürich: How did these projects develop? Your work in film had often sought to draw mythical, historical connections...

At the age of eight—1968—I made a super-8 film with my father's camera, where a farmer had to wave flags and three children in go-carts knocked him down and ran away. There was also a shootout or something similar. I don't want to say that that was political, but something is captured in that image. During my school years, I would always have rows with the teachers because, for me they were too political, one-sidedly political. I once started a row with a teacher and had to leave the classroom, because I said that she only approached things from a left perspective, and that was too boring for me. The Oberhausen Short Film Festival also didn't give me much pleasure because to my mind it was only pseudo political. People were invited from the eastern block to show their boring films. And then our worst film-makers would show their films in Leipzig or somewhere else.

My father always received telegrams from the CDU [Christian Democratic Union] camp. I partly learned their contents by heart so that I—as a sixteen year old at the SPD [Social Democratic Party] voting stands—could use it in an argument against them. Simply as verbal fireworks. I did, however, always read those telegrams. And in Oberhausen, where very little information circulated, I also played around with statistics that they couldn't rebut. Or I worked together with the KPD-ML [The Communist Party of Germany/Marxists-Leninists] because they claimed that an egg should only cost two or three pfennigs. At first I thought it was a great idea until I realized: the chicken doesn't get anything out of it. So it was quite clear that I hadn't really become political at all—it was rather something like an overarching need for recognition.

Later as a student in Munich, I began to develop a sense of antipathy toward the Film Academy. At that time I became interested in the films of Werner Herzog, because they were so detached. They were so strange. *Even Dwarfs Started Small* was the kind of film I liked. I found it political. In contrast, I found these explicitly political films by Reinhard Hauff, Margarethe von Trotta and others to be no good at all. I also felt, in part, extremely aggressive towards Wenders: reproducing stupid crap from America, but so badly. But I liked *The American Friend*, and I thought *Alice in the Cities* and *The State of Things* were great. I liked, in a sense, their avowal that someone had failed. That one can't leave the city. Or that one has cancer and wants to rescue the family.

I actually felt at home with Werner Nekes for whom I worked as an assistant, and I gathered ammunition from experimental films that could be used against mainstream cinema. i.e. Stan Brakhage and Andy Warhol. For me, that was political enough. My work only became politically explicit with *Menu Total*—that was in 1986. In this film, Helge Schneider—who was unknown back then—ran around playing a young boy who wanted to become Hitler, and who wiped out his family. And later they all rise again and are redeemed…

Where did your interest in Hitler and National Socialism come from?

Well, I don't quite know anymore. I think Dietrich Kuhlbrodt somehow pointed me in that direction[2]. He thought *Tunguska* was good because he found Nekes and all that fuss about avant-garde filmmakers to be rather caricaturish. I turned up at the right moment. And then suddenly he would start telling me things. He was a lawyer for Nazi crimes, always travelling around, and he talked about it.

I think Nazis were always an interesting theme for me because I also found camps so interesting…obviously I liked to watch Pasolini's films, I liked *Sodom*…they were films that presumed to have people in their grip and to confine them…and from there to build Nationalism. Aesthetically, that was, for me, eerily appealing: humans under observation, humans in camps, humans in their little nests. Or maybe like me here now in my little cancer room.

Menu Total was a complete failure then. My father said, the film is terrible, Nekes thought it was fascistic, and the newspaper only printed small comments such as 'pubertal crap'. The film was a goner—nobody was interested. It was shown at the Berlinale but flopped. But for me the film is essential, more so now than before. It's gotten better over time—it stands on its own. From there things went on with the Chainsaw film[3]: I saw the fall of the wall on television and then people called me up, 'Did you see that, the reunification, we're celebrating it here in Berlin, it's absolute madness!' And I was in Mülheim sitting in my little cubbyhole and I thought to myself: 'what a load of shit!'. Then I sat down and wrote the screenplay—we had just shown *The Texas Chainsaw Massacre* in the cinema downstairs. And that was then the film that got a sensational reception in Hof.

Figure 3: Schlingensief and camera. © Christoph Schlingensief

What about Fassbinder whom - through your choice of actors alone - you repeatedly quote? How did he come into play?

He was always important. I was once permitted to watch him through a pane of glass and see how he was directing *Maria Braun* or *Lili Marleen*...even then I felt quite a lot of enthusiasm for his work. I thought *Satan's Brew* was incredible and *Fear Eats the Soul*. And then all the discussions about him—one noticed that Germany was processing itself through them.

And there was also Joseph Beuys who appeared in my life when I was sixteen because I had the opportunity to see him. I liked it that the well-off old gents at the Lions Club, where my father was a member, invited Beuys but were then shocked when he said: 'In seven years this social system will be completely destroyed.' Before that, he had spoken about something or other that they found boring. They were all half asleep. When he said that, they all woke up and started to collectively bellow. From that I noted that there are sentences that make such an impression on people that they simply become afraid. Fassbinder was also someone who said such things. That interested me.

So were you mainly interested in Fassbinder's gestures or was there something in his films that you could use as a tool?

I was actually fixated on Herzog. Herzog was, for me, the one who introduced a kind of mythical madness. I was interested in Fassbinder but was not so politically engaged. Parallel to his work, I saw films by John Waters and Kenneth Anger…completely messed up films…at that time I was in the cinema three or four times a day, no joke, for around two or three years at the film museum. It began at noon and in fact I didn't study at all. The politics that I heard were always such an either/or affair. To be totally involved or not at all was too abhorrent to me. I found what Fassbinder said important and that became increasingly the case. However the political side really got started for me at the Volksbühne, with the actor Bernhard Schütz and also with things like *100 Years CDU*.

So the step into the specifically political and the step into the performative went hand in hand?

I can't really explain how that happened. However it has to do with the fact that I did not do it out of resolve. It simply turned out that way. Also, the motivation to found a political party arose only because I simply thought: that's quite enough of Kohl now. How does one found a political party? And above all, the slogan 'Vote for yourself'—I found that interesting! Beuys had previously come up with the slogan, but I didn't know that…Perhaps I was always already political but just from an aesthetic point of view. And what I am doing now is perhaps even more political because it assumes that the individual can't deal with himself.

The move out of film and into the performative—can you describe why film was no longer sufficient? What made you seek out the live event and direct contact with the audience?

It was already the case for me while making films as a youngster: When I got a helicopter to fly up and down in front of a bank with the camera trained on it and actors from the Oberhausen City Theatre running around under it—and we were sixteen or seventeen years old—it was naturally a sensation for the place! The moment was priceless; one was suddenly a film director! I think that for me the film work was about the adventure of shooting. The greatest thing—including the crises and so on—was that one was really trembling and shaking. It nearly made you an addict, the shot of adrenalin you got when there was a bit of fluff on the film or when material was returned that was out of focus or developed incorrectly.

Nonetheless you stopped making films for a while.

The free form of working that I had envisioned simply didn't work out. I thought that the funding bodies would gradually realize that I was serious and would finance my projects, but it became more and more difficult. Then – at some point – they said yes, they would give me money again, but I would have to promise not to make any more films. That was meant humorously, the way everything is always supposed to be funny. But it hit me rather hard. So, nothing worked anymore, although the *Terror* film was co-produced, it wasn't shown on television. Not even now! So I sort of gave up and worked on films for schools.

So you stopped making films more for financial reasons and not out of the desire for another medium. Rather a less-than-ideal solution?

Yes, after I shot *Terror 2000* in 1993, the Volksbühne called. *Terror 2000* was a very important film for me. It also resulted in punch-ups in the cinema. The Berlinale turned it down and so people showed the film in rented cinemas. My films were considered scandalous anyway—and I liked playing along with it. It was fun for me because I found the films to be honest—they really portrayed how Germany was at the time. Frank Castorf, head director of the Volksbühne, and dramaturge Matthias Lilienthal liked the film, and Lilienthal phoned and asked if I would like to come. I didn't know the Volksbühne and so I called friends who said: 'you have to go, that is *the* theatre' and 'wow, crazy, insane'. So I went there and saw *Clockwork Orange*[4] where Herbert Fritsch was hanging on a plank that rose up higher and higher and he hung on—three metres, four metres and, at some point, I left the room because I thought: 'I can't watch that anymore'. The guy is half mad and I am absolutely not interested in seeing whether he falls down. And then Lilienthal caught me in the stairwell and asked me where I was going, and I said to him quite openly that that wasn't for me. But then he started yacking away...anyway I said to him I must have my team with me. At the time, they did all that stuff. We were all living in a huge flat in Charlottenburg. There were, I think, fifteen of us and a tiny toilet. Actually it was pretty bad but it was, of course, a great space to try things out in. And the production *100 Years CDU* came out...and in fact only Marianne

Hoppe thought it was great. She thought it was like theatre in the twenties, a revue. The others ripped it to shreds and I was actually disappointed as well, but Lilienthal wanted me to continue.

Making theatre is always for the moment. Was it sometimes too ephemeral for you?

I always have the feeling that film people know that films can also be seen later. One can get hold of them in ten or in fifty years. A film critic knows that when he writes something now, he has to stand by it or admit that his opinion changed over the course of time. Film people have a different rhythm in consideration to, and in defence of, their work. And theatre people know; ah well, fine. If it's crap today, then tomorrow there'll be *Hamlet,* and then that and then that…that's the difference. In theatre I grasped more and more that it only made sense if I could take something away with me, if I developed myself. I certainly believe, and one can see it in my work more and more, that I am a repeat offender.

During that period, you deliberately expanded your stage activities to include the press. Sometimes one had the impression that you were playing with the media more than they were playing with you.

That appeared to be the case at the time, above all in relation to the party *Chance 2000.* There I obviously pulled out all the stops that I could think of. We would laugh ourselves silly at night about the reports that came out and stuff that was printed. But in other respects, I am still surprised at how some things were blown up out of nothing. Sometimes I hadn't done anything at all except that destiny had perhaps sorted the cards that way. For example, some years ago, *Der Spiegel* wrote an article saying how dilapidated, washed up, and lacking in ideas I was. That came out the week before I did the container in Vienna [*Please Love Austria*]. And afterwards, everybody wanted to hug me; people turned up at the airport and wanted autographs. And today, in regard to my illness, one sees people who celebrate me because they can suddenly find a way to understand my work and recognize something in it…like honesty and so on—but I was always honest. They are only noticing it now. Only when one has had a syringe in the arm or has gone through three withdrawal treatments is one considered to be a decent person. In any case they, themselves, are the purest. And now the *Bild Zeitung* [tabloid newspaper] wants to do home stories and talkshows are calling me up…and everything I say is blown up and turned into a political issue, even when I'm just being silly. I think to myself: What a shame, I can no longer say nor do something simply normal. And then I just shut up and don't do anything. My illness gives me the advantage of saying: I don't want to talk to you, or, I am tired. That is also different from before.

But in contrast, critics or journalists feel themselves to be part of the production—as if there were no outside perspective from which to report about the work… That is a great effect because the boundaries between art and non-art, between production and reception are fluid. I like the notion that everyone is contributing to my artwork, including the critics and journalists and also the audience, so that it assumes its own independent existence.

When your work is discussed, mention is soon made of the way in which boundaries between art and life are blurred. When you were directing in Bayreuth, an analogy was made—by the media, but also by you yourself—between Parsifal and Schlingensief. When you became ill, that was taken to a new level. It actually seemed as if the narrative were scripting your life and not the other way around, as if your life were retrospectively heading towards this moment, and everyone was writing as if your life were a novel.

I often thought in terms of film when I was young—a walk with my parents through the forest in Duisburg existed only insofar as I considered possible plots and characters. Then, things partially began to take on a life of their own and something would occur that I had previously seen in a dream or fantasy, but only because the possibility already existed anyway. That is not artificial—and it is simply logical that such things happen. But this Bayreuth story is more difficult—also for me personally—to comprehend. I had dreamt of the phone call asking me to direct. Then it actually happened. I thought that it was somebody playing 'Candid Camera'. And now with the illness, I sometimes think that perhaps I instigated it somehow. That I was really thinking of Heiner Müller's fate, or said at some stage: 'After this it's all over, then I will get cancer'[5]. But this illness is not just my concern. Rather, it is also related to society and not only because we are all breathing in the same toxins, but also because we don't know what we have to defend anymore. Our immune system is—and here I am not being esoteric—one body and in itself has to be very finely calibrated. The human being must be considered in its entirety. And one forgets that when he allows himself to be constantly distracted and has to permanently enact a role as if he were somebody that he is in fact not, then, he cannot protect who he really is. He just lets it all go and loses himself—and that paves the way for such low immunity problems. I fear that that is what I practised myself: All doors wide open and we are producing the greatest things the world has ever seen! And, to top it off, the *Parsifal* material; I wasn't the right person for it until I got myself so worked up about it. And out of the wound of Amfortas came my illness. Maybe, maybe not. Maybe that itself is the old megalomania, if I think that even the illness is my fault.

Through your work on Parsifal *it also became clear that there were strong leitmotifs present in your work that had reoccurred over many years…*

…exactly, for example 'redemption'. It's lunacy! It was already there in *Menu Total*: 'Your Saviour has come'—and Helge then kills them[6]. At the end they are all redeemed and run around in a circle and the family is together again. It is the performance of a system. And I also believe that Opera is well suited as a performance of a system, but a system that is transformed through music with its rhythms teased out. So whoever is not softened up after four and a half hours of *Parsifal,* to the point where they are totally wiped out, is extremely resistant. Wagner did that in a highly skilled way. Of course, there are people who are not remotely interested in it, thank God! I now also have a distance from it. I liked it very much, but it was probably the worst work I have ever done which, perhaps, drove me – healthwise – into this hole because I did not have my immune system under control and was preoccupied with idiocy such as: This is now 'the last time' and 'this will probably be my greatest work' and 'after this I will die…'. 'Here it is, you asked for it'—So I was also traversing this horrible territory.

You say redemption is a motif – are there others?

When I was sixteen I met a producer who saw *Hey Mummy, we're making a movie*[7] and then said to me: 'One can see from this film that you will never be able to love anybody…you are not interested in the characters.' But that was just a gag, Grandma riding a motorbike into the henhouse and all that stuff. I suffered so much because of that—I had problems with girls, I couldn't approach them and was very shy—all that led to having relationships that were fine, that were good, but that somehow just died. They just didn't work out anymore. And even then, when I became ill, I tried to get rid of Aino in line with the notion: Don't burden anyone else, I'll see it through alone. And something has come from this that I have never experienced before where I believe: I have now found love. There is someone who makes it extremely clear that she loves me which, for her, is a fact that she is sticking to and that's the end of it! That, however, is quite unbelievable. And I am happy about this miracle.

Perhaps that is also connected with the way in which your parents continually appear in your work. Is the analysis of family also a leitmotif?

Yes, that is something strange. I have never separated from my family. Everything continues to happen in the form of this Father—Mother—child triangle. I will simply never grow up. Why the family has shaped me so strongly and why even today, I participate in an argument with my Father, who died three years ago, and why—if all goes well with me—I have to clear things up with my Mother, I don't know. That's just how it is.

Apart from your biological family, there is also a family, or perhaps more correctly, several families of people, with whom you have worked—in mutual trust—often over many, many years: Actors such as Irm Hermann, Margit Carstensen, Udo Kier, who have often appeared in your films. But also the disabled people, who have had an important influence on your work.

I believe that it is a type of mutual trust that I need, a kind of trust that was perhaps also cultivated by Fassbinder. There is a long-term continuity that, for me, is very natural.

Alongside actors, you have always included lay people in your work. How did that come about—did you want more 'reality' on stage? Or did their disruptive presence interest you, as counterparts to the more routine actors?

The so-called lay people play themselves rather than roles on stage. It is always exciting to watch them and they are also a challenge for the so-called profis. There are professional actors who can't stand being together with lay people on stage. It plunges them deep into self-doubt…

For a long time now Africa has also been a recurring motif in your work. Is that an exotic place of longing or is it somewhere that really exists, somewhere that you really found on your travels?

For a long time now I have felt deeply connected to Africa. I have shot films in different African countries and I frequently feel more at home there than I do in familiar Europe. The idea for an opera house with a school and a church and a hospital ward is moving closer to being realized in Burkina Faso. The money and the support are there. I am obsessed with this anti-colonial cultural exchange of life forms. But that is a big topic and we will have to speak about it another time …

– Translated by Anna Teresa Scheer and Tara Forrest

Endnotes

1.   *Translators' Notes:* Schlingensief and Aino Labarenz were married in August 2009.

2.   Dietrich Kuhlbrodt was a lawyer at the Hamburg District Court for the persecution of crimes under National Socialism. In addition to working as a film and theatre critic, he has also performed in many of Schlingensief's films and stage productions.

3.   Schlingensief is referring here to his 1990 film *The German Chainsaw Massacre: The First Hour of Reunification.*

4.   *Clockwork Orange* (1993) based on the novel by Anthony Burgess (1962), was directed by Frank Castorf and featured a scene in which actor Herbert Fritsch (known for his risk-taking) was suspended on a plank that was raised 5 metres above the stage with no safety net or railings to grasp.

5.   Dramatist and director Heiner Müller directed Wagner's *Tristan and Isolde* (1995) at Bayreuth and subsequently died of cancer in the same year.

6.   Here Schlingensief is referring to the unconventional film *Menu Total, Meat Your Parents* (1986), which he made with German comedian Helge Schneider in the main role as a crazed character who kills his parents.

7.   *Mensch, Mami, wir dreh'n 'nen Film* (1977) was a humorous short film made by Schlingensief.

SELECTED READING LIST

English language texts

Books

Koegel, A. and König, K. (eds.) (2005), *AC: Christoph Schlingensief: Church of Fear*, Köln: Museum Ludwig and Verlag der Buchhandlung Walther König. [Text in English and German.]

Chapters and Essays

Dapp, G. (2006), 'Christoph Schlingensief—Bambiland (Inszenierung Burgtheater Wien)', in G. Dapp, *Mediaclash in Political Theatre: Building on and Continuing Brecht*, Marburg: Tectum, pp. 118–134.

Forrest, T. (2008), 'Mobilizing the Public Sphere: Schlingensief's Reality Theatre', *Contemporary Theatre Review*, 18:1, pp. 90–98.

Gade, S. (2005), 'Playing the media keyboard: the political potential of performativity in Christoph Schlingensief's electioneering circus', in R. Gade and A. Jerslev (eds.), *Performative Realism: Interdisciplinary Studies in Art and Media*, Copenhagen: Museum Tusculanum Press, pp. 19–49.

Hughes, D. (2006), 'Everything in Excess—Christoph Schlingensief and the Crisis of the German Left', *The Germanic Review*, 81:4, pp. 317–339.

Irmer, T. (2002), 'Out with the Right! Or, Let's Not Let Them in Again' (trans. C. Wilsch), *Theater*, 32:3, pp. 61–67.

Jestrovic, S. (2008), 'Performing like an asylum seeker: paradoxes of hyper-authenticity', *Research on Drama Education: The Journal of Applied Theatre and Performance*, 13:2, pp. 159–170.

Langston, R. (2008), 'Schlingensief's Peep-Show: Post-Cinematic Spectacles and the Public Space of History', in R. Halle and R. Steingröver (eds.), *After the Avant-Garde: Contemporary German and Austrian Experimental Film*, New York: Camden House, pp. 204-221.

Parsley, C. (2005), 'Public Art, Public Law', *Continuum: Journal of Media & Cultural Studies*, 19:2, pp. 239–253.

Thomas-Vander Lugt, K. (2007), 'Better living through splatter: Christoph Schlingensief's unsightly bodies and the politics of gore', in S. Hantke (ed.), *Caligari's heirs: the German cinema of fear after 1945*, Lanham: Scarecrow Press, pp. 163-184.

Varney, D. (2007), 'Gestus, affect and the post-semiotic in contemporary theatre', *The International Journal of the Arts in Society*, 1:3, pp.113-120.

German language texts

Books

Gilles, C. (2009), *Kunst und Nichtkunst: Das Theater von Christoph Schlingensief*, Würzburg: Königshausen & Neumann.

Heineke, T. and Umathum, S. (eds.) (2002), *Christoph Schlingensiefs Nazis Rein/Torsten Lemmer in Nazis Raus*, Frankfurt am Main: Suhrkamp Verlag.

Koegel, A. and König, K. (eds.) (2005), *AC: Christoph Schlingensief: Church of Fear*, Köln: Museum Ludwig and Verlag der Buchhandlung Walther König. [Text in German and English.]

Kotte, A. and Gerber, F. (2007), *Theater im Kasten: Rimini Protokoll—Castorfs Video—Beuys & Schlingensief—Lars von Trier*, Zürich: Chronos.

Lilienthal, M. and Philipp, C. (eds.) (2000), *Schlingensiefs Ausländer Raus. Bitte Liebt Österreich*, Frankfurt am Main: Suhrkamp Verlag.

Lochte, J. and Schulz, W. (eds.) (1998), *Schlingensief! Notruf für Deutschland. Über die Mission, das Theater und die Welt des Christoph Schlingensief*, Hamburg: Rotbuch Verlag.

Maubach, B. (2005), *Christoph Schlingensiefs Deutschlandtrilogie – Geschichts – und Gesellschaftsdiagnose im Film*, Norderstedt: Grin Verlag.

Schlingensief, C. and Hegemann, C. (1998), *Chance 2000: Wähle Dich selbst*, Köln: Kiepenheuer & Witsch.

Schlingensief, C. (1998), *Talk 2000*, Wien: Deuticke.

Schlingensief, C. and Stüttgen, J. (2000), *Zum Kapital: Als Christoph Schlingensief Das Unsichtbare Gesucht Hat*, Wangen: FIU Verlag.

Schlingensief, C. (2002), *Rosebud*, Köln: Kiepenheuer & Witsch.

Schlingensief, C. (2009), *So schön wie hier kanns im Himmel gar nicht sein: Tagebuch einer Krebserkrankung*, Köln: Kiepenheuer & Witsch.

Chapters, Essays and Interviews

Diedrichson, D. (2002), 'Magie und Massenarbeitslosigkeit, Christoph Schlingensiefs "Chance 2000" im "Prater" in Prenzlauer Berg', in A. Wewerka (ed.), *Zeichen 4, Engagement und Skandal*, Berlin: Alexander Verlag, pp. 99–122.

Hoffmann, A. (2000), 'Scheitern als Chance: Zur Dramaturgie von Christoph Schlingensief', in P. Reichel (ed.), *Studien zur Dramaturgie: Kontexte, Implikationen, Berufspraxis*, Tübingen: Gunter Narr Verlag, pp. 217-311.

Kluge, A. and Schlingensief, C. (2001), 'Ein Kaktus für Richard Wagner: Schlingensiefs *Ring des Nibelungen* in Africa', in C. Schulte and R. Gußmann (eds.), *Alexander Kluge, Facts & Fakes, Fernseh-Nachschriften 2/3: Herzblut trifft Kunstblut—Erster imaginärer Opernführer*, Berlin: Vorwerk 8, pp. 4–8.

Kluge, A. and Schlingensief, C. (2007), 'In erster Linie bin ich Filmemacher: Begegnung mit Christoph Schlingensief', in S. Huber and C. Philipp (eds.), *Alexander Kluge: Magazin des Glücks*, Wien: Springer-Verlag, pp. 109–114.

Lau, M. (1998), 'Der Dilettant als Medienphänomen—Über den Regisseur, Moderator und Hauptdarsteller Christoph Schlingensief', in *Theater Heute*, 5, pp. 4–11.

Löhndorf, M. (1998), 'Lieblingsziel Totalirritation', in *Kunstforum*, Vol. 142/ Issue 10, pp. 94–101.

Schößler, F. (2006), 'Wahlverwandtschaften: Der Surrealismus und die politischen Aktionen von Christoph Schlingensief', in I. Gilcher-Holtey, D. Kraus and F. Schößler (eds.), *Politisches Theater nach 1968. Regie, Dramatik und Organisation*, Frankfurt am Main: Campus Verlag, pp. 269–293.

Roselt, J. (2000), 'Postmodernes Theater—Subjekt in Rotation', in M. Lützeler and I. Hoesterey et al. (eds.), *Räume der literarischen Postmoderne: Gender, Performativität, Globalisierung*, Tübingen: Stauffenburg Verlag, pp. 147–166.

Umathum, S. (2003), 'Christoph Schlingensief: Regisseur der schnellen Reaktion', in A. Dürrschmidt and B. Engelhardt (eds.), *Werk-Stück. Regisseure im Porträt*, Berlin: Theater der Zeit, pp. 141–151.

Alexander Kluge is a German film-maker, political activist and theorist. Trained in law, he turned to film in the late 1950s at the suggestion of his friend Theodor Adorno, co-directing with Peter Schamoni *Brutality in Stone* (1960), a reflection on the Nazi atrocities. In 1962 Kluge signed the Oberhausen Manifesto, which declared a new freedom for cinema from convention and commercial concerns, and soon after, co-founded Germany's first film school in Ulm. Kluge was awarded the 'Golden Lion' for lifetime achievement at the 'Venice Film Festival' in 1982. As a fiction writer and member of the legendary post-war literary circle *Gruppe 47*, he won Germany's highest literary award, the 'Georg-Büchner-Preis', in 2003 and will receive the 'Theodor-Adorno-Preis' in 2009.

Tara Forrest is Senior Lecturer in Cultural Studies at the University of Technology, Sydney. She is the author of *The Politics of Imagination: Benjamin, Kracauer, Kluge* (2007), and the editor of a special issue of *Cultural Studies Review* on the topic of 'History Experiments' (2008). Her current research focuses on the work of Alexander Kluge.

Anna Teresa Scheer studied theatre in London and worked as a performer and director in the United Kingdom and Germany where she lived until 2006. In Berlin, she co-founded the award-winning homeless theatre group *Ratten 07* with the support of the Volksbühne theatre where Christoph Schlingensief was engaged as an in-house director. She is currently a Ph.D. candidate at the University of Melbourne and her research interests include contemporary German theatre, politics, performance and social dramaturgy.

Richard Langston is an associate professor of German at The University of North Carolina at Chapel Hill (United States). He is the author of *Visions of Violence: German Avant-Gardes after Fascism* (2008). In addition to several articles on Schlingensief's works, he has also recently published essays on the post-industrial transformation of labour and the work of art, the aesthetics of shock in the digital age, and German performance art of the sixties.

Kristin T. Vander Lugt is Assistant Professor of German Studies at Iowa State University in Ames, Iowa, where she teaches courses on twentieth to twenty-first century German-language literature, film and cultural studies. Her research focuses largely on issues relating to the 'undead'; she has written on topics ranging from revenant bodies in the work of Elfriede Jelinek to the hyper-live corpses of Gunther von Hagens' 'Body Worlds'. Currently, she is completing a book on representations of the German in the mode of horror (from German horror film to horrific Germans), tentatively titled *Horrific Germany: Haunted Screens from Lotte Eisner to the Hitler Channel*.

Sandra Umathum is a theatre scholar at the Freie Universität Berlin and the coordinator of the International Research Center 'Interweaving Performance Cultures'. She was a member of the Collaborative Research Centre 'Aesthetic Experience and the Dissolution of Artistic Boundaries' (2003–2006). In 2000 she finished her studies with a master's thesis on Schlingensief's *Chance 2000* (1998). In 2008 she completed her dissertation on intersubjective experiences in contemporary exhibition art (in press). Between 1998 and 2002 she participated in several projects by Schlingensief, such as *Chance 2000*, *Bitte liebt Österreich!* and *Hamlet*. She is co-editor of *Schlingensiefs Nazis Rein/Torsten Lemmers Nazis Raus* (Frankfurt/Main, 2002).

Solveig Gade holds a Ph.D. in contemporary theatre and visual arts from the University of Copenhagen. She has published a number of essays on contemporary art and theatre in Scandinavian journals and anthologies, and she is a co-editor of the Danish theatre journal *Peripeti*. She currently works as a dramaturge at The Royal Theatre of Denmark.

Denise Varney is Senior Lecturer in Theatre Studies in the School of Culture and Communication at the University of Melbourne. She is the co-author with Rachel Fensham of *The Doll's Revolution: Australian Theatre and Cultural Imagination* (2005) and editor of *Theatre in the Berlin Republic: German Drama Since Reunification* (2008). She has published on feminist theatre, Brechtian and contemporary German theatre, documentation of performance, and Australian theatre.

Brechtje Beuker is a Franklin Postdoctoral Fellow and Visiting Assistant Professor in the area of Germanic and Slavic Studies at the University of Georgia. Her teaching and research interests include twentieth and twenty-first century German and Austrian literature and culture; theatre and performance theory; the intersection of aesthetics and violence, and Dutch literature and culture. Beuker received her Ph.D. from the University of Minnesota in the fall of 2007. Her dissertation, 'Stage of Destruction: Performing Violence in Postdramatic Theatre', examined the critique of violent ideologies in the written and performed works of Elfriede Jelinek, Heiner Müller, René Pollesch and Christoph Schlingensief.

Morgan Koerner is an Assistant Professor of German at the College of Charleston in South Carolina. He received a Ph.D. in Germanics from the University of Washington (Seattle) in 2007. His research focuses on intermediality and laughter in contemporary German theatre performances after reunification.

Roman Berka studied Art History at the University of Vienna (MA) and attended the postgraduate course ECM—Exhibition and Cultural Communication Management at the University of Applied Arts Vienna (MAS). He wrote his Masters theses on 'Schlingensief's Animatograph' and 'Oscillating Science Communication: Dialogue and Participatory Procedures at the Gallery of Research in Vienna'. He has worked for the art association 'museum in progress' (www.mip.at) in Vienna as project manager, lecturer and curator as well as project coordinator of the social organization 'one world foundation—free education unit Sri Lanka' (www.owf.at).

Florian Malzacher has worked regularly as a freelance theatre journalist for major daily papers and international magazines. He is a founding member of the independent curators' collective Unfriendly Takeover and has, since 2006, served as co-programmer of the festival 'steirischer herbst' in Graz/Austria. He has co-edited several books, including *Not Even a Game Anymore—The Theatre of Forced Entertainment* (2004) and *Experts of the Everyday—The Theatre of Rimini Protokoll* (2008). Since 2009, he has worked as a dramaturge for the Burgtheater in Vienna and as a member of the advisory board of DasArts – Master of Theatre, Amsterdam. He lives in Zagreb and Graz.